Toward a Cultural Theory of Education and Schooling

World Anthropology

General Editor

SOL TAX

Patrons

CLAUDE LÉVI-STRAUSS
MARGARET MEAD†
LAILA SHUKRY EL HAMAMSY
M. N. SRINIVAS

MOUTON PUBLISHERS
THE HAGUE · PARIS · NEW YORK

Toward a Cultural Theory of Education and Schooling

Editors

FREDERICK GEARING
LUCINDA SANGREE

MOUTON PUBLISHERS
THE HAGUE · PARIS · NEW YORK

ISBN 90–279–7760–7 (Mouton)
0 202–90068–1 (AVC Inc.)
Jacket photo by Cas Oorthuys
Cover and jacket design by Jurriaan Schrofer
Indexes by Society of Indexers, Great Britain
Printed in Great Britain

General Editor's Preface

When supporters of "pure science" need to justify it, they point to later applications to human welfare which could not be foreseen, as, for example, in medicine. Anthropology may someday trace back to the present book benefits to society which have come from substantial improvements in education. If so, the book will also be analyzed for the way it documents (almost like a good mystery novel) precisely how creative editors put together two and two and two to get an answer much more interesting than six or eight. If the result turns out to have universal significance, it will also be noted that the initial clues were sifted through an international group brought to an unusual Congress.

Like most contemporary sciences, anthropology is a product of the European tradition. Some argue that it is a product of colonialism, with one small and self-interested part of the species dominating the study of the whole. If we are to understand the species, our science needs substantial input from scholars who represent a variety of the world's cultures. It was a deliberate purpose of the IXth International Congress of Anthropological and Ethnological Sciences to provide impetus in this direction. The *World Anthropology* volumes, therefore, offer a first glimpse of a human science in which members from all societies have played an active role. Each of the books is designed to be self-contained; each is an attempt to update its particular sector of scientific knowledge and is written by specialists from all parts of the world. Each volume should be read and reviewed individually as a separate volume on its own given subject. The set as a whole will indicate what changes are in store for anthropology as scholars from the developing countries join in studying the species of which we are all a part.

The IXth Congress was planned from the beginning not only to include as many of the scholars from every part of the world as possible, but also with a view toward the eventual publication of the papers in high-quality volumes. At previous Congresses scholars were invited to bring papers which were then read out loud. They were necessarily limited in length; many were only summarized; there was little time for discussion; and the sparse discussion could only be in one language. The IXth Congress was an experiment aimed at changing this. Papers were written with the intention of exchanging them before the Congress, particularly in extensive pre-Congress sessions; they were not intended to be read aloud at the Congress, that time being devoted to discussions — discussions which were simultaneously and professionally translated into five languages. The method for eliciting the papers was structured to make as representative a sample as was allowable when scholarly creativity — hence self-selection — was critically important. Scholars were asked both to propose papers of their own and to suggest topics for sessions of the Congress which they might edit into volumes. All were then informed of the suggestions and encouraged to re-think their own papers and the topics. The process, therefore, was a continuous one of feedback and exchange and it has continued to be so even after the Congress. The some two thousand papers comprising *World Anthropology* certainly then offer a substantial sample of world anthropology. It has been said that anthropology is at a turning point; if this is so, these volumes will be the historical direction-markers.

As might have been foreseen in the first post-colonial generation, the large majority of the Congress papers (82 percent) are the work of scholars identified with the industrialized world which fathered our traditional discipline and the institution of the Congress itself: Eastern Europe (15 percent); Western Europe (16 percent); North America (47 percent); Japan, South Africa, Australia, and New Zealand (4 percent). Only 18 percent of the papers are from developing areas: Africa (4 percent); Asia-Oceania (9 percent); Latin America (5 percent). Aside from the substantial representation from the U.S.S.R. and the nations of Eastern Europe, a significant difference between this corpus of written material and that of other Congresses is the addition of the large proportion of contributions from Africa, Asia, and Latin America. "Only 18 percent" is two to four times as great a proportion as that of other Congresses; moreover, 18 percent of 2,000 papers is 360 papers, 10 times the number of "Third World" papers presented at previous Congresses. In fact, these 360 papers are more than the total of *all* papers published after the last International Congress of Anthropological and Ethnological Sciences which was held in the United States (Philadelphia, 1956).

The significance of the increase is not simply quantitative. The input of scholars from areas which have until recently been no more than subject matter for anthropology represents both feedback and also long-awaited theoretical contributions from the perspectives of very different cultural, social, and historical traditions. Many who attended the IXth Congress were convinced that anthropology would not be the same in the future. The fact that the Xth Congress (India, 1978) will be our first in the 'Third World" may be symbolic of the change. Meanwhile, sober consideration of the present set of books will show how much, and just where and how, our discipline is being revolutionized.

Readers of this book will also be interested in a variety of books in this series which deal with primate and human interaction and communication, including linguistics; with general theory in culture and history, and with the worldwide variety of sociocultural forms.

Chicago, Illinois   SOL TAX
September 13, 1978

Preface

The Center for the Study of Man of the Smithsonian Institution requested and received support from the National Institute of Education for an International Conference on Education. The conference was held in Oshkosh, Wisconsin, August 28–30, 1973, under the auspices of and immediately prior to the IXth ICAES held in Chicago, Illinois, September 1–8, 1973.

The Oshkosh Conference, as it came to be called, brought together twenty-two social scientists (two from Africa, four from Asia and Oceania, four from Europe and Great Britain, and twelve from the United States). Their purpose was to consider cultural transmission viewed as the broad interest within which the specific interest in formal education or schooling has been variously defined and researched. The conference was principally devoted to presentations of a series of empirical papers which have since become a volume in this World Anthropology series, *The anthropological study of education*, edited by Craig J. Calhoun and Francis. A. J. Ianni. The need for, and possibility of, developing a general theory in the area of cultural transmission formed a second focus. The participants organized part of the conference around one attempt to formulate such a theory. This attempt, Frederick Gearing's "cultural theory" of education at an early stage of development, was presented for examination to those behavioral scientists invited to the conference.

This aspect of the conference, in spite of its brevity, produced two results. First, discussions helped shape the reformulation of the theory, known as Working Paper 6, which is found in Part One of this volume. Second, four conference participants, because their interests were strong

Support for the International Conference on Education from the National Institute of Education, grant number NE–G–00–3–0220, is gratefully acknowledged.

and because their working lives permitted, have joined others in writing the contributions which constitute Part Two.

The Center for the Study of Man desired a faster assessment of this theory than would be possible by waiting for completion and publication of research projects that utilize the theory and then publication of critiques. Therefore, the Center with additional support from the National Institute of Education has cooperated with Gearing in sending Working Paper 6 to a number of individuals who have done research in relevant fields with the request that they respond to the theory. Copies of the Gearing et al. manuscript were sent to selected individuals, and, of those invited, twenty have sent their reactions.

This volume contains three major sections. Part One is the Gearing et al. theory, as formulated in Working Paper 6, which was sent to the invited commentators. Part Two contains the commentaries received by the Center for the Study of Man. Part Three is the current formulation of the theory that was written partly as a response and, in some instances, incorporated the criticisms and other directions suggested by the commentators. Also in Part Three is Gearing's discussion of further theoretical and practical issues that have been raised in the critique.

The personnel of the Center for the Study of Man expect that the Oshkosh Conference and the subsequent efforts reported in this volume will be instrumental in bringing about: (1) further refinement and the use of Gearing's cultural theory of education and schooling and (2) increased efforts by other theorists and research scientists to contribute to building a unified theory or approach to the study of cultural transmission that will be applicable cross-culturally. Such a theory or theories will allow the students of informal education and formal schooling to take full advantage of the large body of ethnographic accounts of these processes in various societies.

State University of New York   LUCINDA SANGREE
Genesco, New York

Table of Contents

Introduction

FREDERICK GEARING

This volume reports on exercises of the curiosities of several social scientists, principally anthropologists, about how it comes about that, in any community, every person comes to learn some things, and different persons come to learn different things; that is curiosities about the general nature of education and of schooling. That curiosity can be phrased differently: Why, in any given community, doesn't almost everyone come to know almost everything? This form of the question is less perverse than it may seem. It is a genuine question, and it has no very obvious answer. Imagine a real community, your town or neighborhood, perhaps. Think of that community as a population; in your mind, put aside the geniuses and near-geniuses and the extreme mental cripples, and put aside the very young who do not yet talk; there remains "almost everyone." Think, further, of all the kinds of knowledge and skill that can be displayed, verbally and otherwise, by these people; put aside the altogether trivial, such as tying one's shoelaces, and put aside rather advanced or bookish know-hows, such as high school algebra or playing well a rock guitar or chess; there remains "almost everything," the community's pool of commonplace know-how. I repeat the question: Why doesn't almost everyone come to know almost everything?

The question deserves an answer. This volume is an attempt to formulate that question in such a way that it can be seriously answered, with respect to your town or ours, and with respect to all communities comparatively. Three evident facts necessarily bear. First, a person can be said to "know" some know-how when, and only when, he or she can be seen to display it, to verbalize or otherwise act it out in some fashion. Second is the fact that commonplace know-hows are often propertylike; that in any community the members agree that only certain persons, and not others, have the *de facto* "right" to display this or that specific bit of know-how, according to age, sex, and a host of such attributes by which they socially identify themselves and are identified by their fellows. And third is the evident fact that few items of such commonplace know-how, simply because these are commonplace, would appear to put an average person's cognitive or motor abilities to any severe test; typically, commonplace know-hows are easy "to get."

Thus, the question here will take this general form: in any community, items from the community's pool of commonplace know-how would in principle diffuse randomly through the community's population, with some persons displaying this, others displaying that, everyone displaying a lot, unpredictably and without discernible pattern. In fact, as evidenced by the display of these know-hows in the normal course of events, those commonplace items diffuse through the population selectively, predictably and according to pattern. How does this come about? The question, more exactly, is *what constraints*, necessarily noncognitive and nonmotor in nature, *reduce the expectable randomness*?

This question, so phrased, also will be directed at other know-hows that are not commonplace, such as knowing how to do algebra. It will thereby come to address the kinds of issues that preoccupy education researchers, — issues concerning the nature of formal instruction and learning in schools. These more complex know-hows, it would appear, are preeminently propertylike, even explicitly negotiable in the market place. Our question will remain: what noncognitive and nonmotor constraints — alongside other constraints that are cognitive and motor but which are not mentioned here — reduce randomness?

Readers will have recognized in the above paragraphs the idiom of cybernetics. This book follows that idiom. The efforts reflected here would, however, be utterly idle, an exercise in futility, except for a development in the recent history of social science. Reasonably frequently from somewhere in the social science community, an unusually powerful fact emerges. A pair of such powerful facts of late have emerged. They provide a factual basis and thus encourage and guide reconsideration of a task that has long been enticing but most elusive; namely, the application of the notion of "constraint" to the analytic description of the behaviors of humans in groups, including an aspect of that application — the use of that notion to the analytic description of education and schooling.

The two facts are these. First, whenever humans meet face-to-face and talk, dancelike behaviors unfold between speaker and listener, some behaviors of each being synchronized with split-second precision with behaviors of the other. The dance follows the beat established by the voice of the speaker of the moment and is made up of, on the one hand, his speech and his blinks, twitches, gestures, gaze directions, and bodily movements generally, and, on the other hand, the analogous body movements of his listeners, plus their verbal interjections and overtalk (see, among others, Kendon 1970, 1972a). For example, in a well-established and smooth-running casual conversation among five or six persons, the speaker would not begin any utterance and most probably would not finish any utterance (quite possibly, given the split-second precision of the synchronies involved, would not finish the next word) except for the fact that the listeners, through their synchronous body movements and verbal accompaniment, participate throughout in the creation of the thoroughly collective product, which is those utterances by that speaker.

Second, sets of such synchronized speaker-with-listener behaviors unfold in strong patterns, and these patterns make up a multiplicity of simultaneous and largely tacit messages passing between each party and every other (among others, Kendon 1967, 1973; Kendon and Ferber 1973). In the example of a small group in casual conversation, as the speaker talks, he and the listeners are simultaneously negotiating, through these dancelike acts, so as to determine how long he will speak and who will speak next. Through other such dancelike behaviors, they are simultaneously negotiating or maintaining a quite large number of additional *de facto* agreements, whereby the event is a casual conversation and not some other kind of face-to-face talk and whereby the participants assume contrasting roles in the conversation and make the conversation group an organized group, not an aggregate.

In short, whenever humans meet face-to-face and talk, through such multiple messages, they jointly create limits as to the content of their talk and other enactments. They establish that some utterances and acts can appropriately occur and some cannot. And control is brought to bear through those synchronies in speaker-listener behaviors, through the power each listener thereby has over any speaker — a power frequently sufficient to permit any listener to stop any speaker in midsentence, with or without consciously intending to do so, mainly by falling out of synchrony with him or her and the rest of the group. Put otherwise, when people come together and talk, it takes joint effort by all parties to define and create the event and to sustain it. And it seems almost as certain that, under many conditions, any one of the participants can momentarily stop the talk. If that occurs, it again requires joint action by all to recreate the event, or to reconstitute it as an event of another kind, or indeed, comfortably to dissolve it. The presumption is strong that the same general facts prevail in face-to-face interaction where there is little or no talk.

All these dancelike communicative behaviors are tacit in large measure. The participants in such face-to-face interaction are aware in a general way of the influences they exert on each other and are to that degree aware of the multiplicity of messages and of their powers of control. But they are aware only in the sense that they can later report with some accuracy on instances of such influences they have exerted or felt; they are not at all aware, in that same sense, of the specific behaviors themselves — the synchronies and patternings. The presumption is strong that synchronies and patternings of this general kind are culturally universal, that only the particular behaviors and messages vary among cultural groups.

This pair of facts has become known largely through fine-grained, frame-by-frame analysis of filmed specimens of human interaction, often called microanalysis. The wide range of such studies is represented selectively by the following materials. Anthologies and overviews: Birdwhistell (1970), Kendon, Harris and Key (1975), McQuown (1971b), Scheflen (1973); studies treating segmentations of behavior principally: Condon (1970), Condon and Ogston (1966, 1967), Crystal (1969), Ekman and Friesen (1969), Kendon (1973, 1975, in press), Kendon and Ferber (1973), Scheflen (1964); studies of synchrony principally: Condon and Sander (1974), Kendon (1967, 1970).

These and other studies have generated the pair of facts named, and these facts in turn make constraint empirically graspable, especially those forms of constraint that are generated in face-to-face interaction — interactional constraint.

Face-to-face talk is made up of actions unfolding within the confines of preexisting limits and within the confines of other limits established in the course of the encounter itself. People who come together are limited in their options, first, as to the kinds of face-to-face talk that, in their community, can sanely unfold. Second, they are more drastically limited to the kinds of face-to-face talk that can plausibly occur in the particular place, at the particular time of day, and among the kinds of people they are; that is, the mix of age, sex, prior acquaintanceship, and so on, among them. Usually, some options remain: to join in talk or not to, and, if so, to engage in some one kind of talk out of the few or many kinds that are, within the above limits, plausible. Choice among these options requires negotiation, and, if one kind of talking is negotiated, that choice in principle can be renegotiated within those preexisting limits, as when a conversation becomes an argument but not (without going outside) a fight. Once established, the kind of talk creates a new set of limits as to the kinds of topics that can be talked about or otherwise dealt with; options remain within those limits, and these must be negotiated and will normally be frequently renegotiated, as occurs with topic shifts. A specific topic established, this creates still further limits. And so on.

A moment's reflection suggests that all the above must go on simultaneously: those preexisting limits are real because, and only because, they are usually honored, and because, when they are occasionally violated, visible consequences follow. Therefore, in any particular face-to-face talk, whatever else is going on, those preexisting limits are being enacted. And while that enactment continues, negotiation is underway as to which particular kind of talk is to be established; and with that determined, its enactment continues, and so on. The number of simultaneous messages is great indeed, but one does not compile a mere list, because it is evident that the messages are organized: limits nesting within limits nesting within limits.

All these limits are embodied in the patternings in the interaction, and all are made real by the powers inherent in those synchronized, dancelike behaviors by virtue of which (by disrupting them) a listener often can, without conscious design, stop the speaker in mid-sentence.

This implication of the pair of new facts is evident and broad: face-to-face talk and other interaction can be well described as a system of interactional constraints. Put more broadly, this means that much of human life that finds expression in face-to-face interaction can be so described. This very clearly includes informal education and formal schooling.

All this is to say that the pair of new empirical facts provide new encouragement and guidance to take up yet again the task that Bateson (1936) anticipated and which has ever since been to many anthropologists and others most tempting and yet most elusive: namely, the application of what came to be known as the notion of cybernetics — that epistemology — to the description of the behavior of humankind in groups.

The idea of interactional constraint transforms one's perception of the behaviors called education and of those called schooling, as will be evident in the pages that follow.

As noted, this volume reflects the exercise of curiosity by a few anthropologists about education and schooling. It reflects, additionally, a rather disparate body of information about various behaviors in diverse places worldwide, put down by many persons, only a few of whom imagined, when they thought and wrote, that they were dealing with education or schooling. Principally, this book is a synthesis. It is an attempt to gather, articulate, and reapply that large and varied body of information.

PART ONE

Working Paper 6

Working Paper 6

FREDERICK GEARING
with
THOMAS CARROLL, LETA RICHTER, PATRICIA
GROGAN-HURLICK, ALLEN SMITH, WAYNE HUGHES, B. ALLAN
TINDALL, WALTER E. PRECOURT and SIGRID TÖPFER

1. OUTLINE

When men have thought about those behaviors they call education, their thoughts have been rather consistently shaped by an image.

Some men, usually adults, have items of information and skill in their heads; they seek to get those into the heads of others, usually children or youth, and they engage in various utterances and other acts to that purpose; but human heads are complex and incompletely understood things, and the task is therefore difficult; thus successes and failures follow; the cumulative result is a world peopled by some who know and can do a lot and others who know and can do less.

The image shapes thought by influencing persons to conclude, before they really begin to think, that education is to be understood by examining the varying conditions of men's heads and the causes of those conditions. The image defines in advance the "differences which make a difference" and thereby makes some thoughts thinkable and effectively disallows many others.

To a student of culture, the consistency of that image strongly suggests that it is a folk image, a broadly shared, internalized cultural construct, probably Western in cultural origin but much wider in contemporary usage. By allowing some thoughts and disallowing others, this folk image helps coordinate men's everyday actions, which is important social work. But the same folk image, at work in the context of serious thought about the nature of things, may do mischief.

The theory of education as outlined in the following pages is an attempt to become disabused of that folk image. In its place will stand another image of the behaviors called education. We know that the members of any society possess in aggregate a pool of information and skill, and of this pool, it may be assumed, the large majority of items are quite simple in terms of the mental and motor operations involved in understanding them. Thus, this image, which may seem perverse (in principle, *should* at first blush seem perverse):

Any item of simple information or simple skill can move from any physically normal adult or child to any other without special effort, virtually automatically; where such items do not move, tangible barriers exist; these barriers are raised by the parties themselves, conjointly; the barriers, once raised, also block the movement of more complex items; the cumulative result is an uneven distribution of all information and skill.

Thus, by this image, the differences that make a difference are the barriers that get raised, causing the flow of simple information and skill, otherwise assured, to be blocked.

This image derives in no direct sense from the Western cultural tradition or from any other culture known to us, but rather, from cybernetics and from efforts, principally those of Gregory Bateson, to apply cybernetics to cultural studies. On this basis, information and skill, in the absence of restraints, diffuse randomly through any population. However, much information and skill in any population can be seen to be systematically, not randomly, distributed. The empirical task is to identify and map the constraints that reduce randomness and, through analysis, to understand the processes by which those constraints are generated and through which they do their work.

This image is only an image, not amenable to proof, but it is, as it turns out, theoretically interesting. It has evoked a chain of reconceptualization of process, plus new inferences from old data and has stimulated collection of new data in modest amounts. These altered conceptualizations of process are the general cultural theory of education here proposed, in the rather primitive form it can now be offered.

This paper discusses a "general cultural theory of education." A theory of *education*, informed by the above image, must predict that items of identified categories of information and skill will or will not regularly pass between members of identified categories of persons, and it must explain how that regularly occurs. A *general* theory of education must be able to so predict and explain for any human society, from a hunting band to a highly industrialized society, or for groups within these, or for wider networks among these. A general *cultural* theory of education proceeds to such prediction and explanation by employing analytic categories whose contents are solely cultural things, ascriptions of meaning established and daily re-established among the actors themselves in the course of their everyday lives.

The theory deals with a limited kind of phenomena, identified as follows: Where two or more persons come into a face-to-face exchange, and where any two or more of those same persons do so recurrently over some duration, they are engaged in an encounter; the education system of any society (or smaller group or wider social network) is the totality of all such regularly occurring encounters. From a judicious sampling of theoretically salient encounters, relative salience becoming evident in the course of investigation, the phenomena of any selected facet of an education system (or, in principle, of the system as a whole) can be captured for description and analysis.

The theory deals with some of the behaviors occurring in those encounters, those behaviors caught up by four pivotal elements of analysis. First, the behavioral units of description and analysis are "turns"[1] that unfold in any encounter. These include speaking turns, and also acting turns accompanied by little or no speech. Turns may alternate rapidly or slowly, smoothly or awkwardly and abortively. Taking turns entails verbal and nonverbal signals and rules. Turn-taking is humanly universal, but signals and the rules of turn-taking that are cued by those signals are culturally variable. Second, a pattern of turn-taking forms a "public dyad." Any encounter involving more than two persons is a complex of public dyads, each pair behaving with an eye to each other and with an eye to audiences physically present or remote. Third, the same pattern of turn-taking, as between the two parties in a dyad, may consitute a "transaction." A transaction is any interchange between parties wherein the relationship between them changes. The activities that make up transactions are in part conscious and purposeful and in part unverbalized and unverbalizable. They involve communications through verbal and nonverbal channels and simultaneously generate a muliplicity of changes in the relations between the parties. Fourth, what the two parties of any dyad regularly transact are education "agendas." An agenda is a patterning of reciprocal behavior, and parties simultaneously look backward and forward at the kinds of relationships and communications they have just experienced and may immediately anticipate in the interchange, that is, an education agenda is parties-at-education-work. In short, in the course of any encounter, the parties engage in some pattern of turn-taking, thereby forming a public dyad or a set of dyads. The parties transact first one agenda, then another, for the duration of the encounter, and all the while, education work is occurring.

The general cultural theory of education consists of eight propositions, as follows:

The nature of any education system is revealed in outline by a mapping of some of the work it has done, namely, by a mapping of the distribution through the population of items of simple information and skill.

---

[1]   Technical terms appear in quotes when first introduced and are included in the glossary.

1. At any given moment in any society, the distribution of items of simple information and skill falls into three major patterns: for some classes of items, distribution is random throughout the population; for some classes of items, distribution is systematically selective, the members of some categories of persons regularly having items of the class, members of other categories regularly not; and for some classes of items, distribution is systematic to the members of some categories of person, and items are largely but unsystematically not distributed to members of other categories.

Classes of items, to these purposes, are classes as perceived by the population. Categories of person are those established by categories of age, sex, and major hierarchical criteria (social class, ethnicity, etc.) as used by the population. Between items of simple information or skill and complex items, no clear boundary can be drawn by us. Knowing the names of things is knowledge of simple information safely distant from that boundary. Appropriately saying "please" at the dinner table is possession of a simple skill. The ability to read, in the sense of decoding from print to voice, moves toward the boundary, and the comprehension of a written narrative is across the boundary.

Simple information and simple skills are variously distributed in any society. Examples include the widely distributed names of things, as well as various jargons such as street talk, youth slang, this paper; simple technological skills, such as changing light bulbs, diapers, or crankcase oil; the names of athletes, of musicians; rudimentary sex information; etc.

Observers mapping the distribution of simple information and simple skills proceed inductively. Items from any selected class of simple information and skill are mapped as to presence or absence in each of the array of categories of person, and any category of person is mapped as to the array of classes of information or skill enjoyed by persons in that category. The investigator goes back and forth, subclasses of information and identity thus being generated inductively, e.g., occupation specializations, to whatever degree of elaboration desired, necessarily stopping far short, however, of the society's total inventory.

The discovered distribution of simple information and skill describes education work already done. To discover how that work gets done is to look at the education system directly. Particularly, it is to predict when and how barriers to the movement of information and skill are raised. Most particularly, it is to predict the occurrence of certain education agendas.

As parties to encounters do education work, they arrive at agendas of three contrasting kinds. Two kinds indicate the presence of barriers, and one does not. Which agendas will arise in any encounter is predicted by a proposition, best phrased in two parts:

2a. Where parties come together in one or another of two identified classes of encounter, and where they there handle one or another of two identified classes of simple information and skill, contrasting kinds of education agendas are generated. Schematically:

	Information is deemed property	Information is not deemed property
Encounters are between persons within the same categories of social identity	Open agendas	Open agendas
Encounters are between persons who are not members of the same categories of social identity	Agenda types which in common filter information and skill	Open agendas

Encounters may occur between parties with like social identities, as defined by the major categories of age, sex, and hierarchical stratification employed by the population in question; encounters also may occur between parties with identities that contrast as to age or sex or strata or any combinations of these. The members of all societies so sort themselves, with details varying as cultural systems vary. In either kind of encounter, parties deal preponderantly with items of simple information or skill, and these may or may not be deemed by the group or groups involved to be like property. When an item is directly used to produce wealth or power (as is technological information or skill), or when an item is indirectly used to produce wealth or power (as where possession of it serves as a marker of a status with entailed privileges), such items may be deemed propertylike. Members of all societies treat some information as property. Details vary as cultural systems vary; determinations entail ethnosematic analysis.

An agenda is an open agenda when, by the past experience and future anticipation of the parties involved, all items introduced by either party regularly flow freely to the other. It is a filtering agenda when, by experience and anticipation, the exchange of information is selective. For example, both parties recognize areas of information to be things they do not talk about, or perhaps there is discrepancy in the way the parties see the matter, and if one party raises such an item, the other party becomes embarrassed or angry and changes the subject. Where encounters are between members of one category of identity, and where information or skill is not propertylike, open agendas prevail. Where encounters are across categories, and where at any juncture of some duration information is not propertylike, open agendas again prevail. Where encounters are across categories, and where at any moment information is deemed as property, filtering agendas of two different kinds emerge. Agendas in which barriers are raised are of central interest.

2b. Among encounters across categories of identity, and where information is property-like (in the lower left box above), there are, in turn, two subclasses of encounter and two subclasses of information, and these regularly generate two kinds of agendas, in both of which flow of information, and skill is filtered as follows:

	Exchange of information is clearly privileged or clearly proscribed	Exchange of information is problematic
Encounters where mobility between involved categories will clearly occur or will clearly not occur	Stable agendas	(Absent)
Encounters where mobility is problematic	(Absent)	Troublesome agendas

In encounters between parties of contrasting social identity, it may be clear to the group or groups involved that the future social identity of one party will, in the normal course of events, change and become the current identity of the other party (as where the sole contrasting attribute is age), or that in another case, in the normal course of events, it will not so change (as where one of the contrasting attributes is sex). The various attributes other than age and sex that consitute hierarchical status may in clarity entail virtually automatic mobility or mobility between them may be virtually impossible. All these constitute one subclass of encounter, in contrast to a second subclass where such mobility is seen as problematic and unclear by members of one or more of the groups involved. This is typically seen in the context of protest, reform movements, and other social changes. Similarly, in respect to items of propertylike information and skill, the exchange of an item may be deemed by the groups involved to be unambiguously privileged or unambiguously proscribed; these are one subclass, as against a second, where the matter is problematic.

Where clarity reigns, both as to mobility, or its absence, and as to privileged or proscribed exchange, "stable agendas" are regularly generated. Here each party, in both experience and anticipation, perceives that his counterpart has exercised, is exercising, and will exercise discretion and prior censorship as to items introduced; he perceives that with respect to most items thus introduced, germane talk therefore follows. He perceives that, where slips occur, these are quickly corrected with little embarrassment or discomfort.

Where both mobility and exchange are problematic, "troublesome agendas" regularly emerge. Here, through experience and anticipation, parties perceive the frequent introduction of noisy items and resulting disarrays. The two remaining combinations probably do not occur.

In all stable agendas, there is some array of subtypes. Conspicuous among them is the polar contrast between behavior patterns established in the handling of prevailing privileged exchange as opposed to the prevailing proscribed exchange, and within the latter, the contrast between the handling of temporarily proscribed information (as with information or skill proscribed to one age category but not another) as opposed to information permanently proscribed (as to a sex). One special implication of the proposition should be especially noted: in most concrete encounters, agendas typically shift, often between open agendas and stable agendas, or less frequently, between open and troublesome agendas, but in principle, agendas cannot shift between stable and troublesome agendas in the course of an encounter.

Agendas are sets of reciprocal behavior, plus experience and expectation. We have identified three kinds and given them verbal labels. In any society, these three agendas, and only these three, will be found predictably to arise. (Each agenda is divisible into subtypes.) Agendas at this level are explicit. The parties can talk about them in some fashion and can at will enact them. Simultaneously, as parties to an encounter transact these explicit matters, they transact as well reciprocal patterns of behavior at a second, tacit level about which they do not and normally cannot talk, even though they do subliminally perceive and regularly enact these patterns. Parties, in the course of encounters, simultaneously transact some pattern of tacit "initiation and response."

Transaction at this tacit level gives to agendas their real power. At explicit levels of transaction, parties may frequently delude themselves and each other. Thus, we find this proposition, best phrased in two parts:

3a. Where, in an encounter, a stable agenda is in the process of becoming established, concurrently, a settled pattern of tacit initiation and response is becoming established; where a troublesome agenda is being established, erratic patterns of tacit initiation and response are concurrently being established; where discrepancies may appear, as between these explicit and tacit levels, the patterns of initiation and response define the agenda.

An encounter, as noted earlier, consists of primitive units called turns. A turn may be an initiation, or it may be a response, or it may be neither. Initiations and responses are constructions by the actors. A command, for example, is usually read by the involved parties as an initiation; compliance to it as a response. But that command, the identical utterance, may be a cry for help, and very probably would then be construed as a response. By the same token, a question may be an initiation, its answer a response, but the reverse construction may also occur. Turns are construed as initiation and response in all societies, but the signals that identify each form vary culturally and include patterns of synchrony between speech and nonverbal behaviors.

Thus, parties in the course of an encounter may transact the shared sense that, whenever one initiates, it is so perceived by both, and when the other regularly responds, it is so perceived by both. In some patterns — the rare extreme — all initiation might be ascribed to one party, all response to his counterpart. As stable agendas take form, reciprocal perceptions of patterns of initiation and response simultaneously emerge. And as troublesome agendas arise, parties arrive at a tacit sense that neither knows what the other imagines he has done, is doing, or will do next. When that fact becomes sufficiently uncomfortable, the encounter may itself be ended or, more frequently, where the parties are constrained to continue, the interchange becomes pro forma.

Education agendas at both explicit and tacit levels are best revealed to the observer through microanalysis of monitoring processes whereby discrepant behaviors are identified and perhaps corrected by the parties and their audiences.

Encounters occur in all societies, in bureaucratically organized contexts and in such contexts as family, peer group, and neighborhood. In the former, patterns of initiation and response tend to assume special features, thus:

3b. In bureaucratically organized contexts, when stable agendas arise across the hierarchical levels of organization, patterns of initiation and response tend toward wholly asymmetrical form, one party consistently initiating and his counterpart consistently responding; this induces interludes of "liminality" of varying duration.

In such contexts, insofar as such monolithic forms of initiation and response develop, the party who is of the higher level of organization is the initiator; his lower counterpart, the responder. But as between two parties in an encounter, initiation evokes response evokes initiation, which if not interrupted, forms a runaway schizmogenetic cycle, role elaborations tending toward forms not different from those attaching to formal statuses of master and slave. Liminality may occur in any context where some are up and others are down. It is a process by which the latter band together and, in some form, quit playing the game. In these encounters in bureaucratically organized contexts, liminality acts as a degenerative loop that periodically breaks the established agenda with its runaway features and reinitiates transaction.

Open agendas, as noted earlier, do not involve barriers and are thus theoretically peripheral. Wherever they prevail, simple information and skill diffuses randomly. Stable agendas and troublesome agendas both involve barriers, but of contrasting kinds, and thus, we find two kinds of education work going on in these agendas. This education work unfolds along three analytically separable axes, as shown by three additional propositions.

4. Insofar as stable agendas prevail, the resulting pattern of distributed items of simple information and skill is systematic; where troublesome agendas prevail, distribution shows that information has been massively but unsystematically blocked.

This is merely to confirm that education work somehow was accomplished (Proposition 1) and was, in fact, done in the course of transacting the named kinds of agenda (Propositions 2 and 3). One salient disclaimer: it should *not* be supposed that agendas are transacted and then do this work in so simple a sequence. The education work *is* the transaction of the agenda *is* the work.

Agendas are transacted in the context of the handling of items of information and skill where any such items are simple. We have seen the work those transactions do in respect to those items. By the sheer numerical preponderance of such items, agendas are generated and sustained in these handlings. The contrasting agendas, so transacted throughout the course of an encounter, involve contrasting work with respect to other kinds of information and skill as well, including the handling of complex information and skill. The exchange of complex information and skill always requires some regularity of joint effort; this is to say, it requires a settled pattern of initiation and response between parties to an encounter. Thus:

5. Where in any encounter stable agendas prevail, items of complex information and skill are being selectively but regularly introduced and, other things being equal, successfully communicated; where troublesome agendas prevail, such items are capriciously introduced and communication is regularly abortive.

These troublesome agendas also involve the raising of barriers to the sharing of "cultural premises."

6. Where in any encounter stable agendas prevail, the parties share (i.e., regularly enact) the same cultural premise or premises; where they do not, a cultural premise may newly be communicated by one party to another. Where troublesome agendas prevail, cultural premises are not exchanged or shared.

By cultural premise, we mean those phenomena variously called themes or motifs or unconscious canons of choice, insofar as these phenomena, in content, entail unspoken assumptions as to both the nature of things and as to the value of things. They also simultaneously entail unspoken assumptions as to relations both among men and between man and nature. An example would be this formulation derived from a tacit premise in this Western cultural tradition: "Men have minds; natural things do not; men control nature." Premises are tacit, are normally unverbalized and unverbalizable; humans regularly act *as if* they were thinking such thoughts, and any man's departure from such enactments would seem to his fellows conspicuous and odd.

Such premises are tacit. Thus, they are not verbally taught. Rather, in the contexts of encounters, they may be conveyed through joint participation by the parties in education "protocols." Like protocols in international diplomacy, education protocols are explicit guidelines that define, for purposive occasions of some duration, appropriate sequences of events and behavior. The familiar demonstration experiment in school is an education protocol often selected in this and other societies. An example is the demonstration of the expansion properties of gases by a series of heating and cooling experiments. Every education protocol allows an enactment of some cultural premise, just as the demonstration experiments allow enactments of the premise of man's control over nature.

Agendas, we saw, have pivotally to do with patterns of initiation and response. He who initiates, controls. A stable agenda is some settled pattern of initiation and response; it is thus some pattern of control; it is thus some patterned opportunity for one party or the other recurrently to organize the interchange according to some protocol. A stable agenda is a pattern of occasion for tacit communication, through joint enactment, of the corresponding cultural premise. A troublesome agenda is the opposite.

Stable agendas, we saw, involve selective blocking of the flow of items of information; a similar selective blocking does not occur in the communication of cultural premises. In any cultural system, there are many items of information but few cultural premises (and few corresponding protocols). Several different protocols may serve equally to organize exchange as to any item or array of items. Thus, applied cumulatively over an array of stable agendas — regardless of the selective blocking of items of information — all protocols sooner or later get used, and all premises are thereby enacted.

In short, with respect to the communication and sharing of cultural premises, stable agendas never involve barriers, and troublesome agendas always do.

From all that has preceded, it is broadly evident that any education system is a regular series of reenactments of the wider social system. Parties do not come to education encounters innocent of expectation. They come to any encounter as members of an ongoing social system; each party brings a broad prior sense of his own identity and the identity of his counterpart, and each party has some broad sense of what information is property and what is not. Such prior understandings consist of expectations that, perhaps sharpened in detail, are concretely reenacted in the course of these encounters and become those three saliently contrasting states of relationship and communication called agendas. The wider social system is so reenacted, not only in terms of the formal lumpings and separations of the population by identity, but also in terms of qualitative differences in those lumpings and separations. Stable agendas prevail where parties, however variously joined and parted, are relatively at peace with each other; troublesome agendas prevail where parties are not at peace.

Where those troublesome agendas prevail, the flow in either direction of discrete items of simple information is being rather massively but haphazardly blocked. More dramatically, where troublesome agendas prevail, the flow in either direction of complex information and the sharing of premises are being almost totally blocked. This, in effect, precludes reciprocal access to preeminently negotiable properties and assures reciprocal alienation. All this together virtually guarantees that the parties will declare war — a war with precisely that alignment of contenders by which the sectors of the society at and near the centers of power are assured of winning.

One can presume that, through both the habituating and the constraining forces generated through such regular reenactment of the wider system, any education system regularly functions to prevent social change. It strongly appears that, not only in tribal societies (as we might have supposed), but also in highly industrialized societies, parties to encounters, whatever they may imagine they are about, regularly behave as if their overriding assigned task were perpetually to recreate the wider social system unchanged. The major division of the society and the major tensions between such divisions are conspicuously included.

Normal constraints to research preclude direct examination of a society over twenty year spans of time. Yet the following contains many thinkable propositions, any one of which, if demonstrated, would indirectly suggest that education systems overridingly serve as brakes against social change.

7. Where open agendas, stable agendas, and troublesome agendas obtain, role enactments and role elaborations and thus, role learning, across the full array of the society's repertoire of roles, are in force. Where open agendas and stable agendas obtain, invidious distinctions between roles is covert or absent, and where troublesome agendas obtain, invidious distinctions are always present and always displayed in the behaviors of the parties involved.

If all these things are true, why is there the illusion in some societies that education is a vehicle, even the principal vehicle, of social change? In part, this is because there is always new information and new skills, and education systems always deal with these. But we offer the following proposition:

8. Where, in any society, any new item of information or skill arises and becomes identified as belonging to a category of information, or where an old item is reidentified as to category, the flow of such an item is regularly blocked

by the education system, just as all other items in that category are regularly blocked.

Bodies of information and skill are, in fact, perpetually changing in all societies, but how this gets distributed, as well as the wide-ranging implications of its distribution, remains, by the regular operations of education systems, unchanged.

The scientific worth of a theory is principally measured by the number and interest of the testable hypotheses it generates. None of these key propositions have been proved; quite possibly none can be in any direct and compelling way. All, however, generate hypotheses that can be tested. And as such hypotheses are tested and confirmed over time, a structure of conviction builds that the theory is correct.

Let us now turn to a recapitulation and discussion of the theory.

2.   DISCUSSION: ENCOUNTERS

The general cultural theory of education sets out to "identify and map the constraints that ... reduce randomness" in the distribution of information and skill "and through analysis, to understand the processes by which those constraints are generated and through which they do their work." The theory, as noted earlier, deals with a limited kind of phenomena — events where two or more persons come into recurrent face-to-face interchanges. Such events are encounters. An encounter is here a notion rather than an analytic concept; it reflects an educated guess that, to the theoretical purposes at hand, one must attend to face-to-face interchange, and one may safely attend only to that.

That guess is informed by a body of research by and following after Goffman (1964: 135). He has said that encounters arise where two or more persons "jointly ratify one another as authorized co-sustainers of a single, albeit moving, focus of visual and cognitive attention." He names as examples "card games, ball-room coupling, surgical teams in operation, and fist fights." Elsewhere, Goffman (1967: 142–143) says that what is distinctive about face-to-face exchange is the reliance on messages "that can be transmitted only because the body of the transmitter is present," that is, messages where communication moves simultaneously in verbal and nonverbal modes and is "very rich in qualifiers" and where there is "considerable feedback opportunity."

The inclusion in this theory of face-to-face interchange is plausible enough. The educated guess that all else, most conspicuously the mass media, can be safely excluded from the theoretical purposes at hand, may seem implausible and, in fact may, prove costly. Yet this idea gains some plausibility through the following assumption: However an item of information or skill may come to impinge on a man's central nervous system, that item gets reworked in face-to-face interchange; its meanings there become established; and thereby, and only thereby, it comes into that person's repertoire of socially deployable information and skill.

In no society do humans encounter one another at random. In any society, constraints operate so as to enjoin regularly occurring encounters between and among some kinds of persons and to hinder or disallow encounters among others. In principle, this makes it possible to map, for any society, group, or wider network, an encounter profile.

Encounters are defined by the social identities of the parties; namely, by the mix in age, sex, and social strata. An encounter profile is a mapping of all such encounters in terms of their approximate relative frequency. An early imperfect mapping is a prerequisite to other data collection and analysis; additional information accrued in the course of analysis permits periodic correction of a profile that is increasingly correct and useful in the final stages of analysis.

An encounter profile serves as a rough guide for the selection of encounters for analysis. In the final stages of analysis, it also serves to reduce the possibility of overgeneralization by making evident whether the research has embraced some approximation of the total education system, or only a definable sector of it, or, perhaps, a mere dabbling. These are logistic concerns; fine precision does not seem necessary.

3. DISCUSSION: TRANSACTING EDUCATION AGENDAS

The first four key propositions must be discussed together. These phenomena move forward together, and they constitute transactions of education agendas.

1. At any given moment in any society, the distribution of items of simple information and skill, falls into three major patterns; for some classes of items, distribution is random throughout the population; for some classes of items, distribution is systematically selective, the members of some categories of persons regularly having items of the class, members of other categories regularly not; and for some classes of items, distribution is systematic to the members of some categories of persons, and items are largely but unsystematically absent in other categories.

2a. Where parties come together in one or another of two identified classes of encounter, and where they there handle one or another of two identified classes of simple information and skill, contrasting kinds of education agendas are generated. Schematically:

	Information is deemed property	Information is not deemed property
Encounters are between persons within the same categories of social identity	Open agendas	Open agendas
Encounters are between persons who are not members of the same categories of social identity	Agenda types which in common filter information and skill	Open agendas

2b. Among encounters across categories of identity, and where information is propertylike (in the lower left box above), there are, in turn, two subclasses of encounter and two subclasses of information, and these regularly generate two kinds of agendas, in both of which flow of information and skill is filtered as follows:

	Exchange of information is clearly privileged or clearly proscribed	Exchange of information is problematic
Encounters where mobility between involved categories will clearly occur or will clearly not occur	Stable agendas	(Absent)
Encounters where mobility is problematic	(Absent)	Troublesome agendas

3a. Where, in an encounter, a stable agenda is in the process of becoming established, concurrently, a settled pattern of tacit initiation and response is becoming established; where a troublesome agenda is being established, erratic patterns of tacit initiation and response are concurrently being established; where discrepancies may appear, as between these explicit and tacit levels, the patterns of initiation and response define the agenda.

3b. In bureaucratically organized contexts when stable agendas arise across the hierarchical levels of organization, patterns of initiation and response tend toward wholly asymmetrical form, one party consistently initiating and his counterpart consistently responding; this induces interludes of "liminality" of varying duration.

4. Insofar as stable agendas prevail, the resulting pattern of distributed items of simple information and skill is systematic; where troublesome agendas prevail, distribution shows that information has been massively but unsystematically blocked.

3.1. *Sharing*

This is a cultural theory of education, but culture here is not something in the head of the "omniscient informant." It is evident in the first proposition, and less self-evident but still true for the other propositions, that cultural variability is the matter of principal theoretical interest. It is thus especially necessary that terms, such as "sharing" an item of culture or "not sharing" it contain as much precision as can be had.

A measure of precision is gained by two assertions that hold, in principle, throughout the theory. First, at no point does the theory suppose it is necessary to know what is going on inside any individual's head. Thus, to report in this theoretical context that some array of persons share an item of information is *not* to claim that one individual has it, and another, and another. Rather, they share it, sharing being an activity that goes on between them. Second, when humans share, they behave, which is to say, they speak and they otherwise act, reciprocally. More narrowly, to report that individuals share an item of information is to report that each is behaving as if he or she has seen no reason to suppose that his counterpart is intending, through the use of words or other acts, anything different than he intends. In short, sharing between two parties here means merely the absence of behavioral indications by either party that he perceives that they do not share (Lyons 1968). More must not be assumed.

3.2. *Information and Skill*

In any society, items of the aggregate body of simple information are variously shared and not shared. Any such item is explicit, which is to say, it is adequately verbalizable for normal communicative purposes among persons who share it. The body of simple information in any society includes the categories, in terms of which people perceive their surroundings, categories of natural things, man-made things, super-natural powers, time and space, insofar as these categories have names generally known to the people. The body of simple information also includes constructions as to physical connections (A causes B), logical connections (A and B), and social connections (A has authority over B) between and among any of these categories; insofar as these connections are named. The body of simple information also includes exemplars of beauty or ugliness, or goodness and badness.

Parallel to the body of simple information, in any society, there exists an aggregate body of simple skill, items of which are unevenly distributed. Any such item is explicit, which is to say, it can be demonstrated at will. The body of skill includes simple performances in technology, ritual, folk art, and highly standardized performances whereby information and skills are socially deployed, as in etiquette or in religious and political practice. All these are included insofar as items are by some men, few or many, readily demonstrable through performance.

3.3.   *Categories of Identity and Mobility*

The prediction of types of agenda outcome (Proposition 2a and 2b) requires four sets of discriminations. Among them are determinations as to whether any encounter is among persons within one category or among persons in differing categories of identity and also determinations as to clarity or ambiguity with respect to mobility between the categories. The identification of such categories of person draws on the most extensive body of literature in anthropology. Yet such identifications to these theoretical purposes require trial and error restrained by the principle of parsimony. For example, with respect to age and sex, there is in any society a modest number of major classes and some proliferation of subclasses, and with respect to other hierarchical strata, the major divisions are frequently many and the proliferation vast. The problem is to find that modest number of categories that are salient to the actors.

These are matters of group perceptions. Berreman's work (1972) forewarns that these perceptions, like cultural phenomena generally, are quite probably not shared throughout the total population. Thus, the relevant perceptions in respect to any encounter are probably those of the major reference groups of the parties to the encounter.

3.4.   *Propertylike Information or Skill, and Privilege or Proscribed Exchange*

There is in the literature a wealth of indications that much information and skill in any society is propertylike. Examples of these are the information and skill entailed in various divisions of labor items involved in initiations and other rites of passage, sex roles, and the behaviors that have been called conspicuous consumption by Thorstein Veblen. The key question, as yet unanswered, is whether propertylike information constitutes an identifiable cognitive domain (or domains) in a society. The theory does not appear to stand or fall on the matter, but it is made more elegant to the degree that domains of this kind are found with regularity, and it is made more intriguing to the degree that these are structurally deep. In any event, these cognitive domains, together with the matter of clarity or ambiguity as to the appropriateness of exchange of such items, are group phenomena; thus, the above forewarning from Berreman (1972) applies here.

3.5. *Turns*

The theory shifts now to examine the behaviors of the parties themselves, that is, to the patterns of interchange that are transactions of education agendas. Analysis of these behaviors requires a corpus of encounters recorded on film or videotape. These behaviors, verbal and nonverbal, are subjected at many junctures to microanalysis.

The behavioral units of transactions include turns. For one cultural system at least, turn-taking has been revealed through microanalysis (Duncan 1972) of a system of verbal and nonverbal cues and signals passing between parties to an interchange. Such behavior is based on rules that, when followed, cause turn-taking to proceed smoothly, and when not, cause it to break down, at least momentarily. The theory assumes that turn-taking is humanly universal, though the cues, signals, and rules will vary as cultural systems vary. If this assumption should prove wrong, the theory would cease to be a general theory, and would apply only to those cultural systems that have turns. Chapple and Coon (1942) have noted what appears to be a biological level of the same phenomena. They describe action-inaction rhythms, which are products of some nature-nurture mix and vary among individuals. These rhythms, to the degree they are violated (as where one party to an encounter is kept in an inactive state beyond his tolerance), evoke behaviors of characteristic kind. The behaviors may or may not contain the turn-taking cues and signals recognized in the cultural system; in either event, they would presumably affect the turn-taking pattern. Frederick Erickson (n.d.) has microanalyzed filmed sequences of hand-shaking within and between ethnic groups. The analysis shows turn-taking proceeding on a predominantly nonverbal level; as would be supposed, the sequences go smoothly within ethnic groups and rather abortively between such groups.

3.6. *Public Dyads*

The device of analytically separating an encounter of more than two parties into a set of dyads is common enough. This theory of education, however, requires that these be handled as public dyads; that is, that the two parties be seen as acting not only with an eye to each other, but with an eye to various audiences only some of which may be physically present. And this requirement threatens to swamp any analysis in the sheer multiplicity of conceivable impingement. Thus, by some device, relatively salient audiences must be brought into focus, while others are left to one side. We can tentatively entertain a model that radically simplifies the problem.

Parties to an encounter transact with an eye to salient audiences, physically present or not, and construe themselves-with-the-audiences in the following patterns of "we-they" alliance and apposition. Where A and B are parties to an encounter, A has the option of construing himself with B as allied in apposition to two sets of audiences, c and d, or he has the option of construing himself and c in alliance as against B and d; B has parallel options. At any moment, A's constructions and B's may or may not be congruent (see Figure 1.)

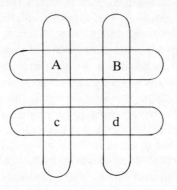

Figure 1.

The content of those constructions is revealed, if it is, in the examination of transaction interchanges themselves.

3.7.   *Transaction: Explicit Role Elaborations*

Transactions, as noted earlier, are interchanges wherein the relationship between the parties changes in some identifiable fashion. In the course of any encounter, interludes can be expected where transaction is proceeding and other transactionless interludes can be expected where the relationship is holding steady. These are the transacted education agendas.

Two kinds of change in relationship are at issue. The first is explicit, which is to say, the actors can and do talk about these facets of the relationship. We here follow Barth (1966), who describes the process as the transaction of role elaboration. In his analysis of the crew of a fishing boat, he traces how the formal statuses (skipper, net boss, fisherman) and the formal rights and duties that attach to these statuses become elaborated into the stable relationships that one sees regularly enacted among the men. In the analysis, Barth pivotally uses Goffman's notion (1959) of impression management, wherein parties in the course of transaction engage in over- and undercommunication, thereby defining and establishing the role elaborations at issue. The role elaborations are also sustained during nontransactional interludes.

Between parties to an encounter, role elaborations include those that establish patterns of rewarding and punishing, telling and listening, modeling and imitation, as well as others that set tones of deception or trust or cooperation or opposition. Still others project short- and long-term purposes and reciprocal concerns. Transactions and ensuing changes in relationship are always reciprocal.

Bernstein (1964: 59–60) has shown that a "restricted" code characteristically prevails during the earliest phases of an encounter (because language is thereby made maximally redundant); the parties gain time while communication unfolds through non-verbal channels.

3.8.   *Transaction: Initiation and Response*

Transactions also critically involve interchange that proceeds at a tacit level — interchanges which parties do not and typically cannot verbalize. The parties are arriving at patterns of initiation and response. These patterns are fully tacit. That is, parties may in full awareness settle into patterns of question-and-answer, or I-talk-then-you-talk, or I-model-you-imitate. These would in all probability be talked about by the parties as initiations and responses, if they chanced to fall into that vocabulary.

In any interaction, every utterance or other act is objectively both a response to something that preceded and an initiation of something that will follow. Thus, initiation here deals with tacit constructions by the parties to an encounter that segment the flow of interaction — that is the unverbalized tacit construction, "He initiated; I am responding" (Bateson, 1972: 298ff.).

Transactions tacitly proceed through prestations and counterprestations of the thing itself — that is, enactments of initiation and response wherein the part preferred by either party is overcommunicated in his enactment, and the other, less desired part is undercommunicated. Communication is nonlinguistic in the sense that an initiation or response is itself not verbally stated, but rather is (over- or under-) communicated through speech in conjunction with paralinguistic, kinesic, and proxemic modes.

Several microanalysts have examined this type of communication patterns: Duncan (1972), Condon and Ogston (1967), Kendon (1970, 1972a); others have considered patterns wherein verbal behavior anticipates or lags behind nonverbal behavior, synchrony and nonsynchrony in speaking-listening behavior as between the parties, and contrasts between a person directly addressed and another who is present and only listening. None, to our knowledge, have sought to identify the contrasts in clues and signals between initiating and responding.

Bateson (1972) had dealt with these phenomena rather programatically and without microanalytic examination of such behavior.

If these tacit phenomena do not exist, if they cannot be empirically identified, or if they do not become patterned in mappable ways in the course of transaction, then the theory is most fundamentally weakened; it would then be necessary to fall back on turn-taking plus role elaboration. These together seem less powerful in bringing about effects such as those named in propositions 5 and 6.

3.9.   *The Steady States that Emerge in the Course of Encounters are Education Agenda*

An agenda, as we said earlier is "a patterning of reciprocal behavior, and parties simultaneously look backward and forward at the kinds of relationships and communications they have just experienced and may immediately anticipate in the interchange." And these agendas are of three kinds: open, stable, troublesome.

While examining verbal interchanges among strangers in an Israeli immigration center, Handelman (1973b) identified some seven contrasting frames of offers and responses. These frames, unfolding in some series, might constitute the repertoire of verbal behaviors enacted in that cultural system and in the course of transaction. Two would seem to be modes of enactment of a transacted stable agenda, should that emerge, and the remaining modes would seem to be modes of enactment of a troubled agenda should that emerge as the experienced and anticipated pattern in the encounters involved.

Erikson (1975) has analyzed a filmed interview between a white college counselor and a black student on the student's career. It is virtually a classic case wherein transaction proceeds to a troubled agenda and the interchange thereupon becomes pro forma and remains so until its conclusion. The student has said he wanted to become a counselor; the counselor was listing the difficulties of being a counselor.

Agendas are identified in part by observing patterns of reciprocal behavior between the parties themselves. (When an item is raised, is subsequent talk and other action germane? Are classes of items consistently avoided?) Yet, agendas are more compellingly identified by observing monitoring activities, especially those that follow departure from established behavior patterns (Scheflen 1964). In the context of an open agenda, having secrets is a departure; in a stable agenda, not censoring some items is a departure; in both, corrective monitoring is normally quickly effective; in a troublesome agenda, withholding items is massive but erratic and monitoring is normally ineffective. All this is subject to various empirical tests.

3.10. *Liminality*

In encounters across levels of bureaucratic organization, the patterns of initiation and response tend to be monolithic: where a stable agenda prevails, one party initiates with high regularity and his counterpart regularly responds. In such contexts, reciprocal prestations form potential runaway cycles; initiation evokes response evokes initiation, tending toward total dominance and total submission. Moreover, liminality (V. Turner 1969) behaves as a governor checking runaway tendencies as follows. Where parties to an encounter are peers, and where both are of low status and participating in concurrent encounters with those of high status, the peers will periodically activate a liminal relationship between themselves and against their superiors and sustain that liminal relationship or condition for a while, then drop it and later reactivate it. This process continues in cycles of varying frequency and scale up to, and including, revitalization movements and mass protests. In an education encounter, where the "lows" have become actively liminal, they figuratively or literally drop out. In effect, they quit responding (or quit responding consistently) and, thereby, dampen the runaway cycle inherent in formal education contexts. Stable agendas between persons of contrasting levels in formal contexts run cyclically through alternating runaway and liminal phases. Whyte (1949) has described reactions of employees in a restaurant when they are perpetually caused to respond to others' initiations. He described, for example, the behavior of cooks, who were forced perpetually to respond to the dinner orders of the waitresses. He described a condition of liminality. Bernstein (1964: 65–66) has noted that parties tend to shift to the restricted code when the situation causes them to seek to emphasize their we-ness *vis-à-vis* others. Lacey (1973) has shown the polarizing processes among students in a British secondary school where academically low students establish an identity group in apposition to both the high students (similarly grouped) and the staff. And Turner's original study (1969) made reference to a very wide array of contexts in which liminality processes emerged.

These special features assumed by stable agendas in bureaucratic contexts take on salience in broadly comparative studies, e.g., studies comparing very small societies where formal organization is minimal with very large societies where it is massive. They also assume special salience in historical development analyses wherein the expanding role of bureaucratic organization and its implications are typically a conspicuous feature.

4. DISCUSSION: COMPLEX INFORMATION

5. Where in any encounter stable agendas prevail, items of complex information and skill are being selectively but regularly introduced and, other things being
equal, successfully communicated; where troublesome agendas prevail, such
items are capriciously introduced and communication is regularly abortive.

4.1. *Sharing, Again*

The proposition asserts that, where stable agendas prevail, parties may or
may not communicate and come to share complex information or skill,
and where troublesome agendas prevail, they surely will not. The latter
occurs because this communication requires concerted joint effort,
which, in turn, requires some settled pattern of initiation and response,
the absence of which is the key defining feature of troublesome agendas.

Sharing means here what it meant in the context of handlings of simple
information and skill: the absence of any indications by a party to an
encounter that he perceives his counterpart to be intending anything
different than he intends by the involved utterances or acts, whatever
they may be.

4.2. *Complex Information*

There exists in any society an aggregate body of complex information and
skill that grades into specialized information and skill as acquired and
deployed by literati, technological, and professional specialists, and vir-
tuosos in art as well as religious, athletic and scientific specialists. The
body of special information and skill is topically like the bodies of common information and common skill (see section 3.2).

Complex information and skill, it seems clear, always involves numerous items interconnected in some fashion; these items, one by one, may
frequently be simple, but the interconnections among them make them
jointly complex. In all languages, names of things are names of classes;
this is simple information. Such classes are themselves assembled hierarchically in wider classes sometimes named; the hierarchies form taxonomies or paradigms or other forms. An organized set of items is
complex information. In all languages, constructions regarding physical,
logical, and social connections are likewise named; usually this is simple
information. But operations that employ named categories and connections (as in Piaget's conservation principle) are complex information. All
names range along a continuum whose poles are digital and typologic.
Insofar as names are digital, a concrete item belongs to a class when it
displays each of the attributes that define the class; the decision as to each

attribute is yes or no; the summative decision as to ascription of the item to the class is yes or no. Insofar as names are typologic (Heider n.d.), some item stands as the prototype of the class, and other items are ascribed to the class according to the degrees of similarity they exhibit to the prototype. Thus, an item is ascribed more or less to the class. An example is that the class "apple" may (though it seems improbable) be construed digitally by parties to an encounter — shape, color, skin, seeds, size, weight, and taste will be the defining attributes. Or it may be construed typologically, as where the Delicious apple may be the proto-type and other apples are seen as more or less applelike, and some, such as crabapples are so dissimilar as to fall (almost) out of the class altogether. All such named classes, one by one, are items of simple information; how they are joined together and thereby become complex information, in part, depends on their kinds of names. For example, typologically apples, pears, and walnuts do not join easily to form a principle of plant propagation.

Analogously, performances of skills range along a continuum from digital to typologic. As an example, where parties to an encounter ask whether a ballet performance is technically correct, they may construe the performance digitally, the attributes of each movement being defin-able by action and the complex performance being definably correct or incorrect. If they ask whether any movement or the total performance is dance, or what "danceness" is, the matter requires prototypical exemp-lars, and thus, is construed typologically.

4.3. *Specialization*

Complex information grades into and becomes part of specialized infor-mation (Goodenough 1951; Gladwin 1970; Tschopik 1938). Thus, the theory at this juncture deals with those processes that open up or close off the possibilities of specialization. What is predicted is clear: Between those sectors of the society at relative peace, stable agendas prevail. Complex information and skill may selectively flow and corresponding specializations are accessible. Between those sectors not at peace, troublesome agendas prevail. Complex information and skill cannot flow and specializations are not accessible. This is to say that each such sec-tor retains what it has.

The effectiveness of the latter half of the prediction is less clear. In the statistical sense of most instances, most of the time the prediction almost certainly holds but it appears to be too soft, with many diverse exceptions not easily accounted for. It may be that the men in any society who command extensive complex information tend with some frequency to be unusually unruly types who willfully treat matters of social identity and mobility (those predictors of agendas) differently than do their fellows and sometimes thereby succeed in transacting stable agendas where troublesome agendas would be anticipated. Predictive propositions about unruly men seem possible in principle, but they are elusive in fact.

4.4. *Education Research*

By the theory, some parties — where stable agendas prevail — may have access to complex information and skill and related specializations, and if the information or skill is privileged, they certainly will have access. Yet they may not get the information or skill; they may simply try and fail. These are, of course, the phenomena that preempt most of the attentions and intellects of the men of schools and colleges and of most of the men who study those places. Such preoccupations are not trivial, of course, but that focus of interest, seen in the context of this theory, does point up the fundamental contrast between this theory and studies of education as currently pursued.

By the theory, when the regularly occurring denials of access have been accomplished, some homogeneous array of prospective specialists remain; and in terms of effects on the wider social system, it makes little difference who comes to specialize in what, as long as someone does. The key phrase, of course, is "effects on the wider social system."

5.   DISCUSSION: CULTURAL PREMISES

6. Where in any encounter stable agendas prevail, the parties share (i.e., regularly enact) the same cultural premise or premises, or, where not, a cultural premise may newly be communicated by one party to another. Where troublesome agendas prevail cultural premises are not exchanged or shared.

5.1. *Cultural Premises*

By cultural premises, we mean those phenomena variously called themes, motifs, or unconscious canons of choice, insofar as these phenomena, in content, entail unspoken assumptions as to both the nature of things and as to the value of things and simultaneously entail unspoken assumptions as to relations both among men and between man and nature. The example given was this constructive formulation derived from a tacit premise in this Western cultural tradition: "Men have minds; natural things do not; men control nature."

Such premises are tacit, and one rarely attempts verbal formulation, yet these premises are commonly and frequently reflected in verbal glosses. Example: to *wrest* a living *from* the land, which glosses the example given above. Other expressions common in Western cultures that would seem to be glosses of this kind are: any person has a *psyche* that he can *will* to *work* and through *exerting energy* can *alter* the course of natural events and *affect* the psyches of other men, which efforts make for *progress* at home and in *other lands*; on the other hand, any man can will at intervals *to play in order to replenish* his *spent* energies, thus later to work more *efficiently*.

Cultural premises are variously treated in a quite large body of literature. Hallowell's excellent Ojibwa research (reprinted in Diamond 1964) dealt with the Ojibwa notion of person, which entailed all the above-named features of a premise; Yaker (1972) deals with schizophrenic conceptions of time; Emiku Ohnuki-Tierney (1972) deals with Ainu spatial concepts; Dorothy Lee (1949) in her well-known work deals in part with Trobriand conceptions of causality and being. There are many others. Similarly, two studies, one by Rosalie Cohen (1969) and one by Bernstein (1964) have quite different orientations and can quite easily be seen as dealing with cultural premises. There is also a feature of added interest since both are treating contrasting premises that coexist in single societies. Cohen's studies deal with two cognitive styles, analytic and relational, and Bernstein's with two linguistic codes, restricted and elaborated.

5.2. *Education Protocols*

"In the contexts of encounters, it was noted, [premises] may be conveyed through joint participation by the parties in education 'protocols.' Like protocols in international diplomacy, these protocols are explicit guidelines that define, for purposive occasions of some duration, appropriate sequences of events and behaviour." The example given was familiar demonstration experiment showing expansion properties of gases by a series of heating and cooling experiments. This protocol enacts the premise of man's control over nature.

The most extensive discussion of protocols and how they enact premises (our terms, not his) is Bateson (1972), in his treatment of Learning II. Starting from a list of four basic kinds of learning experiments employed by experimental psychologists, Bateson imagines it is possible to generate many hundreds of possible contexts of learning (protocols). Cohen (1969) and Bernstein (1964) suggest that the cognitive styles and linguistic codes they treat behave as protocols by shaping interaction patterns in the home, at school, and in society. Warren (1967) has shown for a village school in Germany and Singleton has shown (1967) for a village school in

Japan regularities of patterned behavior (protocols) that appear to derive from and, in turn, convey pervasive cultural themes (premises). Philips (1972) clearly documents contrasts between protocol-like inter-personal styles at home and at school for Indian children in Oregon; Howard (1970) has shown analogous patterns for Rotuman children and also explicitly has drawn the premiselike messages; Burnett (1969) has shown for high school ritual and Tindall (1972) for Utes and Mormons playing basketball, that participation in these protocol-like activities are in effect lessons in wider cultural matters that are part-premises.

5.3. *Sharing*

Sharing means here, as before, the absence of indication that either party to an encounter sees evidence of the absence of sharing. Particularly, this most frequently will mean that both parties by such evidence feel comfortable in their joint participation in the protocol prevailing at that juncture. If so, they share the premise the protocol enacts.

Incompatible premises and protocols regularly coexist in a society. By the theory, where troublesome agendas prevail, premises are not shared and do not come to be shared.

6.   DISCUSSION: EDUCATION AND THE WIDER SOCIAL SYSTEM

7. Where open agendas, stable agendas, and troublesome agendas obtain, role enactments and role elaborations, and thus, role learning, across the full array of the society's repertoire of roles, are in force. Where open agendas and stable agendas obtain, invidious distinctions between roles is covert or absent, and where troublesome agendas obtain, invidious distinctions are always present and always displayed in the behaviors of the parties involved.

8. Where, in any society, any new item of information or skill arises and becomes identified as belonging to a category of information, or where an old item is reidentified as to category, the flow of such an item is regularly blocked by the education systems as all other items in that category are regularly blocked.

6.1. *Reenactment*

That education systems are somehow at work recreating the wider social system is rather massively indicated in the literature. Very selectively, with respect to social class or ethnic contrasts, see Bernstein (1964), Cohen (1969), Gumperz (1969), King (1967), Parsons (1965), Philips (1972), Rist (1970), Rosenfeld (1971), and Wax et al. (1964). With respect to sex roles, see Brophy and Good (1970), Rattray (1932), Talbert (1970), and Underhill (1936). With respect to prevailing norms of interpersonal behavior, see Fortes (1938), Henry (1957, 1959), Herzog (1962), Howard (1970), Singleton (1967), Warren (1967), and Williams (1958).

6.2. *Gatekeeping*

If the habituating and restraining forces engendered by sheer reenactment are not enough, there still remains a failsafe device. The education system, principally through testing and issuing of credentials in whatever form these take in the society, acts as gatekeeper, selecting persons for life careers in the various sectors of the society. Such testing attempts explicitly to measure the party's current share in the society's body of information and skill; it also predicts and determines that share. Further, the testing act itself entails the transaction of an agenda, and it assumes some cultural premises and not others. The overriding fact is redundancy: The testing simply asks the party to do once more what he has been doing all along. What he has been doing is participating in one particular manner in the society's education system, what he does during the test is to so participate, and what he will do as a result of the test is to continue so to participate. Testing is a replay. Cohen (1969) has shown this. It concerns many.

It should additionally be mentioned that, in the course of doing education work, parties also generate an additional kind of social identity — smart and dumb — in the variety of ways that may be phrased and perceived. In large part, this is role elaboration, i.e., new attributes are attached to existing identities. This does not occur randomly as the first set of studies (above) invariably shows. In some part, it is independent of this and especially applies to that selected, homogeneous body who pursue complex information and skill and the corresponding specializations.

7. SUMMARY

The general cultural theory of education is here summarized and contextualized as tersely as can now be done. This will perhaps serve as a step toward a more formalized statement that may prove possible at a later time.

7.1. The cultural system of any society, or smaller group, or wider social system, is a structure of equivalence (here unexamined) of which the surface manifestation is an aggregate body of information and skill that is systematically distributed among the population according to the major contours of their social organization.

7.2.   The education system of any society is a regular series of processes whereby that body of information and skill is perpetually redistributed according to the social organization. Such redistribution is perpetually required by the succession of the generations.

7.3.   The processes of the education system move under restraints generated by the nature of the body of information-and-skill-cum-social organization, namely, that some information and skill is deemed property; some is not; and some categories of persons are deemed properly to possess such property, and some are not.

7.4.   Under such restraints, as men meet and handle simple information and skill, three kinds of agenda are regularly transacted: open agendas during which such information and skill is randomly distributed; stable agendas during which the movement of such information and skill is selectively passed and blocked; troublesome agendas during which the movement of such information and skill is massively but unsystematically blocked.

7.5.   Under restraints established in those agendas, complex information is respectively randomly distributed, selectively passed and blocked, and totally blocked.

7.6.   Under restraints established in those agendas, cultural premises are respectively randomly distributed, systematically passed, and totally blocked.

7.7.   By cumulative processes occurring in contexts of the various types of agendas, the systematic distribution of information and skill according to the contours of social organization is, in its form, perpetually recreated. Items that were randomly distributed remain so; items confined to categories of persons are kept so, and the major points of tension in the social organization are perpetually regenerated as well.

APPENDIX A: GLOSSARY

AGENDA   Parties in the course of a face-to-face encounter may be moving toward a pattern of reciprocal behavior (*see* transaction). Or they may be sustaining an established pattern of reciprocal behavior of some brief or extended duration; in this event, they have established an education agenda (*see* open agenda, stable agenda, troublesome agenda).

CULTURAL PREMISE   An unstated assumption involving simultaneously the nature of human and natural things and their value, and relations among nonhuman things and between those things and men. Cultural premises are rarely verbally formulated in naturally occurring events, but they are enacted consistently, and behavioral departures are highly visible.

INITIATION AND RESPONSE   Interchanges among parties to an encounter are segmented by them (*see* turns). Of these minimal segments, some are construed by the parties to be initiations, some responses, some neither. Initiations and responses are fully tacit, that is, are not and cannot be talked about or willfully enacted. These involve involuntarily given and subliminally perceived verbal and nonverbal signals, which presumably vary as cultural systems vary and must be sought through microanalysis.

LIMINALITY   When monolithic patterns of initiation and response occur (one party initiating consistently, his counterpart responding), liminal episodes of greater or lesser duration may be generated by the responding parties conjointly; such episodes are evidenced by displays of solidarity and principally include collective moves that interrupt the established patterns of interchange.

MONITORING   An established agenda, during the period of its duration, is not sustained solely through habit. Parties are variously adept, and for this and other reasons, there are disruptive departures from the pattern. These departures evoke monitoring behaviors by the parties and their physically present audiences and principally include overcommunication through enactment of the "correct" behaviors.

OPEN AGENDA   An established pattern of reciprocal behavior wherein the parties to an encounter perceive that neither is censoring items of information or skill.

PROTOCOL   An explicit set of rules that establish stereotyped patterns of interchange as a norm, for an encounter over some duration or for a series of encounters. These rules establish expectations as to speaking and listening, modeling and imitating.

PUBLIC DYAD   A face-to-face encounter of two or more persons is analytically separable into public dyads, each party in dyadic interchange with every other party, but the parties behaving with an eye not only to their counterparts but with an eye to salient audiences physically present or not.

STABLE AGENDA   An established pattern of reciprocal behavior wherein the parties to an encounter perceive that both parties have been, are, and will be dependably censoring items of information or skill; patterns of tacit initiation and response are regular.

TRANSACTION   Occurs during an encounter as long as the relationship between the parties is unsettled and changing; that is, in the course of an encounter, there may be (1) a transaction episode leading to (2) a settled pattern of behavior, an agenda of some kind, the latter interspersed with (3) monitoring interludes, and as the situation may later shift, a new transaction episode leading toward a new agenda. Transaction always proceeds at both explicit and tacit levels, always involves both verbal and nonverbal communication, is always constrained within broad limits by the formal statuses and roles of the parties.

TROUBLESOME AGENDA   An established pattern of reciprocal behavior wherein the parties to an encounter perceive that both parties have not been, are not, and will not be dependably censoring items of information and skill; patterns of tacit initiation and response are erratic.

TURNS   The minimal segments of behaviors in the course of encounters are speaking-and-acting turns. Turn-taking is subject to rules and signals that presumably vary as cultural systems vary and must be sought through microanalysis.

PART TWO

Commentaries on Working Paper 6

Introduction and Acknowledgements

LUCINDA SANGREE

We have arranged the invited responses in sections, according to what seems to us the major thrust of each author's commentary. Our arrangement introduces the reader to the critiques in a way that points up facets of each commentary which uniquely illuminate as well as criticize or support the theory of cultural transmission presented by Frederick Gearing and his associates in Working Paper 6. We recognize, however, that each author has made several different points which could be read in connection with the comments of respondents located in other sections. For example, John Herzog's commentary examines the scope and usefulness of the theory and is appropriately placed in the first section, "Principally on the Scope and Content of the Theory." In addition, Herzog's paper also points out the difficulty of operationalizing the concepts "stable agenda" and "troublesome agenda" in ways that would facilitate the study of social change. The respondents dealing primarily with operationalization of terms and development of appropriate research techniques are found in the second and third sections, "Principally on Interactional Analysis" and "Principally on Micro versus Macro Levels of Analysis." Herzog's comments are thus seen to be relevant to these concerns as well as to those of the first section. For cross referencing we rely on the reader's powers of discrimination and association.

The first five commentaries pose the following questions. What is the scope of this theory presented in Working Paper 6? Are the authors actually offering a *general* theory? Are they offering a *cultural* theory? What do Gearing and his associates mean by the phrase "a theory of education"? Is this the education we think of in its specific reference to bureaucratically structured organizations which present certain information to a specific clientele (usually children)? Does the phrase "theory of education" refer to that which philosophers have broadly defined as the "school of life"? In the area of anthropological research on cultural transmission, what could be the future of a theory that emphasizes flow of information in face-to-face interaction? What is the relation of this theory to the research and theory concerned with child development and learning processes? In addition to these questions, the contributors in the first section emphasize the need for definition of the terms utilized in Working Paper 6 such that direction can be given to persons who may want to undertake research on specific hypotheses derived from the theory.

The fourteen remaining commentaries are arranged in five groups: commentaries principally on interaction analysis; on micro and macro levels of analysis; on inductive method; on formalization; on inter- and intra-psychic analysis.

Several of the contributors ask whether we have the techniques in social science to do the kind of research that this theory demands. A description of the various ways the commentators have considered this problem in relation to the theory presentation in Working Paper 6 is unnecessary here. Since the posing of this question has had an important influence on the revision of the theory, this will be apparent to the reader. We direct attention especially to the paper by Frederick Erickson in the second section which focuses upon successes and problems in the observation of interaction, and also to footnote three at the end of Craig J. Calhoun's commentary which emphasizes the difficulty of assessing "knowledge gained."

John J. Gumperz, Carol Talbert, and Ward Goodenough question the assumption that one can view information as flowing unless blocked. They point out certain implications for research that follow from the flow perspective taken by the authors of Working Paper 6. Gumperz and Talbert, in addition are concerned with the relation of macro social phenomena to micro (that is interpersonal interaction) phenomena. The comments of Gumperz indicate that extant research does not allow us to relate data generated by attention to gross social indicators to data generated by observing face-to-face interaction. Sorting people into macrosociological categories of social identity that are assumed to persist is not an answer, says Gumperz. Talbert's research, as she describes it, illustrates this point, for it is apparent that the speech activities of interest to her do not relate in a systematic way to the gross categories of social identity that she and others had predicted would be relevant. Goodenough's emphasis on the ordering of experience by the individual leads us to place his commentary in the last section, "Principally on Inter- and Intra-Psychic Analysis."

A record of the seminar led by Madeleine Mathiot and Paul Garvin illuminates the research stance taken by them and their students in contrast to the stance taken by Gearing and the other authors of Working Paper 6. The placement of this discussion immediately after the preceding emphases on interaction analysis and the difficulties of relating micro to macro analysis serves to illustrate some of the difficulties raised by those preceding commentators. This seminar record also serves to point up the rationale behind several changes included in the revision of the theory. For example, there are no "categories of information" in the revision. Instead, the interactional emphasis is pressed consistently. The impact of the insistence by Mathiot and Garvin that constructing a reference model can be an important early step in conducting research will be evident to all who read Part III.

Thomas R. Williams gives a brief history of the anthropological approaches to the study of cultural transmission in addition to his specific comments on Working Paper 6. We feel it is appropriate to place this history just preceding the revision of that working paper which has now become "A Reference Model for a Cultural Theory of Education and Schooling."

My contact with the authors of Working Paper 6 has been brief. I was brought to the scene by the Center for the Study of Man of the Smithsonian Institution as an interested but uninvolved individual. My responsibilities were to collect and edit the contents of Part II, edit contents of Parts I and III when requested to do so by the authors, and to assist in readying the entire volume for publication. I was employed by the Center for the Study of Man as a research associate for these specific tasks. I am grateful to Sam Stanley and his staff at the Center, especially Jennifer Stephens and Diana Parker, for their aid which made it possible for me to contact the invited respondents and carry out other aspects of the tasks necessary for the presentation of this set of critiques. The fact that I was located in Buffalo and the Center is in Washington did not prevent their extending to me any assistance I needed at any point in this undertaking, an undertaking which had begun almost a year before I joined the enterprise.

I have conceived my task to be the presentation of the critiques in a manner which both highlights each contributor's unique perspective and exposes certain critical threads that weave through many of the separate communications. It has not been my responsibility to offer a criticism or body of suggestions. The communication of John J. Gumperz comes close to expressing my own thoughts on Working Paper 6.

My work was greatly aided by the then-chairman of the Anthropology Department of the State University of New York at Buffalo, Erwin Johnson, who smoothed out potential knots in the bureaucratic red tape. I am also grateful to the Technical Assistant of the Anthropology Department, Wendy Seubert, whose help in locating recording and typing equipment was essential to me. I also appreciate her assistance in helping keep our financial records straight.

Miriam Norris and Marie Varga, who were employed in the office of what soon became the Center for Studies of Cultural Transmission, an interdisciplinary group on the Buffalo campus, helped with the early stages of manuscript typing; but, more important, their knowledge of university and office procedures saved this novice hours — which means they saved the project a considerable amount of money. The extremely swift and skillful manuscript typing of Martha Cosentino played an important role in finishing up the early draft of this volume within the time allotted for its completion.

Special gratitude is due Gregory Bateson. Conversations with him both on the phone and in person were of great value to me in at least two ways: (1) in my work as editor; and (2) in perception of the worth this editorial task has had and will have for me in my own research. I am also aware that his conversations with Gearing and Gearing's associates encouraged them in their view that the negative cybernetic view of distribution of information and skills is an interesting and probably useful one. Bateson's enthusiasm in pursuit of the application of impeccable logic and the perspective of communication theorists to various fields of research is inspirational to all who are fortunate enough to engage in face-to-face encounters with him.

SECTION ONE

Commentaries, Principally on the Scope and Context of the Theory

COMMENT *by Robert J. Havighurst*

If I grasp the main idea about Gearing's general cultural theory of education, it is that it is more useful than what he calls the folk image of education. The folk image, or the ordinary, naive Western theory of education is that the educational process — the passing of information and skill from one group to another or from one generation to another — is facilitated or impeded by the quality of the material inside the heads of people. This material is an entity that we call intelligence or mental competence. It is located in the brain and central nervous system. Since people obviously differ in their information and skills, and since information and skills exist in the brain and the central nervous system (CNS), we can best learn about education by studying the various conditions of the brain and the CNS and the causes of those conditions. This is the folk theory.

Gearing proposes that a more useful theory of education will focus on the process of communication of information and skills between people and between groups of people. He postulates certain barriers to communication that are cultural barriers rather than biological barriers. These barriers or restraints on the free flow of information and skill between persons and groups can be studied and understood as cultural phenomena. His cultural theory of education should "predict that identified categories of information and skill will or will not regularly pass between identified categories of persons and must explain how that regularly occurs."

I understand him to offer his theory as a useful way of understanding the process of education in any human society, complex or simple. I do not read his theory as a denial of the existence of differences between people in respect to their brains and central nervous systems on the ways that such differences facilitate and impede the flow of knowledge and skill. But he believes that his cultural theory is at least as useful, or perhaps more so, in understanding why some people learn so much more than others and why they learn such different things.

The educational system, for Gearing, is a gatekeeping or filtering institution that facilitates the flow of information and skill between certain categories of persons and impedes the flow of certain kinds of information and skill between other categories. This flow is impeded for certain kinds of information and skill between sexes, age groups, ethnic groups, social classes, and occupational groups. The educational system tends to be conservative, a protector of the status quo.

It will be interesting to study systematically in various societies the three kinds of agenda or patterns of reciprocal behavior: open agenda, where communication is full and free; stable agenda, where certain items of information or skill are regularly censored or not communicated between certain groups; and troublesome agenda, where the persons or groups involved are erratic in their communication efforts and, therefore, do not trust each other and do not cooperate well in the educational process.

I should like to see this theory applied to the educational system of a complex metropolitan area, where there are blockages in communication between ethnic groups, social class groups, and residential area groups (suburbs versus central city).

I would also like to see how Gearing's theory would work in the communication between the faculty of a university and a group of their students who have committed themselves to the counterculture. What agendas remain open in this situation, and what agendas become troublesome?

The Case of Cultural Pluralism

Of special interest might be an application of the Gearing theory to the attempt of a dominant Anglo culture group to communicate educationally with a native culture group that has been systematically subordinated throughout a century or more, but which is now being set "free" by the dominant group to determine its own lifestyle and its own future social and economic structure.

There are three strikingly parallel examples of this situation, all involving the settlement by Great Britain of Anglo people in a land inhabited by a Stone Age native society: the United States, Australia, and New Zealand. In all three cases, there has been the same sequence of events and policies, commencing with the taking of land by the Anglos; then conflict and war, in which the natives were defeated; then the withdrawal of the natives to reservations where they were presumably protected by the Anglo government; then a policy and program of assimilation of the native group into the dominant society; then a realization that this would not work out, followed by a program and policy of cultural pluralism. Cultural pluralism was intended to mean a fair degree of self-determination by the native society, together with a policy of mutual appreciation and understanding between the dominant and the subordinate culture groups.

As a means of putting policy into practice, the dominant society provides an educational system for the subordinate group. Whether the policy be assimilation or cultural pluralism, there are bound to be a number of troublesome agendas in the educational system that the dominant group sets up and maintains. Where there is a policy of cultural pluralism, the dominant society has tended to offer support with only a minimum of direction for an educational system that is to be developed and maintained autonomously by the native society.

Thus, there is now in the United States a program of Indian education in which Indians are increasingly in charge. In New Zealand, there are Maori educators with substantial influence in school districts with Maori students, although there are no segregated Maori schools. In Australia, there is the beginning of a system of schools for Aborigines, with a policy of increasing the numbers of Aboriginal teachers and developing advisory councils made up of Aboriginal parents. Furthermore, in all three countries, the native groups have been provided with funds that they may use as they see fit for the development of their society.

In all three cases, the educational system for the natives is evolving away from domination by the Anglo society. But the native leaders and teachers have been educated in Anglo school systems, certainly with a number of troublesome agendas. One interesting question has to do with the cultural premises concerning the relation of the cultural group to the land. The native societies all have the outspoken cultural premise of tribal or societal ownership and use of land, to which individual rights to occupy and use land are subordinated. On the other hand, the Anglo society has the cultural premise of individual or family ownership and use of land. The Anglo-dominated educational system during the program-period of assimilation attempted to teach the natives information and skills that would make them competent individual farmers. This produced a troublesome agenda. Now that the native societies have control of land (more the case in the Australian and the American than in the New Zealand situation), it will be interesting to see whether stable agendas will be produced by the native educational systems with respect to information and practices concerning the use of land.

COMMENT *by John D. Herzog*

Fred Gearing has earned the gratitude of his colleagues for taking on a task that many have deemed essential but none until him have seriously assayed. A theory of *education* (in all its manifestations) that is *general* (applicable in all human groups) and that remains consistently on the *cultural* level of analysis: mind-boggling! Gearing must also be complimented for his earnestness and openness in presenting his theory in various forums over the last few years, for the forthright manner in which he has clarified points and dealt with criticisms as the theory has evolved, and for his success in attracting able graduate students to derive and test hypotheses based on the theory.

With this introduction, perhaps what follows will be taken altogether in the spirit in which it is intended: as an attempt to be helpful to a colleague who has undertaken a nearly impossible challenge, but one that must be faced and effectively discharged before the study of education, anthropological or otherwise, can move beyond the natural history and tinkering stage in which it is now mired. Anthropologists who have not seriously studied education will not recognize what I am talking about; those who view the potential contribution of the discipline as the upstaging of charlatan schoolmen will also lose patience. So be it! Gearing is not addressing these people either.

Indeed, as I thought and rethought what I would write in these pages, it became increasingly clear that Gearing and I share a basic perspective on education. The differences with the present formulation that I express below assume the validity and usefulness of the general cultural theory and are attempts mainly to redirect elaborations of it in forms that I deem more telling and parsimonious. It makes sense to me to conceive of education as patterns of transactions taking place in encounters; the metaphor has the virtue of encouraging us to consider the possible educational spin-offs of almost every human interaction sequence while not overlooking the likelihood that more "education work" is done in specifiable subtypes of encounters, e.g., initiation ceremonies, in some schools, than in others. The time is long overdue for serious students of education to adopt this broad view, which is integral to Gearing's theory.

One of the strengths of this paper, for me, is the clear and useful link early forged in it between Gearing's notions and the earlier formulations of Bateson and other information theorists. The perspective of cybernetics has been available for almost two decades, but very few people concerned with education (as opposed to mental illness, for example) have been brave enough to attempt an accommodation of it to this data realm. I suspect that equally pregnant for the elaboration of the present theory would be Anthony F. C. Wallace's notion (1970) of "equivalence structures" especially for the realization of Gearing's intention to do no psychologizing.

After his very catholic first pages, it was disappointing to discover that Gearing gravitates to the use of the terms "education" and "education agendas," which connote "school" or even "classroom." This comment may surprise Gearing, but it is one that demonstrates how hard it is for even a first-rate scholar to free himself from the conventions of his culture sufficiently to theorize about *education*. Analysis of this tendency in Gearing's thought may help us to strengthen and more thoroughly to generalize his theory.

Perhaps the clearest indication that Gearing is thinking primarily of schools when he writes about education agendas is the stark and unexplained statement that "open agendas are of peripheral interest." With this fiat, perhaps the largest class of educational encounters is eliminated from further consideration. Gearing, at least, should have explained why he feels that open agendas are so unimportant; his way of handling this point contrasts with his careful discussions of much more obvious issues. Surely the workings of open agendas could be illuminated through the application of Gearing's core analytic concepts, and through such analysis, one might obtain a general notion and many specific ideas as to how most people learn most of what they know. This was the initial appeal of Gearing's theory to me; it promised to liberate from the confines of the folk image so well conjured on the first page. It can still liberate, if Gearing will reconsider his abnegation of open agendas. (Parenthetically, it is not clear to me what Gearing means in saying that "for some classes of items, distribution is *random* [emphasis added] throughout the population" (Proposition 1). Does he mean unpatterned in the statistical sense, or merely widely distributed?)

The corrollary to Gearing's disinterest in open agendas is his fascination, in light of his original definition of the term, with stable agendas in which communication occurs, as opposed to those in which it is blocked. As first explained, stable agendas emerge in encounters where exchange of information is either clearly privileged or clearly proscribed, but in Proposition 5, we learn that "where in any encounter stable agendas prevail, items of complex information and skill are being ... successfully communicated"; that they are also being blocked in their movement is no longer noted. Gearing then emphasizes that stable agendas are typical of "bureaucratically organized contexts." What we are observing, I think, is a back door accreditation of formal education encounter settings as the sites in which the really important education business of a society occurs. Gearing seems to forget that by his own definition communication of some sorts is proscribed in stable agendas. Whence this lack of concern with limits placed on the circulation of information?

A partial answer to this can be adduced from Gearing's declaration that "any education system regularly functions to prevent social change." He is here indirectly facing the supposed discovery of the last decade that a society can be changed very little, if at all, by intervention in the content and dynamics of its open and stable education agendas. Gearing's theory explains this failure by underscoring how closely related the education agendas of a society are to the social structure and cultural premises of the society. The reasoning is plausible, but Gearing owes us answers to at least two further questions. First, is the goodness of fit always as total as the theory implies? (I do not think that the "unruly men" argument of section 4.3 is a sufficient response). Is it not possible that "revolutionary" information and skills may be unwittingly transmitted in both open and stable communicating agendas, e.g., revised conceptions of politics via post-Watergate television or literacy in a peasant village? Second, and more interesting, what permutations of agenda types into other agenda types are possible, and, if they do occur, under what conditions do such transformations occur? This is an undeveloped aspect of Gearing's theory, a critical one that should not remain uncultivated.

I am, in fact, concerned about the social policy implications of Gearing's doctrines, especially the uses that might be made of his conclusion that education normally or inevitably (which?) functions to prevent social change. If this is so, there is little reason for spending money to improve schools or other education agencies. Social investments should be made in other sectors, and even meliorist-gradualist views of the role of education in society should be abandoned. Is this an accurate summary of the thrust of Gearing's ideas? If so, we may see a new name in the roster of revisionist critics of education: Moynihan, Greer, Jencks, Jensen, and ... Gearing. If this interpretation of his views is incorrect, Gearing owes it to himself more than anyone else to set the record straight.

To move on to a separate issue, it is possible that the theory at the moment may be overrich in technical terms. Specifically, Gearing does not convince me that cultural premises are anything other than items of highly complex information not transmitted at the conscious level. So far as I can determine, Gearing does not define information in a way that requires the parties in an encounter necessarily to be aware of all the items that they may be exchanging. The theory is not strengthened by thus etherealizing perhaps the most important items, cultural premises, transmitted by the education system — largely in *open* agendas, I'll wager! Second, it does not seem that the term "protocol" adds anything that a phrase such as "formalized turn-taking," an adaptation of one of the theory's core concepts, could not handle equally as well. Compare: "Turn-taking is subject to rules and signals that presumably vary as cultural systems vary," and "A protocol is an explicit set of rules that establishes stereotyped patterns of interchange as a norm ... " Both sentences are taken from the glossary. The plea of this paragraph is for parsimony in terminology; presumably, other prunings are also possible.

Furthermore, there are two areas in which the present statement should be more thoroughly elaborated. First, in its present form, the theory is very heavily cognitive; I would like to know Gearing's ideas on the cultural channeling of feelings and emotions (the affective education dear to the hearts of certain educational reformers) as well. Emotion could be treated entirely in its public aspects, permitting the theory to retain nonreductionistic purity. Second, the validity of the theory will be more firmly established if a place is found within it for a modified concept of development, by which I mean allowance for the fact that the capabilities of the parties in any encounter vary predictably according to the state of biological and cognitive maturation each is in. It is absurd to pretend that "any physically normal adult or child" is the *de facto* equivalent to any other such person (his nonfolk image). We know that, at age five, for example, most children are incapable of receiving certain kinds of complex information, and that at age 70, perhaps less regularly, most adults are not able to acquire the skills of a ballet dancer. The parameters of such an enrichment of the theory would have to come from developmental psychology, perhaps a sticky prospect, but they could be easily couched in the language and perspective of information theory. After all, cyberneticists routinely allow for variations in the capacities and characteristics of transmitters and receivers, which are analogous to the parties in an encounter in Gearing's theory. As with the channeling of emotion, only the public aspects of development need be dealt with.

In closing, I want to return briefly to the theme of the first few paragraphs. The general cultural theory of education is an ambitious undertaking and also a powerful vehicle for thought that will increasingly influence, and perhaps even dominate, anthropological research on education in the next decade. Gearing has developed it at a time when interest in education is growing among anthropologists, and when there exists no rival formulation of equivalent elegance and scope. Much work remains to be done in extending, revising, and refining the theory, as I have tried to point out in the preceding paragraphs. The present work is clearly a tour de force of which the author may be justifiably proud and toward which the profession, if it attends to its own best interests, will be appreciative and eagerly exploitative.

COMMENT *by A. Richard King*

My comments on Working Paper 6 are influenced by two biases. The first is that I have a high respect for Gearing's earlier work, including "Where we are and where we might go: steps toward a general theory of cultural transmission" (1973). The second is that my student audience is composed mostly of teachers and students training to become teachers — a population for whom anthropology has a powerful and useful set of conceptualizations, as well as a certain amount of scholastic nonsense not always apparent as such to anthropology students required by rites of passage rituals somehow to incorporate the words of the masters into some rationalizable framework.

Gearing's present paper comes to us not as something completely new, but rather, as a continuation of conceptualizations to which he and others have earlier contributed. I find the present paper inappropriate as a general cultural theory of education, and sincerely hope it will be withdrawn as such, perhaps to be reformulated within a context of extending and refining the potentially useful but certainly underutilized methodology of encounter analysis. An interesting possibility for so doing might be to back up slightly to Goldschmidt (1972) and to consider the congruences, divergences, and other implications to be derived from his paper and the commentary by seven others. It appears odd that Goldschmidt is not even mentioned in Working Paper 6; further odd that so little is common in the reference systems for the two papers. The *Current Anthropology* bibliography contains fifty-eight references besides Goldschmidt; Gearing et al. contains forty-nine. Only two common sources appear; only seven author's names are common to both bibliographies.

Student reactions to the two Gearing productions might illustrate broadly my point. When we discussed the Council on Anthropology and Education paper — treated as a methodological formulation despite its title — we found not only a high interest factor, but several students were able to utilize it in their field studies. The present paper, which is but a sophisticated expansion of the first, elicits little but negative reactions, ranging from feigned inability to find any meaning ("What *is* he talking about?") through various specific criticisms of implied but unsupportable conceptual linkages, to perceptions of a latent political motivation and identification of this paper as an attempt by the authors to make some statements about an oppressive, dysfunctional school and social system.[1]

Our sympathies are entirely with such efforts, but not to the extent of discarding some fairly sound theoretical formulations which have served

---

[1]   The research associate, in a cover letter requesting reaction to the paper, reinforces this latter notion by saying, in part: "The authors see cultural transmission as involving systematic inadvertent censorship ...", a loaded terminology in our world today. Among other things, such definitions establish an immediate barrier to research undertakings. Gearing has already written lucidly about the problems of anthropologists and professional educators in establishing acceptable working relationships for research; imagine the response sets established when the anthropologist presents himself to the educator with a request to make a study of the systematic inadvertent censorship system in *this* school.

over time and which deserve at least the dignity of recognition and decent burial if they are to be discarded.

A basic criticism of this paper is that too much is subsumed as education, and phenomena that probably must be included in whatever emerges as the domain of education are excluded, either explicitly or by implication. Although the term is not included in the glossary, education is defined in text as a function of " ... regularly recurring encounters (involving) ... two or more persons ... (coming) ... into face-to-face exchange ... recurrently over some duration ... " No attempt is made to establish a conceptual differentiation among the terms "enculturation," "socialization," "education." In his earlier paper, Gearing stated his disclaimer for boundaries most succinctly. He asserted that transaction and equivalence as analytic concepts will replace class concepts and that, while boundaries are "a problem, ... establishing such boundaries is a nuts-and-bolts logistic problem. The implication is that one wisely leaves it at that — and copes." This is an acceptable methodological position that is unsupportable as a general theory proposition unless the concept of theory itself is to be modified radically.

We are all too familiar with the problem of dealing with classes of abstractions; the more one deals with them, the more tortured the defining attributes seem and the less faith one has in concept boundaries. Consider for example, the problem of coping with socialization as defined by Mead (1963) and by Cohen (1971). Regardless of precise definition and without need for firm boundaries, important distinctions of the processes and contexts for learning cultural symbols and symbolic behaviors are identifiable within the concepts of enculturation and socialization as conceptually distinct from what is called education.

The present definition of encounters as the totality of the education system ignores these established concepts. One is left with the impression of intent to elevate education to a metalexical level referring to learnings (mappings?) acquired from regularly recurring interaction of one and all classes. Furthermore, one is left with the notion that regularly recurring interactions are primarily education behaviors. We are then required to include in the category of education (encounters) not only all formal and informal instructional situations and all the goal defining and instrumental activity developmental situations during human maturation but also such additional variable encounters as: the mother-infant nurture relationship; identification of significant others (kin, peers, we-they); procreative and recreative sexual encounters; a drink at the pub after work; adult utilization of institutionalized services (encounters with bus drivers, bank tellers, priests, bureaucrats, etc., *ad infinitum*), and avocational pursuits of leisure or retired members (chess, golf, card games, etc., again, *ad infinitum*).

All are encounters by terms of the definitions and disclaimers provided by Gearing et al. If we are expected to accept that all are thus, by definition, portions of the education system of the society, we move rapidly to the all-inclusive philosophical premise that "education is life" (learning?). That is nice cocktail party conversation, but hardly a serviceable theoretical construct for social science perspectives.

Even common usage has long since gone beyond the point of equating education with formal education (schooling). Yet, for all the broad and non-class-defined scope Working Paper 6 gives to the term, we find in the summary pages a strong assumption of the formal system as the education system. (We also find a minor but bothersome problem with useages such as parties for people, humans, individuals; with "concrete encounters" as a subset; and with the use of "education *work*." Implications of the last term are especially troublesome.) The question is whether or not there is a place in analytic terms for education? If so, in relation to other existing conceptualizations of learning, is education a parallel level of abstraction, a subset, or a replacement?

However and whatever else is included in a conceptualization of education, a pervasive connotation of preparation is included, either explicitly or implicitly; perhaps most often both (Herskovits 1947). This seems to be an essence of differentation from other developmental learnings. As one small illustration, consider the acquisition of language competence by a maturing neophyte. Control of the native language is acquired as a normal, although subculturally variable, developmental process. The multiplicity of forms and contexts for language performance and the attendant identity and aspiration learnings, whether acquired in school or elsewhere, seem to be another order or process; the multiple implicit cultural patternings inherent in the categorizations, order and structure of language (e.g., in English, the active-passive implications; the past-present-future time differentiations) constitute yet another order of adaptive pattern. Functioning as an adult in any given society may well include further "education," but it will be uniquely and systematically patterned partially as a result of variables in the preparation language experiences provided during maturation.

Reference to the learning experiences provided leads to the second level of problem presented by the definition of education as exclusively a function of face-to-face interchange (encounters), specifically, Gearing's "educated guess" (one wonders peripherally which encounters "educated" that guess) that ". . . mass media can be safely excluded . . . [because] . . . however an item of information or skill may come to impinge on a man's central nervous system, that item gets reworked in face-to-face interchange, its meanings there get established . . ." Elsewhere, the working paper acknowledges that learning results from interaction with the environment. But the model as presented appears to ignore the domains of introspection, projection, fantasy, and dream, to say nothing of the multiplicy of nonverbal message systems (Hall 1959), which may consitute important learnings, especially about behavioral limitations. Such learnings are not necessarily reworked in face-to-face interchanges in order to become portions of shared and transmitted repertoires. The formulations presented are useful for analysis of interaction and encounters as social processes, but the general cultural theory of education refers to the totality of distribution of information and skill. Particularly in relation to mass media, it seems unsupportable to assume that information acquires meaning only by being "reworked in face-to-face interchange." This is not to say that encounters are not powerful verification contexts in shaping patterns of adaptations, but rather, to point out that encounters cannot be isolated as the necessary or sufficient categories of contexts for provision of education in a cultural system if one expects to make any specific sense out of the concept of education. Herskovits, in his above cited classic and widely reprinted definitive work, provides a caution particularly relevant to Gearing's paper. "We must, therefore, be as cautious in evaluating definitions of education that are too inclusive, such as that which holds this process to be 'the relationship between members of successive generations' as in accepting definitions that are drawn too narrowly."

Numerous other comments that could be made are within a context of further definition and refinement of the methodology of encounter analysis which I continue to feel has a high potential and about which Gearing has said a lot that makes good sense. My essentially negative response thus far is mostly confined to the level of assumptions implied by presenting this as a *general* cultural theory. My projections of the best possible outcome is that rather than establishing *theory* by the simple process of assertion, disclaimer, and selective ignoring, it would be preferable to see a major effort of reexamining concepts of culture and education within the context of a growing body of data derived from encounter analyses. One might begin with Chapman and Counts' (1924) naturalistic conceptualization of the evolutionary patterns of education among human cultures and identify conceptual threads of culture and education to Weaver and White's (1972) analysis of the potential and shortcomings for uses of anthropological (and sociological) theory in urban complex societies. Further, one could turn to Bohannan's (1973) proposal for rethinking the concept of culture.

A lot of theory has been generated; much of it is discarded or reformulated. A great deal of theory that is reformulated is susceptible of verification or further reformulation by means of encounter analyses.

COMMENT *by Gerard Rosenfeld*

> One afternoon Gerard Rosenfeld and one of the editors discussed "A General Cultural Theory of Education" as presented by Gearing et al., in Working Paper 6. The transcription of that tape-recorded conversation presented below is taken from that discussion. In the early part of the conversation, Rosenfeld addresses the subject, and then, toward the end of the discussion, he is questioned by the editor. Rosenfeld's comments, in some parts have been edited, and portions of the tape recording have been omitted. We are grateful to Rosenfeld for his assistance in helping us prepare this version of our discussion and his patience with any stylistic changes in his presentation that resulted from our need in some instances to summarize rather than to transcribe.

It is a very serious undertaking, and Gearing et al. are certainly to be commended for such a monumental effort. There's a problem involved, however, in taking on the totality of human life when you call what you're doing a general theory of cultural transmission. The implication, even in the title, is that you're going to give an explanation of what it is generically to be human. The theory does not do that.

I could ask, should this be called a theory of cultural transmission? Should it be called a theory of social structure? For that's one of the things that the theory purports to speak to — the unequal distribution of propertylike and non-propertylike (to use their terms) bits of information. Should it be called a theory of knowledge? Well, it is not any of these, and that is why it is not being called that. But I think that even what it is being called is a little too embracing and a little too large, given what at this point their information is. What the theory, I think, does is explicate process.

What I get from the theory is the following: People engage in certain kinds of encounters. The nature of human life is such that you have to be made human in order to be human, so these encounters begin from one's earliest experiences. One could specify in some typical order, the stages of the life cycle, either in one culture or across cultures, facilitating talk about how these encounters and transactions take place. In other words, they speak of them in vague and broad and undefinable terms. There are encounters. Well, between whom? The answer could be "between anybody." The point is, are these encounters characteristically the same or different throughout the life cycle? Is the encounter between a mother and a child the same as between a mother and a mother or is it the same as between that mother and child twenty years later? These are the kinds of filler, or what I could call content, that are not yet, as best I know, part of the data from which the theory has been built.

In my judgment, the theory needs more cross-cultural and culturally specific ethnographic examples of what is meant.

The authors do not suggest in Working Paper 6 what the societal task is.

What are the things that all peoples must accomplish to survive? What I'm suggesting is that there are categories of information that all peoples must pass on to members of the group. We should identify those (and implicit in what I'm saying is that others have tried to do so). We could then try to apply the theory to these areas of content and see if this theory, which is process, matches up with these areas of content. This would then also give it cultural context. In other words, can we identify categories of information and actions that characterize human life? If so, then the encounters, the agendas, the transactions, and the other things they say have contextual meaning; they can be seen against specific and particular kinds of conditions historically, presently, and cross-culturally. This is not evident in Working Paper 6.

Gearing suggests that educational systems are essentially conservative. According to him, educational systems apportion information and delegate privilege in order to reenact a given social structure. I think we could all accept that. But how does it get that way? There is no discussion of cultural antecedent, of historic process. The differences among people are, we often say, a result of differentials in their experience. What Gearing et al. are trying to do is apply a theory across cultures without examining the differential in those cultures' historic experiences. And if I wanted to consider the dialectic as spoken of by Marx with respect to knowledge and political structures and so forth, then I would probably denounce the theory as totally irrelevant. It does not take up those issues at all. In other words, it does not answer the question — why? Why is this so? Why do cultures apportion knowledge and privilege and skill? Is it a conscious act? Is it something that is part of the biology of the organism? What is it? How information is selected and who will get it is a matter of a group's world view which in turn is a matter of that group's experience. This is not explainable in terms of the theory as it now stands.

Let me mention two pieces of work that, though they do not call themselves theories, speak to some of the same issues and might be taken into consideration in a reworking of this theory for the purpose of making it more formidable.

One work is Jules Henry's article (1960), "A cross-cultural outline of education," which originally appeared in *Current Anthropology*. Henry tries to survey examples from different cultures as they are written in the literature and to describe how people pass on their heritage. He considered not only how individuals become like other members of the group but how these procedures vary in the different cultures. Some of those who have been working on the general cultural theory of education have had specific experiences, e.g., Tom Carroll (1976). Somehow these ought to be incorporated in the theory, and beyond that, generalized to larger instances not solely their own. This brings me to another concern I have, namely, that much of what the theory says is drawn from observations among relatively young people — that is, schoolchildren, basketball players, and teachers. There is a lack of observation of adult and adult, between employee and employer.

Another work to which I would refer the theorists is Melville Herskovits' book (1947), *Man and his works* — the section called "Education and the Sanctions of Custom." In this work, Herskovits made various kinds of generalizations about cultural transmission. But what Herskovits does is absent here, and should be thought about, that is, to define the areas of content that all societies must deal with, the problems that every people must respond to. There are certain things that all people must handle in order to survive. Then one can begin to think how information along those categories of content is passed on. Some of the areas are:

1. All people must respond to their environment; they have to cope with their environment, so all people have technology.

2. All people must handle the problems of communication, verbal and nonverbal; all members of the group must learn how to speak, somehow to communicate.

3. All people must handle the problem of individual and group crisis, whether with respect to illness and health, bodily function, maturation, and so forth.

4. All people are concerned with status acquisition and have certain prescriptions about who will hold what status and at what points in the life cycle.

5. All people have to handle the division of labor along the axes of sex, age, etc.

If we were to take those areas — let us say, bodily function, illness and health, and worldview — if we take those areas of content, does the theory apply? This is what I would like to see done. Then the theory would have some meaning for me.

It is as if they were saying, here are the rules of baseball — there are three outs, there are balls and strikes, and so on. But it does not tell you anything about playing baseball. You have the rules of the game, but you can't really get a feel for it or know what the game is about. That is what I think about the theory. It is a framework, and it needs substance and content. It needs the designation of specific substantive areas to which it can be applied and either verified or not, expanded or not, or abandoned or not.

For me, it is not a theory. It is a set of rules about how educational transactions take place. It is not an explanation of why they take place; it is just how they take place. We have a description of the phenomena as these are played out but no causal descriptions. There is no discussion of historical and cultural antecedent — how do cultural premises (I would call it worldview) come about? Consider the education process "image," that Gearing et al. present:

Any item of simple information or skill can move from any physically normal adult or child to any other without special effort, virually automatically; where such items do not move, tangible barriers exist; these barriers are raised by the parties themselves, conjointly; the barriers, once raised, block also the movement of more complex items; the cumulative result is an uneven distribution of all information and skill.

The implication in that axiom is that inevitably this will occur. That may be the case, and again I would say it does not occur randomly. It occurs because there are historic, political, and economic causes for these things. For example, different peoples perceive childhood differently. Generally speaking, in the United States we perceive children as subadults, incapable of adult tendencies. Other cultures perceive children as miniature adults, capable at their own level of all adult tendencies. The kinds of things that are transmitted to children are transmitted on the basis of that premise. So again, Henry might say, as he has in some of the things he has written, that he has known children who at the age of three and four understood the meaning of death.

My reactions to this theory have remained rather consistent over the months. I still feel with each subsequent phrasing, the same problems have to be addressed. How were the particular events and situations selected? How were the categories of labels for explication chosen; that is, what gave rise to the term "agenda" and so on? Are these in fact the best terms to use?

The authors of the manuscript focus on what is usually referred to as microanalysis. But these processes, defined by the labels they attach to them, agendas, transactions, etc., are they labels that have come out of their observations? Are they the things that typify what they have observed and seen or read about or thought about or, in fact, can they make the distinction any more? The encounters and agendas are extrapolated after the fact and are not necessarily contrived experiences that people consciously bear in mind. Gearing would reply that, we don't say that they are, but that should be made more emphatic. What categories of events and behaviors were omitted that would either support or make the theory more formidable, and which are needed for further examination?

Let me give what may be a strange example: How about an encounter between a person and a ghost? For some people, ghosts live — they are everywhere. The deceased are present. Have we defined every category of encounter or every category of relationship? Could Adam Kendon film the spatial deportment of a man and the ghost to whom he speaks? In other words, the whole area of religion and the supernatural is not necessarily explicable in terms of this theory. Yet we learn about religion and we do derive worldview and so on with respect to it.

The authors have observed a few ethnographic instances bearing on the theory. We need some other comparable instances.

Consider Tindall's work (1975) on Ute-Mormon basketball playing, for example. Examine that in another context. Go down to a playground and watch black kids play basketball to see if the same kinds of things can be applied to their play. For a theory to have wide application, this must be done. If a theory does not have wide application, it is not a theory.

I am especially concerned that the theory does not deal well with social change. Consider, in reference to Proposition 8, the following statement from Gearing:

Where, in any society, any new item of information or skill arises and becomes identified as belonging to a category of information, or where an old item is reidentified as to category, the flow of such an item is regularly blocked by the education system as all other items in that category are regularly blocked.

I think Gearing is bound by his notion of schooling. There can be shifts in who initiates to whom. For example, changes in technology are such that, in a military context, it may now be a corporal who has more knowledge, say, about space technology, than an officer, and thus there may be shifts in who initiates to whom, in encounters between the corporal and a captain or a major. And it is not necessarily true that information that fits one category or another will be transmitted in the same way as that fitting another category. Because the school serves to do that, it is not necessarily the case in other contexts. Consider the women's movement, or the youth movement and the drug culture — or even the entire decade of the Sixties, specifically, blacks and civil rights in the Sixties. What was so troublesome about that whole period to the dominant white society is that blacks were initiating action to the dominant culture, namely whites. There were lunchcounter sit-ins, boycotts, and other similar activities.

I would rather restate Proposition 8 as follows: "As information proliferates, the techniques by which this is distributed equally become proliferated." Even within the context of school, one can talk about peer teachers, paraprofessionals. These are new kinds of accommodations. They may not be significant or profound, but they can take place, and they represent shifts in how information is transmitted.

Sangree: Are you suggesting that sheer mass of new information can be a spur or a trigger of change in the way information is distributed, and that there are probably other such triggers or elements of change as well?
Rosenfeld: Yes.
Sangree: So you have suggested sheer accumulation of knowledge as a factor, and I can understand that in the area of space technology — that is, in discussing the change in initiation patterns between corporal and officer. But what could we pick out as a comparable factor in changes

in who-initiates-to-whom patterns in say the woman's movement or in black-white relations. Could you think of one? I can't at the moment.

Rosenfeld: Let me put it this way. It is probably true to say that cultures are forged by adults. This is true for any number of reasons — for one, they are physically superior to children. In almost no society do you find children telling adults what to do. It is not children who manufacture or contrive a collective worldview and then tell adults they will have to conform to the children. But we have seen at least the beginnings of that in this culture with the civil rights movement and the antiwar movement. Young people were reversing the initiation-response pattern. Where a stable agenda might have existed, a troublesome agenda arose. And the categories of information that were heretofore open only on a particular level, e.g., sex, are now being expanded.

Sangree: Is it possible to draw out of that discussion something comparable to sheer mass as the factor influencing the initiation-response pattern. If there is a switch in the initiation of interaction between generations, what is the factor?

Rosenfeld: The factor is more knowledge.

Sangree: You think, again, it is mass, i.e., more knowledge?

Rosenfeld: Yes, Gearing says, "Bodies of information and skill are in all societies perpetually changing," to which we could add "getting larger." "But how that body gets distributed," says Gearing, "and the wide-ranging implications of that remains by the regular operations of the education system unchanged." And I'm saying that's not true.

Sangree: You're saying that just the change in size of the body of information can cause change in the way information is distributed.

Rosenfeld: That's right. Now, maybe one, in turn, would argue that, as the mass of knowledge increases, the individual experiences a smaller totality or smaller segment of the totality, and selection is even more deliberately and specifically made, that agendas are erected that perpetuate what has been going on. But it doesn't always work that way. There are some things that people learn now that they did not learn before. This is something Margaret Mead (1970) talks about in *Culture and commitment.* There are teaching societies and learning societies. Our society could be thought of as a society where we administer to kids. In smaller scale societies, the individual wants to know that which he must know because he sees the whole model structure before him. As we become more specialized, a smaller totality of that which is available comes to the individual. The techniques by which this will be transmitted begin to vary. And so there are events in the world now, because they are by definition world events, that come to children and adults simultaneously. Heretofore, it would have been adults who decided what came to children and in what sequence.

Sangree: Have we a second factor here in addition to the mass of the information, namely, timing?

Rosenfeld: Timing that is dependent upon the means and media by which this information is transmitted. New techniques of information transmission have as a possible result the imparting of information to adults and children simultaneously, that which had previously been transmitted by adults to children. This could lead to a shift in initiation and response patterns as in the youth movement. Here I obviously have in mind mass media, and Gearing and the others specifically exclude mass media from their consideration. But new techniques of information dissemination lead to new considerations of information. What had formerly been adult knowledge given to children by adults might now be categorized as "world events" that all should know simultaneously. You can see the implications for shifts in patterns of initiation and response. The accumulation of knowledge alone forces shifts in information transmission.

Gearing says, "In no society do humans encounter one another at random. In any society, constraints operate so as to enjoin regularly occurring encounters between and among some kinds of persons and to hinder or disallow encounters among others. In principle, this makes it possible to map, for any society, group, or wider network, an encounter profile." This is a very important notion. Has this been done? Have Gearing et al. tried to map an encounter profile? I think it should be done. Once one maps an encounter profile one can apply all the other processes that the theory claims transpire. Consider for example, child-to-child and child-to-mother encounters. The object would be to see if each of these categorical labels — open agendas, stable agendas, etc. — can be applied. That would be very important. Of course, when you go into a cross-cultural experience, there are different kinds of encounters so you would wind up with a worldwide sampling of encounters. As I said before, we would not speak of an encounter between a person and a ghost, but others would.

If you simply observe two people interacting, they may act as if they accept and understand the nature of their transaction when, in fact, they do not. People may share the labels for what they are doing but not necessarily share their understanding or approval or disapproval of these labels. What is the true meaning of this sharing? Is it what it is perceived to be by the observer on the basis of his interpretation of how people are interacting, or is it the perception of the people actually in the encounter?

Does the theory bring the covert and overt together in some understandable fashion? How do we know when sharing is taking place? The theory does not necessarily tell us. The theory tells us that if there is no troublesome agenda, then we are sharing. Stable agendas imply sharing. But this is not necessarily so. There may, in fact, be a stable agenda because people do not share perceptions but do not want to get in one another's way. And, because they don't share perceptions, they want to avoid problems, and this may seem like a stable agenda. People may share different cultural premises, recognize this, and adjust their encounters so they appear to be experiencing a stable agenda.

Henry has spoken of this. In speaking of spontaneity and creativity in the American classroom — a topic discussed also in Spindler's book *Education and culture* (1963) — Henry presents an anecdote in which children are playing a game called "spelling baseball." One child tells on another for talking. The teacher believes this and punishes the accused, whereas, in fact, the one reporting the infraction was sitting where she could not observe the culprit. What is going on here? Is the child believed because anyone telling on a member of her own team would not be apt to lie? What the motivation is, I can imagine, e.g., ingratiation with members of the other team. The point is that the incident illustrates that a lot is going on in this classroom other than a language arts lesson. This is an example of multiphasic learning. On the surface, it is a language arts lesson, and people may be sharing premises in reference to the lesson — it is good to be able to spell, etc. But all these others things are going on, and Henry's point is that these are the significant things that are being learned. Schooling in these kinds of contexts actually serves to have kids grow away from one another rather than toward each other.

In addition, it is uncertain that the team is itself made up of persons sufficiently diverse, ethnically and in other ways, to take a really wide view of the entire educational transmission process. There are no blacks and no Spanish speakers. This is not said to fault the researchers at all. In fact, their integrity and capability lends more credence to their effort. It is merely that the focus of their concerns is essentially molded by their cultural premises — e.g., a relative absence (or perhaps, it is unstated) of concern for social class as it relates to who gets what information under what circumstances, for what purposes, and with what results. I think their response might be that they were not really concerned with this. If so, I would be correct, I think.

COMMENT *by John Singleton with the Pittsburgh Student Group: Margaret Gibson, Leslie Posner, Alice Troup, Gregory LeRoy, Theodora St. Lawrence*

> John Singleton suggested that he and a number of his students hold a seminar to consider Working Paper 6. The seminar was tape-recorded and transcribed. Singleton and his students and the editor have edited the transcript.

Singleton: This is an ad hoc group of education and anthropology doctoral students and one professor responding to Working Paper 6 by Fred Gearing and his associates. We're sitting in a small room. We are locked in for the next hour and we have developed an agenda for responding to the paper so that we can organize some of our random comments.

The first item is to talk about definitions relating to education and educational systems, since we have seen what we think are some discontinuities in the use of these terms throughout the paper. Second, there are some more concerns about definitions of other terms used — transaction, process, culture, and social change. Third, there is a question about the assumptions underlying the model of social identity presented in the paper. Fourth, there is a concern about formal theory and theory development. Fifth, there is a question about the inclusion of the bureaucratic hierarchy analogy but not the continuation of it into other kinds of organizations. Finally, there is a concern about social change and education.

We begin with the definition of education and the educational system.

Gibson: The authors give the definition of an encounter and then they go on to say that the "education system of any society is the totality of all regularly occurring encounters." Presumably we are talking about education not just within the school system, in schooling, but also in the larger society, so that any encounter that occurs regularly — as when I go to work at the US Office of Education — is presumably within what Gearing calls the education system. But I don't understand why that is a system. Maybe that's education. But is all of education, in his term, a part of a system?

Singleton: As I see it, the basic definition, is that "the education system of any society is the totality of all regularly occurring encounters," and that those encounters occur "where two or more persons come into face-to-face exchange, and where any two or more of these same persons do so recurrently over some duration." That the regularly occurring encounters are equal to the education system is a very interesting concept, however, in a couple of places in the paper, the educational system is referred to differently. At one point, the authors talk about "the illusion enjoyed in some societies that education is a vehicle, even the principal vehicle, of social change" — the authors seem to be switching to the folk view of education rather than making a reference to the educational system which is what I think the authors intended. It seemed to me that the authors were speaking specifically of the schools.

Gibson: I am still having problems with the system. I am thinking somewhat of Dr. Rolland Paulston's terminology (1972b) that there is education that is not systematized, particularly when he discusses informal education versus nonformal education versus formal education — all of which for him is schooling. Informal education as some of the socialization things we talk about is education, but it is not necessarily part of an education system. Do you disagree with me?

Troup: There are some things in the definition that I think have to be brought out a little differently than either of you have done. If you look at Gearing's definition of education as culture transmission, there are two things that are important. One is that he is not talking about content; he is not talking about what *is*. Now, you are suggesting that a system of education is intended learning of some kind, and that is content, a specific piece of knowledge, or whatever; it is part of content. But he is not talking about content; he is talking about the process of education — what goes on in situations or what goes on in specific contexts, when something called transaction, when something called education happens. And I think that it is not a content – it is a process.

Gibson: I am not concerned about the content. I am concerned about the word "system," I guess.

Troup: But system to you implies content, doesn't it? The intended transmission of some content?

Gibson: I am less concerned about the content than about the structure that is.

LeRoy: I suggest that what Greta (Gibson) seems to be saying is that the word "system" in her terms, or the author's terms, seems to be synonymous with some form of institutionalization as opposed to patterned processes. I think if I were writing this paper, at least in these initial pages, I might substitute the word "process" for the word "system" as it is used here. As I see it, what Gearing is talking about is, in fact, a process, as you just said, and not a system, as I understand it.

Gibson: At least Gearing should define how he means to use the word "system."

Troup: I would certainly agree with the idea that Gearing is trying to identify patterned processes, and be those affective, linguistic, or whatever, it is not content, but rather, the processes that go on. Content is irrelevant.

Singleton: I think that content is not in question, but the use of the word "system" by Gearing is as the social scientists' concept of "system," where all things are interconnected. It is not related to the formalization of organizations, even in what we are calling nonformal education; I see that as a kind of sidetrack. I'm concerned when Gearing talks about how the "education system, principally through testing and issuing of credentials in whatever form these take in the society, acts as gatekeeper, selecting persons for life careers in the various sectors of the society." It is not regularly occurring encounters that select people out, but rather, it is schools that select people out. Formal educational institutions, and sometimes nonformal, in the terms that educators are using, select people out and act as gatekeepers primarily for various economic careers. This is a different thing, and you cannot talk about that system in the same words you use when you talk about a process as a regular series of occurrences. You have to, somehow or other, hold back from what appears to be the meaning; a kind of folk definition of education continues to creep in here, namely, that education equals schooling, education equals formal schooling.

Posner: When you keep saying the word "folk image," are you using his introductory usage of it?

Singleton: Yes, I think so. And I like the introductory usage of folk image, because it seems to be very true that there are alternative conceptions. I like very much the suggestion that maybe we ought to look at how information and skills and knowledge are blocked rather than the ways in which they are transmitted. We have always assumed that education is a simple business of pouring something from one pitcher into the next, and we talk as if we operate our schools that way. But the suggestion that we really ought to look at the ways in which we are raising barriers rather than creating channels seems to be highly appropriate. What do schools do? What functions do they perform? Gearing suggests that we ought to look at the functions schools perform relative to hindering the flow of information rather than at the functions they perform in transmitting it. Greta, you wanted to ask about transaction.

Gibson: Where Gearing defines it, he says: "A transaction is any interchange between parties wherein the relationship between them changes." I guess I need to know more about what "changes" means. I am not quite sure how I know when the relationship has changed between two people.

Troup: It could change for the better or it could break off.

Gibson: And in both cases, it would be a transaction. If I knew it had changed, it would be a transaction. Then I could also begin to subdivide or classify types of transactions. But I am not quite sure when something is a transaction versus another exchange that is not a transaction.

Troup: Yes, when we were talking before, I was thinking of a transaction as being a positive thing, something that would only occur when people came closer to each other, but I guess it might be possible to have transactions where people would end up never speaking again. But I don't know if transaction is used that way.

Gibson: What is meant here by transaction may be very different from what I am used to, which is the word "event," used by Jacquetta Burnett (1972) in an article she wrote. With her definition, at least you know when the event begins and when it ends. Burnett also has categories for labelling the people who are involved at the occurrence and for determining whether it happens on a recurring basis. But even this is just, at least for me, sort of mushy — I don't know how to draw a boundary around a transaction — how to recognize it when I stumble upon it.

Singleton: You are looking for a set of criteria to distinguish a transaction when it is occurring in front of you.

Troup: Transaction — there is a whole body of literature on it. It comes out of communications theory, doesn't it?

Gibson: I am not sure it is used that consistently though.

Singleton: Transaction is a scientific term to describe particular kinds of behaviors.

St. Lawrence: But Gearing is using it in a more strictly economic sense.

Posner: I was thinking of one of the papers that the Buffalo group working with Gearing has on teacher education in the Montessori school and the definition about who controls the agenda. It seems that one can't talk about transaction when one person is so much in control. That a transaction is more like information giving, where someone obviously is recognized as having the upper hand, and there is no possibility of change.

St. Lawrence: On the authority's part.

Gibson: But you may change. The person in the subordinate position may be changed. Do you think there has to be change from both sides? Maybe there does.

Posner: No. But it would seem that where somebody is obviously in authority and is giving out information, and where the subordinate person obviously accepts the authority, one would say that the superordinate person is controlling the agenda and that transaction.

St. Lawrence: I think that transaction contains an implication of possibilities for negotiation, possibilities for change, and that a nontransactional situation occurs when somebody is in control to such an extent that no change is possible.

Gibson: This is what I asked Alice (Troup). Do you have encounters when you don't have transactions? And you felt that, yes, it was possible.

Singleton: When we talk about encounters and transactions in those terms, our total life is lived in encounters and transactions.

Posner: Yes, but that is supportive of the whole idea of lifelong education.

Singleton: That was the definition of education, of all of our encounters. We are not talking about education then; we are talking about life.

Posner: I wonder.

St. Lawrence: I remember the use of the word "reciprocal." When the authors talked about reciprocal — there is a lot to play with. You could get into all the material about reciprocity, and when is something a gift, and that kind of thing. That could articulate very interestingly with this hierarchy business.

Singleton: The definition of transaction as given in the glossary does not refer to a kind of economic model. Reading from the glossary, we have the definition: "Transaction occurs during an encounter as long as the relationship between the parties is unsettled and changing; that is, in the course of an encounter, there may be (1) a transaction episode leading to (2) a settled pattern of behavior, an agenda of some kind, the latter interspersed with (3) monitoring interludes, and as the situation may later shift, a new transaction episode leading toward a new agenda. Transaction always proceeds at both explicit and tacit levels, always involves both verbal and nonverbal communication, is always constrained within broad limits by the formal statuses and roles of the parties." I have the feeling that transaction is what Gearing was talking about in the earlier Council on Anthropology and Education paper (Gearing 1973) when he discussed the various areas of communication.

Gibson: He used the term "transaction" in that paper.

St. Lawrence: He talks about agendas as being reciprocal, and then he starts talking about information as property.

Singleton: Information as property is a separate way of classifying information, of understanding what information gets transmitted during a transaction.

LeRoy: It is too bad we don't have a blackboard in here. We could actually draw a hierarchy of these concepts; I think that would be very helpful. I'm not certain, for example, how the word "agenda" as it is being used here relates to the meaning of transaction. For example, Gearing writes: "... what the two parties of any dyad regularly transact are education agendas." I'm not quite certain what that means or implies.

Troup: I did attempt to sketch this out when I was going over it — beginning where he is working with the education process — and he defines it as having to be a face-to-face thing, thereby taking out education that relates to learning through reading. Another characteristic is that education is a turn-taking, and there must be a public dyad. It also involves transaction. I really am not sure how all this comes to be an agenda, but the agenda is the patterning of the reciprocal behavior, how the behavior is patterned in the face-to-face situation — that is the turn-taking part of the patterning. Then there is the public dyad, how one relates to other people in relation to set statuses and to other people looking on. So a transaction has to do with putting all those together. It is an arranging of the agreement about how people are going to interact with each other.

St. Lawrence: The agenda is reciprocal, and in this respect, it makes sense. To become an agenda, there has to be a certain amount of reciprocity.

Troup: Reciprocity may be simply that I give in. I shall accept you as the authority, and I'll give in. That might be the way I reciprocate.

Singleton: Withdrawal from this is, I think, what the authors are referring to as liminality.

Student: I could not understand that very well.

Singleton: Gearing's basic example of liminality is the withdrawal that occurs in a troublesome agenda. Somebody sits back and becomes passive, does not really get involved in changing relationships — refuses to be drawn into it.

St. Lawrence: I'm wondering if liminality is a word that had some other referent. It might help us to understand why liminality was chosen to name this process.

Singleton: While we're looking at liminality, the other definitions that you had problems with are process, culture, and social change. Alice, did you want to speak to those specifically?

Troup: I think I have said quite a bit about process already. I think that the effort is to identify the process of education. And I am not sure that this has been done. The only thing that seems to relate to it is the idea of negotiating the agendas. My notes are directional here, but it seems to me that the agenda model is set up by putting together two contingency tables and thus defining three kinds of agendas — open agendas, stable agendas, and troublesome agendas. An open agenda occurs where simple information and skills diffuse randomly, but I am not sure what that means. I have trouble understanding what random diffusion through a population is (unless you're talking about genetics).

Singleton: How about language?

St. Lawrence: Yes, but that's not random. Language transmission is hierarchical in terms of parents teaching children, and it is systematically done.

Singleton: You talk about this, but parents don't — they really don't — teach. Remember where kids do get language? They learn language from their total environment, from whom ever happens to be around. When parents take the trouble to teach children explicitly, they are not really transmitting anything. They are going through certain kinds of models that they think are important. But the kids really pick up the language on their own, and it is not something that somebody has to devise a school in our society for teaching. Kids come to school already speaking their mother language.

St. Lawrence: Kids get reinforced for talking. If they didn't get reinforced for talking, then we might get something similar to a random distribution of language.

Singleton: There is a random distribution, particularly in the sense of a larger social system in which there may be competing languages.

St. Lawrence: If something is random, does it imply that sometimes it doesn't happen?

Singleton: No, I'm assuming that Gearing is talking about things that are automatically diffused.

St. Lawrence: Oh, but random and automatically diffused are not the same thing. Anything that would be considered automatic, I would also consider systematic. Things that you must guarantee to get done have to be systematized.

Singleton: There is a system. It is this open agenda he is talking about that is the least interesting of the agendas because it automatically takes place. There are no blockages to it, other than extraordinary physical ones, physical handicaps.

Troup: So now, we come to the stable agenda, which is hierarchical and systematic. Finally, we consider the troublesome agenda. A troublesome agenda, interestingly, means partly systematic and partly haphazard. I don't quite understand how, if you are talking about one culture at that troublesome level (which is truly troublesome), part of it is systematized and part of it is haphazard. Yet, that is what Gearing says. That brings in the idea of social identity. The troublesome agenda seems to arise from some kind of conflict or at least miscommunication or noncommunication due to differences in social identity. To me, that was a very intriguing thing to bring in, because I think that I read social identity through differences in age, sex, class, or whatever within the culture. But I think Gearing interprets social identity as also being how one deals with subculture. And when the subcultures are brought into this, one obviously will have a different kind of troublesome agenda, because the larger the social identity is, the greater the potential differences.

LeRoy: I am wondering if perhaps it wouldn't be to our benefit, and also to Gearing, if we could use some concrete examples. I am not quite certain that I grasp what you are saying. I think my most basic confusion relates to the contingency table in which Gearing, dichotomizes the two dimensions that he claims are relevant to the structuring of either open or filtering agendas. I am not certain this is true whether for example, social identity is either a "yes" or a "no" situation. If, for example, I am talking to Greta, obviously Greta does not share certain complements of social identity with me, the sex factor being the most obvious.

Singleton: Interesting —

LeRoy: It may not be, however, salient.

Singleton: Salient identity may change from encounter to encounter.

LeRoy: Yes, but it seems quite possible that, when people share certain relevant social identity characteristics and do not share others, that this would, in fact, affect the encounter situation, the kind of information that is transmitted.

Singleton: What you are saying is that you can't draw up a table of encounters such as Gearing has done because anybody coming to an encounter has a variety of identities, and during an encounter, any one or more of those identities may be brought to the surface depending on what happens within the encounter. We just had an identity separate from education-anthropology doctoral candidate suddenly intruding on us when we said there were sex differences, and the sex differences became relevant as part of the conversation. Other kinds of differences will come in, too. Like when I raise my voice, and everybody else sits down and is quiet because I am the professor. I can use this identity rather than my identity as a colleague. At other times, I can sit back and let you carry the weight of the discussion and not assume this identity.

Troup: I was asked for an example earlier, and I think I have one from some of the material that Jacquetta Burnett has talked about. It has to do with eye contact patterns. I suppose you could look at the fact that in most school systems teachers expect kids to look at them when they're conversing. Maybe this is randomly diffused, maybe it is systematized, maybe my mother said to me, "Alice, look at me when I'm talking to you." Anyway, my looking at somebody's eyes is indicative that I am giving him or her my attention. But, among the Puerto Rican kids that Burnett was looking at — they were *not* looking at her. The respect for adults and authority meant that you kept your eyes down. Therefore, all of the teacher's cues about the communication were missed by these kids; it wasn't a reciprocally transacted thing.

Singleton: It was a troublesome agenda.

Troup: Yes, it was a troublesome agenda. And you see the kids who are looking at their teachers have gotten this idea, randomly or systematically. But the Puerto Rican kids don't have it. If you looked at the environment that the Puerto Rican kids came from, their looking down would be randomly or systematically done, but it would make sense to them. Furthermore, an Illinois farm kid sitting in a Puerto Rican classroom would get in a lot of trouble for being aggressive and threatening toward the teacher. That is what I am trying to say here: It is more than just the social identity. Does this make sense?

St. Lawrence: I think it depends on how you define social identity because one of the identities can be your ethnic identity. The question is whether you want to emphasize that identity or whether you even have the option to not emphasize it. It may not be a conscious thing.

Troup: I think the point I am trying to make is, if you have choice in the social identity that you assume, then you can probably transact or encounter or agenda better than if you don't.

Gibson: But it is not just one thing; it is not that you are going to manifest your maleness versus your professorhood or whatever. They are all together.

Singleton: Exactly. Consider the problem of boy students in a female teacher's classroom. We get the problem of what the boys are learning from the female teacher, although she is not projecting herself as female at an explicit level. Yet, tacitly, as Gearing points out, a lot of things are happening. And it is at a tacit level that the agendas can become troublesome between the female model and the male student.

Troup: Or vice versa.

Singleton: Shall we go on to formal theory development? Teddy (St. Lawrence), you were raising the question about how this theory of cultural transmission and education comes into some kind of theory status. I am not sure how you were raising that question.

St. Lawrence: Well, it seems to me that there is a hole in the middle of the thing. As Alice said earlier, this is, in many cases, a macrotheory, but it is being approached in this paper in some very micro ways. My point is that none of the key propositions have been proved, and quite possibly none can be. This is rather frightening because this project involves a lot of work. I am not sure if it is all going to come out the way it should — the way anyone wants it to come out.

Singleton: Well, is there a problem with definition of theory, with what theory is? Alice was talking about that.

LeRoy: Well, I am sort of thinking out loud. I am not really sure what Teddy is referring to. I would say that one of the fundamental tenets of theory is that the propositions must somehow be linked to the empirical level of analysis. Somehow, the propositions have to be capable of being stated hypothetically. This has been my kind of ideal conception of what theory is all about, and perhaps what is lacking are these linkages to the empirical level. Is that essentially what you're saying?

St. Lawrence: Yes. I see a macro theory, which looks very nice, and I see a kind of micro methodology. But I don't see how you get from point A to point B, because I don't see them necessarily following from one another. More important, I don't see the macro being built out of the micro in any logical way.

Troup: Yes, I think maybe the problem is that the macro theory has a lot of things in it. It has a lot of concepts, or analytical constructs, or notions, or whatever the word is. There are a lot of them there — it is a very wide thing, and you can see how to operationalize very small parts of it. The hypotheses in the other papers that Gearing's students have done involved the operationalization, and they used very small units. The question is whether or not the whole system is ever going to relate to the small hypotheses that we can envision working with. Maybe that overall isn't bad. In fact, working with the micro units may help to redefine the theory. I guess it is possible to summarize Freud's theory in one sentence. I suppose one could say that the subconscious affects human behavior, or something like that. I don't know if the words are right, but one might possibly get Freud's idea across in one sentence. I'm not sure that one can ever get this across in one sentence; there are too many things going on in it.

LeRoy: Well, I am not sure that is what is intended to be done with Gearing's theory. I think you would severely adulterate the meaning of Freud's work if you attempted to reduce it to a couple of key phrases.

Singleton: How about Karl Marx?

LeRoy: The same would be true of Marx, or Durkheim, or of any theorist.

Singleton: There is not a one sentence —

LeRoy: You could say Marx interpreted history in terms of economics.

Troup: Marx said it himself — from each according to his ability, to each according to his needs.

Singleton: But that is not a theory. That was his goal, and you have a whole background of implications of this, as you study economic history. To study education as a form of encounters generally would seem to me to be the purpose here. To get at it and to get down to the level at which we are dealing with education requires a whole variety of steps. This is your macro to micro thread. It requires some kind of thoroughly elaborate interpretation, but no more or no less elaborate than was developed by the theory builders of the past. What we have here, it seems to me, may not be the final model of an education theory. What we have is what it has claimed to be —namely, a working paper aimed toward developing the kinds of thinking that have to go into the development of theory. How does one begin to get at that? With this kind of working theory one of the ways in which it gets built is to have people test it out, to try working with it; whether it's a student developing a dissertation or whether it is a group of colleagues sitting around the table discussing it. You have to find a way to see what the theory implies; work with those implications, and then work back at the theory. Whether this becomes one grand theory building effort or whether it becomes a small step along the way to somebody else's theory is almost irrelevant.

St. Lawrence: In terms of theory building, I guess I would like to see some indication of how the theory is going to be built back up from the micro level. What are you going to do with all this? Where is it all going?

Singleton: At the moment, we're trying to conceptualize it, to categorize it.

St. Lawrence: It seems to me to be overwhelming, so overwhelming that I wouldn't want to become involved with it.

LeRoy: Yes, you speak of it as a single entity, and I am not sure if that is the way Gearing would want students or anyone addressing this theory to approach it. Rather, I would assume, and what I would want done if this were my theory, would be to take it apart piecemeal, to look at each of the components, and to build inductively from there. There is no way to go about it scientifically in any other fashion. There is no way to study this theory as an entity other than via the kind of armchair philosophy that we have done to date on this thing.

St. Lawrence: I think, also, that I'm suggesting that there is an implicit kind of anthropological training in which one takes the empirical, the micro material, and builds up from there. It is not necessary to do this in order to have this theory, but this is the traditional way of doing something in anthropology.

Singleton: Gearing is also trying to describe the ways in which what he has done fits into this theory so far. Granted, it gets strained at times because he is very generous and tries to include everybody, but there is enough data around to begin to do this, not only as armchair theorizing about what might be out there, but also as a synthesis of what, so far, people seem to think is out there, whether or not they have been able to develop a common framework for it.

St. Lawrence: I really don't see this happening in the paper, and I guess that is what bothers me.

Singleton: Anybody have any final words? The bureaucratic model bothered you a little bit, didn't it? Did you want to take that up specifically — bureaucratic hierarchy?

St. Lawrence: It bothered me because it wasn't put in the paper specifically as an example. Yet, I think that it would have to function as an example; otherwise why pick on the bureaucratic hierarchy?

Singleton: What are the other examples of organizations that you wanted? Kinds of systems? Social structure?

St. Lawrence: One thing I was thinking of was male-female. It need not be organizations. It might be ethnic groups. It is very hard to talk about ethnic groups as an organization — unless you are talking politically.

Troup: You mean the formal organization? Or is it always hard to talk about ethnic groups as any kind of organization system?

St. Lawrence: I mean as an organization. I don't know if an organization exists that isn't formal in some way or other. It seems to me to be part of the definition of an organization.

Singleton: Do you mean the explicit acknowledgment that there are relationships and names for relationships?

LeRoy: I just have one further item — I'd like to begin reading a short paragraph and then ask a couple of questions or, rather, throw them out as open questions. Gearing writes: "One can presume that, through both the habituating and constraining forces generated through such regular reenactment of the wider system, any education system regularly functions to prevent social change. It strongly appears that, not only in tribal societies ... but in highly industrialized societies, parties to encounters, whatever they may imagine they are about, regularly behave as if their overriding assigned task were perpetually to recreate the wider social system unchanged. The major divisions of the society and major tensions between such divisions are conspicuously included." I wonder what that says about the process of social change? Does it imply that social change must necessarily include violence of some sort? If so, how does one explain the rather profound social change that has taken place nonviolently in some societies? I don't quite understand how to conceptualize social change in terms of this schema. It seems that the only way in which social change could take place is through troublesome agendas. Obviously, I have not thought this through thoroughly; I am just throwing it out as an open question. It was one of the things that I had questioned when I went through the paper initially.

Singleton: Troublesome agendas are the source of social change. Social change does not come through stable agendas or open agendas because they are system preserving rather than system changing.

Troup: I disagree.

Singleton: You disagree? Good!

Troup: My last comment was going to have to do with that social change paragraph, too. It goes back to the differentiation I made that nobody else picked up on. If you talk about education as content, then it is not likely that social change comes that way. But if you talk about it as process, then I don't see the conflict that Gearing sees in the paper. In other words, I think that you can use the same encounter-education processes, change the content, and accomplish social change. In terms of brainwashing, that happened with the Korean War. The religious fanatics were the people who could best be brainwashed. The religious fanatics were individuals who came out as socialist fanatics or communist fanatics. And the people who changed the least were those who were apathetic or who didn't have a need to be committed to anything. It seems to me that social change was accomplished from radical religious beliefs to radical political beliefs. The processes were the same — interaction processes. If you are focusing on how people transact things, and if the content of what they transact is irrelevant, then the process could be used to accomplish social change. Now I don't think the process is the kind of nonchangeable thing that Gearing suggests it is. But I agree with what you said earlier when you were pointing out that the word "education" is used in different ways. It is a content-process conflict, and you see it as a different definition of education.

Singleton: Yes, I see it as the intentional education system that regularly functions to reproduce the environment, the one where we formalize education in our intentions, which is not taken care of specifically here, but I suspect that what's being talked about are those places where we intentionally set out to educate somebody. In those cases, we are reproducing the society as we see it and very often as we live it, even though we don't see it that way. The school is nearer the defects of the society, even when it claims not to be. The social class hierarchy is reinforced by schooling rather than subverted by it, although we keep talking about the schools as open channels for achievement and success. In encounters we reproduce all the social systems we belong to. We rarely bring to any set of encounters an agenda that contradicts all of the systems that we currently associate with. It has to come from something in our background.

Troup: But those same things that happen in our — you just called them encounters — if the content were changed, we might behave in different ways and still serve coffee, or whatever.

Singleton: But what is content in this case? These are the skills, knowledge, and attitudes that Gearing says are being transmitted.

Troup: Well, it is a very abstract thing. It's just that, if you talk about growth process models in anthropology, you are abstracting from content. And that's what I think Gearing is trying to do; at least, that's what he suggests he's trying to do, to me, when he uses the word "process." And, that's a whole other can of worms to say how to differentiate it from content. I think he doesn't do it. I have another problem with that, in that he talks about process, but he keeps bringing skill and information bits and so forth into it. You have to go the whole way with abstractions. We could all use our same patterns of interaction whether we are discussing a paper for Fred Gearing or whether we are going to decide what course we'd like to have offered next year, or whether we are discussing whether or not we were going to take a political stand on something, or whether we were going to meet at somebody's house for a party.

Singleton: Or whether we were going to go out and create a revolution.

Troup: Yes, our own social encounter, interactions — who listens to whom — would not change.

LeRoy: But didn't we just finish saying that such things do change, depending upon the content of the encounter? I would be willing to stick my neck out and say that, if we were to discuss or plan some form of revolution, some sort of massive revolutionary change within the university or elsewhere, the various perspectives from which we are operating, which are not necessarily manifest in the kind of conversation that we are having now, would come out. That our perspectives — the perspectives out of which we are operating — would change.

Singleton: All right, certain identities would become more salient.

LeRoy: That is right. There are obviously certain topics of conversation where sexual identities are salient, where we would consider our respective sexual identities, and obviously, in something like this, that isn't a factor to be taken into consideration.

Troup: I would agree with that. Yet, among the people who are sitting here now, in the context in which we know each other, our interaction system could be applied to a number of contents. And it's unlikely that revolution would be one of them.

SECTION TWO

Commentaries, Principally on Interactional Analysis

COMMENT *by William S. Condon*

The following comments on *A General Cultural Theory of Education*, by Frederick Gearing et al. stem from the present author's views, which were derived from the analysis of human communication. I find Gearing's theory to be very interesting and a possible basis for a new understanding of education.

The theory concerns education as a human behavioral process. This implies that such behavior is observable and can be subjected to analysis. That which interferes most with analysis is the set of assumptions that the investigator brings with him, often unknowingly. People keep trying to study various areas in terms of the same old perspectives, while new viewpoints are often required in order to gain new information. This is recognized in the Gearing theory, which presents an altered perspective. It is concerned with studying which people and their children get information and skill and which do not. Focus is on the barriers to the flow of information, which are created as a function of forces that are conservative in the sense of preserving ongoing forms and styles, although they are not necessarily political. These three features — flow of information between people, barriers, and a conservative force — constitute the assumptions in terms of which the educational system is to be described. There are subcategories that further delineate the flow field. Simple information, since it is easily available, defines randomness. Difficult information is not readily shared, is nonrandom, and is felt to occur because of barriers. Relationships between people are the behavioral processes that institute the barriers. I have some concern about the assumption that the simple is equatable with randomness and the difficult with nonrandom and that this is a function of barriers. At any rate, the concept of information flow in this theory seems to involve a theory of human communication.

The paper serves an important purpose in calling into question the accepted or mythological view of education. As previously indicated, the difficult task is to break through one's own assumptions that guide inquiry. Such assumptions help to perpetuate the accepted view, and, in that sense, are conservative. The conservative force of educational information flow is an important hypothesis. The goals of this educational theory are not explicitly stated, however. There is a suggestion that the elimination of troublesome agendas might be valuable. There is a sense in which this is to be desired, but also a sense in which it is not desired. Perhaps we need to seek formats for stable agenda through which we can use troublesome agendas creatively.

An analogue to a troublesome agenda may be the process of inquiry itself, or possibly, information seeking in contrast to information flow. (Many areas of science epitomize the theory of education presented. Because of the economic value of information, many subtle barriers develop, hindering the creative flow of information.) One usually operates with a given set of assumptions, epistemological categorizations of the nature of nature. As suggested, these are carried into investigation with conservative force. Much time is spent making the system under investigation fit these categories. Radically new information rarely accrues since the very sets of the inquiry prevent anything from being observed that does not conform to those assumptions. It is only as one is able to relinquish deep-rooted sets (premises) that it becomes possible to see new forms of order. Moreover, it is difficult to give up prior sets — it is very troublesome — and involves much effort and fatigue. Uncertainty is a feature that must be lived with. The restraints or barriers to the dissemination of information may be similar to the barriers in gathering information. (Edmund Husserl, the philosopher, sought to define an assumptionless noetic through a phenomenological "bracking-out" of categorizations. His ideas have important methodological value apart from the idealistic metaphysics propounded.) In a sense, then, troublesome agendas may be desirable. It may be possible for change to occur at the interface of troublesome agendas — where premises are called into question by confrontation with differing premises. It is at this communicational location that the conservative assumptions may undergo change.

People may be much more conservative than we have thought. Repetition compulsion, as described by psychoanalysts, involves the maintenance of patterns of behavior even when these are self-defeating. Encounters and agendas are highly patterned and repetitive. It is difficult to change one's pattern of interaction, and it is at this point that I feel the theory requires change. The description of encounters — the "units" in terms of which they are described — requires more careful assessment. A more organizational approach might be valuable. The whole concept of turn-taking as a kind of basic category for the analysis of communication can be misleading. Twelve years of intensive sound film analysis of human communication by the present author suggests that there are many more important aspects to communication than turn-taking, which is only one feature of a very complex process. The units of a given domain are not what the investigator begins with, but rather, are what he discovers after many exhausting hours of observation. It has been found very useful to talk about multiple forms of order within ongoing processes rather than discrete units between which communications such as "barriers" occur. It would seem, perhaps, important to study how barriers or constraints are created in actual interactions. Different people might and probably do erect barriers in different ways. In this sense, an agenda may have many ranges of important communicational events that cannot be conceived in terms of a turn-taking model. These would become nonobservables in terms of that assumption.

Summary

In conclusion, I find the theory to be important and in line with many emerging observations. The communicational and conservative emphasis, which sees education in terms of flow and barriers to that flow, provides a new and creative perspective. The weakness of the presentation of the theory, from my own background, lies in a need for a more organizational view of communication that will do justice to the complexity of encounters and their varying agendas. I do not wish these minor criticisms to obscure the great importance of the author's views of cultural transmission as involving systematic barriers or censorship.

COMMENT *by Starkey Duncan*

This theory, being based on processes of face-to-face interaction, is naturally of great interest to me as a researcher in that area. Indeed, it is difficult to imagine another appropriate base for a general cultural theory of education. There is, however, a present hazard in the construction of such a high-level theory. The phenomena of face-to-face interaction may be insufficiently understood at this time to permit an empirically sound base for the theory. That is, when adequate research on various empirical issues is not yet developed, a general theoretical statement is forced to make assumptions with regard to these issues, thereby running the risk of being shown to be wrong, both in those aspects and in the logical developments based on those aspects, when more research returns are in.

This general problem may be illustrated by suggesting some potential problems arising at the points of contact between the theory and the phenomenon of face-to-face interaction.

The theory posits "speaking-and-acting" turns as the "minimal segments of behaviors in the course of encounters." Evidence has been presented relevant to the hypothesis of turns as a unit of interaction in dyadic conversations (e.g., Duncan 1972). It seems unlikely, however, that this unit is a minimal one in the organization of those conversations. There is some evidence that units of interaction occur during speaking turns (Duncan 1974), thereby constituting a unit on a lower hierarchical level. And there is no *a priori* reason to believe that these lower level units are any less significant than are turns for interaction or for educational processes based on that interaction. Further, there is no way of knowing at this point in time whether or not other units on a still lower level exist.

Finally, it seems important to emphasize that both speaking-turn units and "within-turn" units appear to be true "units of interaction" (Duncan 1974) in that these units, as presently understood, can be created only through ordered sequences of action involving both participants. Neither type of interaction unit can be created unilaterally.

Interactions involving more than two participants are called "public dyads." While this is clearly one available analytic tactic, the appropriate treatment of three person and larger interactions is ultimately an empirical one; it may or may not prove more effective to regard these larger interactions as unified wholes, as public dyads, or in some other manner.

The treatment of social categories applying to interactions may require more subtle treatment. For example, Friedrich (1972) presents evidence that these categories can be rather finely graded, and that some may change, perhaps frequently, in the course of a single interaction. It would seem desirable for the theory to incorporate in some manner this intuitively reasonable finding.

Ultimately, these considerations do not seem central to the proposed theory. To the extent to which they are, in fact, peripheral, it may be desirable either to eliminate them from the theory or to deemphasize their importance in the presentation.

I would like to make one further comment, realizing that it might arise from an inadequate reading of the paper. Because an important aspect of interaction appears to be the definition of the social situation in which the interaction takes place, it may be desirable to incorporate this consideration into the theory. For example, it is not entirely obvious to me that interaction between two parties defined by the same social categories

necessarily entails open agendas. Might there be certain interaction contexts, involving identically defined parties, in which agendas might not be
open? This question stems from the possibility that a given definition of
social situation, as well as the respective definitions of the participants,
may proscribe certain topics of conversation.

COMMENT *by Frederick Erickson*

The key notion presented by Gearing and his associates, that one should
expect simple information and skill in the absence of restraints to be
diffused randomly through any human population, is intriguing. It may
even represent a Copernican revolution in thinking about cultural transmission. Their cybernetic metaphor does not strike one as completely
new and unique; it has been floating around implicitly for some time
among scholars concerned with anthropology and education. But Gearing et al. have made the cybernetic metaphor explicit and have elaborated
its theoretical implications. They have also sketched exciting prospects
for empirical research in mapping and dissecting the sociocultural
restraints that systematically channel the distribution of information and
skill in human groups of varying size, complexity, and continuity across
time.[1]

I have some empirical evidence to report that speaks to the theory, as
well as some specific suggestions and criticisms regarding the theory in its
present form. The suggestions have primarily to do with terminology and
considerations of the nature of encounters as social situations. I will
present these suggestions first, as they have to do with another of the
author's key notions: the troublesome agenda. The empirical data come
from my own research on behavioral indicators of troublesome agendas; I
will discuss this last.

Before beginning those discussions, I would like to anticipate an obvious criticism that may occur to many readers. By placing occasions of
face-to-face interaction at the center of his theory, Gearing fails to do
justice to other forms and agencies of cultural transmission. Admittedly,
the theory can be criticized on these grounds. It seems to underemphasize
the larger sociocultural structure within which educational encounters
are embedded and to discount the influence of these macrostructures on
the microstructures of face-to-face interaction. The theory also does not
comprehend desociated learning — when children and adults learn some
new information and skill by themselves through discovery as they rub up

[1] The root metaphors of "distribution within a population" and "restraint" are very
similar to those of Bohannan in his recent and controversial piece "Rethinking culture"
(1973), in which he draws an analogy between gene pools and what he calls "culture pools."

against physical (and metaphysical) artifacts and spaces shaped by culture. Clearly, some cultural transmission occurs independently of mediation through social interaction. In our own society a child playing at taking apart a clock would be one example of this; the Plains Indian vision quest is another example of a quite different sort.

I think these lacunae in the theory are just fine for now. In focusing on some theoretical distinctions, one inevitably leaves others blurred. Very little attention has been paid to the encounter by students of cultural transmission, thus it seems high time that the encounter receive central emphasis, as it does in Gearing's theory.

Issues of Terminology

In discussing educational encounters and their constituent elements, however, I think the authors have put together an unneccessarily confusing set of terms and usages.

First, consider the use of the term "education." Because the term literally means directed cultural transmission or enculturation (from the Latin *educare* or *educere*), and because Gearing's theory postulates that cultural transmission is inherently automatic (relatively undirected?) in the absence of systematic restraints, perhaps this is not a theory of education, but of "non-educed" cultural transmission. At least, it is necessary to make explicit where intentional direction of learners by educators (whether they are parents, siblings, teachers, or peers) fits or does not fit into the model.[2]

Next, consider the terms and concepts involved in the four pivotal elements of analysis — turns, public dyad, transaction, and agenda. I will deal with these in an order different from that of the authors, beginning with the simplest issues and moving on to more complex ones.

Public Dyads

Regarding public dyads, I would make just a minor point. While the dyad is clearly the minimal unit of face-to-face interaction, it does not follow that any occasion of interaction "involving more than two persons is a complex of public dyads." Interactions involving three or more persons may for some purposes be analytically divisible into successive pairs of

---

[2]   It is difficult to find a term whose connotations are not at odds with Gearing's root metaphor; e.g., cultural *transmission*, while more neutral than "education," is not exactly suitable either because it connotes a sender who is actively projecting information across some gap to a receiver. Information is not transmitted without some special effort, and Gearing is concerned with the movement of simple information or skill "from any physically normal adult or child to any other without special effort, virtually automatically."

dyads performing before audiences, but this may not be the only useful way to slice the interactional pie. Three persons and more can speak at once, do cooperative work, or join together in rituals. The exchange or transmission of simple information and skill may take place by participation in such conjoint activity. Further, as the authors point out later in their discussion, participation may take place in ways other than by initiating and responding. Therefore, it seems to me unwise to tie one's self at the outset to the dyad as a unit of analysis, since it may turn out at later stages of inquiry to impose unnecessary analytic limitations.

Turn-Taking

It also seems misleading to define interactional behavior in terms of a "pattern of turn-taking." This makes for an overemphasis on interactional reciprocity at the expense of what I call interactional complementarity. To be sure, interaction proceeds according to patterns of initiation and response and reciprocal linkages between behavioral units can be described by various "ping-pong match" models. In addition to considering what happens sequentially (reciprocally) between interactional partners, it is often necessary to consider what happens simultaneously: what the listener is doing while the speaker is speaking, and what the speaker does while the listener is listening. This is what is meant by interactional complementarity, for slow motion analysis of film shows that speakers, and listeners literally complete ("fill up") one another's behavior in an integrated, mutual performance. It is this radical interdependence between speakers and listeners that the work of Birdwhistell, Hall, Scheflen, Condon, Kendon, and Byers illustrates for us, and this is missed by emphasizing only the patterns of initiation and response (unless the authors include simultaneous listening behavior under the category of "response," in which case this should be made explicit.) Condon (1967: 221) refers to interactional complementarity as a process of "whiles" — while one feature of communication behavior occurs in one person, another feature is occurring in another person. Byers and Byers (1972) use mutual cultural performance as their metaphor for interactional complementarity. Interactional partners join together in behaviorally completing a joint performance — the speaker's behavior does not cause the listener's simultaneous behavior, any more than the string bass player's performance of his part in a symphony orchestra causes the behavior of the trumpet player in performing his part. Under conditions of satisfactory ensemble, they perform together.

Leonard-Dolan and I (Erickson 1973) have used the metaphor of a ballroom dance to illustrate the complementarity between interactional partners. When one of the two partners falters (in listening behavior or in speaking behavior), the ongoing symmetry of their performance is disturbed, and a mutual interactional "stumble" occurs. Our recent research (Erickson 1973, 1974) suggests that stumbles are behavioral manifestations of what Gearing et al. call troublesome agendas, and that these momentary interactional lurches or pratfalls function as indicators of trouble to interactional partners and researchers alike. (The empirical evidence will be discussed in more detail in the last section.)

I would guess that Gearing et al. have taken interactional complementarity into account implicitly in their theoretical statement, and that the differences between their terms and perspective and mine are minor. One of the most valuable aspects of the Gearing statement is that it gets us looking at and talking about what actually happens in educational encounters — examining the organization of behavior in face-to-face interaction. This permits us to specify cultural discontinuity between encounter participants in precise ways and to analyze discontinuity in operational terms rather than solely in terms at a high level of abstraction lacking behavior referents, e.g., value orientation.

Agenda

The distinctions between open, closed, stable, and troublesome agendas are useful. But it is not clear from the authors' definition what the term "agenda" means: "Agendas are sets of reciprocal behavior, plus experience and expectation." While one could quarrel with using the term to refer to both behavior and expectation, other more common terms, such as "role," encompass, both behavior and expectation.

Whatever role means, I have a sense of what it can mean and can usually discover quite quickly how an author is using it; whatever "agenda" can mean as used by Gearing, I am not so sure, and it takes me longer to decipher the usage.

It seems to me that more standard terminology would be better. Part of what the authors mean by agenda is encompassed by the term "role set" (cf. Barth 1972; Merton 1958). Despite the checkered career of "status" and "role" as constructs in social science, I think that these and related terms, as recently used by Goffman (1961b), Goodenough (1965), Cicourel (1972), and Barth (1972), are effective in describing dimensions of the social organization of occasions.

An agenda in ordinary usage means a plan or program for an occasion of interaction (cf. Miller, Galanter, and Pribram 1960; Scheflen 1968). I think it would be wise for the authors to limit their use of agenda to the purposes or the sense of program brought to an encounter by interaction partners.

Encounter and Transaction

Yet another aspect of the authors' use of agenda and transacting agendas is what Goffman (1961b) means by encounters. He means more by encounter than the authors give him credit for in their citation. They write: " ... encounters arise where two or more persons jointly ratify one another as authorized co-sustainers of a single, albeit moving, focus of visual and cognitive attention." Goffman (1961b) proceeds further to discuss how encounter participants actually accomplish the interactional work of cosustaining a focus of attention. They do this by continuously defining and redefining the situation they are sustaining as members of a performance team. The definition of a situation establishes which attributes of the various social identities brought by participants to the situation — sex, age, occupation, kinship, physical and emotional state, etc. — that will be relevant or irrelevant. Participants may bring to encounters agreements about what aspects of social identity will be ignored for the purposes of the encounter; these agreements Goffman (1961b: 19–26) calls "rules of irrelevance." If participants do not come to an encounter with such agreements, they must be negotiated, explicitly or implicitly, during the course of the encounter. From my research on American school counseling and job interviews, it seems that, if the social identity of participants and their relevance rules are still under negotiation during the first part of the interview, it is very likely that asymmetric communication behavior will occur. This is behavior of the kind Gearing says is characteristic of troublesome agendas. Behavioral asymmetry may also occur when new and unexpected aspects of social identity are introduced into the encounter, e.g., when one of the participants reveals that he is Roman Catholic, or has received an extremely high or low grade in a course, or has not been attending class. At that moment, the social identity of one participant changes, and a change in the rights and obligations attendant to both members of the interactional status set must be renegotiated. At these points, interaction partners are likely to lose their balance and stumble.

Another source of trouble in encounters is discrepancy between participants in their definition of the interactional task, activity, or occasion at hand (cf. Barth 1972: 208). A good example from American educational encounters are the definitions of work and play — when students define an occasion or key activity of an encounter as play while the teacher defines it as work, a troublesome agenda occurs, marked by asymmetric interactional stumbling behavior.

Thus, encounters are not interactions in which the social identities, roles, and occasions are totally programmed in advance by a culture. Encounters are situational variations on general cultural themes for social relations. The themes are situationally transformed from moment to moment in the process of being performed by agents who are more than sociocultural automata (cf. Cicourel 1972). Handelman (1973a: 211) observes:

Goffman's great contribution is to show that an encounter is not merely a replication of the structure of the setting in which it takes place, but that it is a temporary re-ordering and re-patterning of selected elements of that social structure, which are permitted entry to and expression within the encounter ... The encounter is not a "bridge" which links the individual and the social order, as Goldschmidt (1972: 61) has suggested, but it is a transformational articulation which selectively limits the expression of both individual *personae* and the social order.

While Gearing et al. note that people bring to encounters profiles of social identity and agendas, their model does not account for the creative process of negotiation by which social identity, role, and occasion or task are actualized in a given encounter. Indeed, they assert categorically that, in the final analysis, "the relevant perceptions in respect to any encounter are those of the major reference groups of the parties to the encounter." In my own data, this does not always turn out to be the case, although admittedly, it usually does. A model for interaction in educational encounters must be able to take account of exceptions to general sociocultural rules because situational exceptions are frequent enough to produce ambiguous results if not accounted for.

In general, it seems true that encounters proceed more smoothly between persons who are culturally similar than between persons who are culturally different. This is the point Gearing et al. are making. The reason it is true seems to be not only because persons from the same cultural group are more likely to share conventions about communication style — "patterns of initiation and response" (speaking and listening behavior) — but also because they are likely to share conventions about how to negotiate and renegotiate the definition of a situation throughout the encounter. They seem to be able to recover their balance quickly as interactional stumbles occur. Discrepancies in conventions for defining situations can result in troublesome agendas, and these discrepancies are more likely intercultural, for as Barth (1972: 209) notes, " ... [societies] differ not only in their status inventories, but in ways these statuses can be combined in persons and elicited by alters and in the ways distinctive social occasions can be created."

Sometimes interactional partners of different social and cultural backgrounds can create within the boundary of an encounter the conditions under which differences in style of communicating and in modes of defining the situation do not seem to count so much. A troublesome agenda, if it arises, is a relatively minor one and gets worked through quickly. Perhaps this is because interactional partners fortuitously happen on common aspects of social identity that become so salient that they are willing to overlook whatever discomfort and asymmetry is produced by difference in communication style. Perhaps a strong motivation to find common aspects of social identity increases the likelihood of finding it. Whatever the causes, I have found in my research that differences between encounter participants neither in communication style nor in social identity — in terms of major reference groups such as ethnicity, race, and in the case of school encounters, academic major and grades — can predict the occurrence of troublesome agendas in every case. Sometimes social and cultural difference is creatively transcended by interaction partners.

Empirical Research that Speaks to Gearing's Model

I have pressed Gearing et al. hard on their notion of encounter because it became central to me in my research on naturally occurring gate-keeping encounters — school counseling and job interviews and on arranged encounters between pairs of students who were strangers. This research is reported more extensively elsewhere (Leonard-Dolan 1972; Erickson, 1973, n.d., 1974; Shultz 1974). It was a microethnographic study of interethnic relations in gate-keeping encounters in which a number of interviewers were filmed and videotaped in encounters with students or job applicants of varying ethnicity.[3] After the initial filming, the interviewer and interviewee were shown the videotape of their interview in separate viewing sessions.

My colleagues and I began with a theoretical orientation that resembled that of Gearing at many points. We wanted to see whether interaction proceeded differently and was perceived differently when the interviewer and student were ethnically similar and ethnically different. Our initial working hypothesis could have been generated from Gearing's framework. In interethnic encounters, we expected to find differences in cultural communication style (speaking and listening behavior), and that these differences in style would produce systematic interference analogous to linguistic interference, manifested in various forms of behavior asymmetry, verbal and nonverbal. We proposed that the amount of behavioral asymmetry in a given interview would be associated with less help and cordiality offered by the interviewer to the interviewee. We operationalized behavioral asymmetry in terms of the metaphor of interactional stumbling described earlier.

[3] Sponsored by the Center for Studies of Metropolitan Problems, NIMH and partially supported by the Ford Foundation. The support of both is gratefully acknowledged. Carolyn Leonard-Dolan and Jeffrey Shultz were collaborators in the research. They helped to develop and refine the behavior described here, and Shultz did the statistical analysis reported here.

In Gearing's terminology, we expected to find more instances of communication behavior characteristic of troublesome agendas in interethnic encounters than in intraethnic encounters. (Gate-keeping encounters, especially the school counseling encounters, are relevant to Gearing's theory, since the school counselor functions as the student's "social structure coach," i.e., the counselor teaches about the structure and rules of society, the school the student is presently attending, and the world of work or higher education that may lie ahead.)

Not only did we find more instances of uncomfortable interactional stumbles (troublesome agendas) in interethnic encounters than in intraethnic ones, but it was at such moments of stumbling that both participants in separate viewing sessions were most likely to stop the videotape spontaneously and comment on what they saw happening at that moment, i.e., encounter participants identified moments at which troublesome agendas occurred as emically salient moments. Further, for interethnic encounters, the comments of both participants about the same moment tended to be quite divergent in character, e.g., a white counselor described his own behavior as giving *information* about the student's career goal, while the student, who was black, characterized the same behavior as *insulting* because it contained the implication that the student was not qualified to achieve the goal. In a job interview, a German-American interviewer described his own behavior as trying to put the nervous job applicant at ease, which the Italian-American applicant said the interviewer showed disinterest in what the applicant was saying.

In encounters between persons of the same ethnicity, troublesome agendas occasionally arose, but they occurred less frequently and were marked by less asymmetry in speaking and listening behavior than were the troublesome agendas occurring between persons of different ethnicity. What is especially interesting in the light of Gearing's theory is that, when both ethnically similar participants commented on their moments of stumbling in viewing sessions, they tended to characterize what was happening in ways that were congruent with one another. If the counselor reported that he was trying to help the student, the student also reported receiving help. If the counselor said that he was rebuking the student, the student said that he was being rebuked. This is in sharp contrast to the incongruity found between the ways ethnically different interactional partners characterized identical moments of interactional stumbling.

This suggests that troublesome agendas do interfere with the communication of information in encounters, but that there are some conditions under which the troublesome agenda can occur in which communication is massively blocked or distorted and other conditions under which much less blockage occurs.

The findings reported so far are consistent with our initial working hypothesis and with Gearing's framework. As we looked at the films and coded them in a variety of ways, it became apparent that there were a number of anomalous cases for which the working hypothesis could not account.

In most intraethnic encounters, there were few instances of interactional stumbling and asymmetric speaking and listening behavior. There were, however, some intraethnic cases in which instances of stumbling and troublesome agenda occurred quite frequently. Conversely, in some interethnic encounters, troublesome agendas occurred infrequently, and asymmetry in communication behavior was very slight. This was puzzling. The apparent anomaly was only resolved when we looked at the moments of interactional stumbling in a more differentiated way.

My colleagues and I operationalized behavioral asymmetry in a number of ways, two of which are briefly described here. One way was very simple. We counted the number of interactional stumbles in each encounter, the number of times one speaker interrupted the other, and the number of times both speakers sustained simultaneous talk without interrupting (this last is an indicator of interactional symmetry; the former are indicators of asymmetry). This information was computed for each encounter, and scores for the three indicators were summarized together for each encounter as an Overall Behavior Symmetry Coefficient (OBSC). Encounters were ranked according to their OBSC.

The other way of operationalizing behavior asymmetry was considerably more complicated. Adapting the procedure of Prost (1967), we had coders watch the films frame by frame (at twenty-four frames per second) and chart the beginnings and endings of motion in various body parts of the speaker and the listener. These charts of kinesic activity showed us the timing of body motion down to one-twenty-fourth of a second. A polygraph printout of the sound track was also prepared; from this, the strongest voice accents of each speaker were identified and placed on the kinesic chart, so that the chart gave us a precise measure of speech and kinesic rhythms. Thirty-nine of these Kinesic and Speech Rhythm (KSR) charts were prepared, covering the most extreme interactional stumbles (moments of troublesome agenda) in thirty-nine interethnic and intraethnic encounters. I then developed a procedure for coding the degree and kind of rhythmic asymmetry at the uncomfortable moments.[4] Encounters were then ranked as high, medium, or low in rhythmic asymmetry.

The results for the OBSC and KSR measures of behavioral asymmetry are summarized in the tables 1, 2, and 3, in which encounters are categorized as intraethnic and interethnic.

---

[4] This procedure is described in greater detail in Erickson (1973).

Table 1.   Two measures of interactional asymmetry by ethnicity

	KSR asymmetry		OBSC asymmetry	
	Intraethnic	Interethnic	Intraethnic	Interethnic
Low or none	15	11	7	8
Middle	0	4	4	11
High	0	9	4	10

Key: χ^2 = 12.88;   *P* = <0.01;   N = 39
       χ^2 = 1.60;   n.s.;   N = 44

There is a difference intra- and interethnically for the OBSC scores, but the difference is not statistically significant. The difference for the KSR scores is much greater, and the χ^2 value is six times that for the OBSC, significant at the 0.01 level. It is clear that something quite different is being monitored by the two different measures.

The KSR score is not only a more micro measure of interactional asymmetry than is the OBSC, it is also our best measure of cultural performance style sharing between interactional partners. (We assume that, even given cultural diversity within an ethnic group, intraethnic partners in encounters are more likely to share similar performance styles than are interethnic partners, and even if they bring microculturally different variants of performance style to the encounter, one of the two partners is likely to know how to code-switch to match the style of the other.) The KSR chart measures not only the occurrence or nonoccurrence of interactional stumbles (troublesome agendas) but the quality and degree of behavioral asymmetry when the stumbles occurred. How much asymmetry occurs at a moment of troublesome agenda seems to be related to cultural similarity or difference between interactional partners. Whether a troublesome agenda occurs at all seems to be related to another factor that is not cultural, strictly speaking. This factor is social structural — similarity or dissimilarity in the social *persona* — the composite social identity that is revealed by interactional partners during the course of an encounter (see Goodenough 1965). We called this factor "particularistic comembership" and considered it at three levels of generality and inclusiveness: ethnicity, panethnicity, and comembership. The most specific and restricted category of social identification was ethnic comembership. A more general and inclusive category was that of panethnicity. As we analyzed our data, we realized that encounters between Polish-Americans and Italian or Irish-Americans tended to resemble one another in some ways, and encounters between blacks, Chicanos, and Puerto Ricans also tended to resemble each other. We identified two panethnic classes: White Ethnic, and Third World. Despite cultural differences between ethnic groups in one of the two classes, face-to-face relations were more symmetric intra panethnically than inter panethnically, when interactional symmetry was measured by the OBSC. (e.g., the OBSC score for an encounter between an Italian-American interviewer and a Polish-American student, while not as high as that between that interviewer and an Italian-American student, would tend to be higher than the OBSC for that Italian-American interviewer talking to a black student.)

We used the term "total comembership" to stand for the most general and inclusive category of social identification. This was the sum of all shared, particularistic attributes of social identity (including ethnicity and panethnicity but not limited to those categories of ascription) that were revealed in a given encounter.[5]

Comemberships in whatever particularistic categories of ascription, taken together, are all features of what Gearing et al. call the "profile of social identity." Ethnic, panethnic, and total comembership can be thought of as three different levels of inclusiveness of social classification. When the OBSC and KSR scores are compared according to these three classifications (see tables 2 and 3), it is clear that as the generality of inclusiveness increases — from ethnicity through panethnicity to total comembership — the relationship with OBSC scores increases, while the strength of the relationship with KSR scores decreases. This suggests that some occurrences of troublesome agenda can be accounted for by differences in cultural style, but that other troublesome agendas and more macro features of interactional asymmetry can be accounted for by lack of commonality in social identity. Conversely, similarity in communica-

Table 2. Two measures of interactional asymmetry by panethnicity

	KSR asymmetry		OBSC asymmetry	
	Intra panethnic	Inter panethnic	Intra panethnic	Inter panethnic
Low or none	21	5	12	3
Middle	2	2	7	8
High	2	7	5	9

Key: $\chi^2 = 10.369$; $P < 0.01$; $N = 39$
$\chi^2 = 6.31$; $P < 0.05$; $N = 44$

[5] An Irish-American counselor and a Chicano student revealing in an encounter by the ashes on their foreheads on Ash Wednesday that they are both Roman Catholics, revealing through their talk that had both been wrestlers in high school or both had gotten parking tickets that week, have displayed diacritical marks of comembership in categories of social identity that are ostensibly irrelevant within the frame of a universalistically defined school counseling encounter. Yet these particularistic comemberships are not irrelevant in actual performance in the encounter. (If, in addition to being comembers in Roman Catholicism or wrestling, they were both Irish-American, their total comembership score would be even higher.)

Table 3.   Two measures of interactional asymmetry by total comembership

		KSR asymmetry			OBSC asymmetry		
Comembership		Low	Medium	High	Low	Medium	High
Asymmetry	Low	7	2	6	1	5	9
	Medium	13	1	2	5	7	4
	High	11	1	1	9	3	1

Key: $x^2 = 6.614$ (n.s.)   (N = 39)
$\chi^2 = 15.34$ $(P < .01)$ (N = 44)

tion style accounts for some of the absence of troublesome agendas, and therefore, facilitates the transmission of simple information and skill between interactional partners (or the mutual agreement that the agenda is closed). Commonality in social identity also accounts for an absence of troublesome agendas.

The profile of revealed social identity (or social *persona*) of encounter participants is one aspect of what Goffman (1961b) and Barth (1972) call "definition of situation." Some comembership features of the profiles of social identity of both encounter participants, such as being wrestlers, are situation specific. They are revealed face to face, and their relevance or irrelevance to the encounter is negotiated by interactional partners, as is their salience. The weight of such attributes of social identity as being a wrestler or being Italian-American varies as a weighting factor from one encounter to another. It follows that, for a given encounter, if one attribute from a person's total repertoire of statuses (social identities), such as being a wrestler, has high salience and weight, other attributes from the repertoire, such as being black or being Italian-American may have less salience or weight in that context, than they would have in another encounter.

The OBSC figures are empirical evidence demonstrating that at least one aspect of the definition of a situation — the social profile of participants — is related to the occurrence of troublesome agendas in educational encounters. More interestingly, the figures show that situationally revealed and defined features of social identity (comembership), in addition to features of social identity defined customarily as present or absent as relevant or irrelevant to one's social profile (such as ethnicity or race), are related to the occurrence or absence of troublesome agendas and to their severity when they occur.

Conclusion

Three main ideas have been presented as comments on Gearing's theory: (1) the suggestion that Gearing et al. make their terminology consistent with that of Goodenough (1965), Barth (1972), and Goffman (1961b); (2) an overview of Goffman's notion of definition of situation and its relevance for the kinds of research questions framed by Gearing's theory; and (3) a report of empirical findings that suggest that troublesome agendas can arise in encounters because of differences in the way interaction partners define the situation they are in, as well as because of differences in their patterns of listening and response.

Gearing's paradigm comprehends much of what I and other microethnographers of face-to-face relations have been doing. It is very helpful as a frame of reference for a behavioral anthropology of the educational process. Much work can be profitably done in this area.

But participants in educational encounters not only behave, they act. I have become increasingly convinced that, in order to understand the dynamics of educational encounters, we need to link behavioral studies with a theory of social action in everyday life. This is a big order. It seems to me that Goffman, Barth, and the "everyday life" sociologists give us ways of accounting for how persons who are not social or cultural automata sustain social action face to face, transforming general cultural rules within the frame of the encounter. If Gearing and his associates can comprehend within their paradigm this view of the creativity of interaction partners in generating social performances, then we will have a fully differentiated model for the study of educational encounters — encounters in which the medium of behavior and action, rule governed but also improvised from moment to moment, is the message of cultural transmission.

COMMENT by Adam Kendon

Insofar as I understand what Gearing and his associates at Buffalo are getting at, I like it very much. I am pleased with the way in which what they are doing provides a broad context for the sorts of things I am doing. Most of the time I am simply fascinated with the minutiae of face-to-face interaction — suffering continuously from a sense of puzzlement and wonder at just how given occasions of face-to-face interaction are brought off, with all the complexity of behavioral interrelationship they involve. It is important, however, for one to be able to see the significance of what one does in a wider perspective. Gearing's perspective provides such.

I share Gearing's belief in the value of what he calls a radically interpsychic perspective. From my point of view, I find that occasions of face-to-face interaction cannot be accounted for unless one sees that one is dealing with systems of behavioral relationship which are jointly participated in by members, but which are the exclusive product of none of them. I am pleased with the centrally important place that Gearing gives to the face-to-face encounter, including the point that it is through face-to-face interaction that items of information or skill acquire meaning and are made available as socially deployable. As I see it this is a central tenet of Gearing's position and there are many questions that can be explored as to how this happens. Some of these Gearing et al. explore, but to a large extent this emphasis on face-to-face encounters operates as an assumption in the discussion and there is much more to be said about it.

There are numerous points I could take up. However, I will just refer to one or two matters that directly involve my work. First, a general point. Gearing has said in conversation that the principal empirical fact that has emerged from the microanalysis of interaction is the "massive redundancy" of face-to-face communication. Now I may misinterpret what he means here, but in saying this, it seems to me, he is referring, at best, to only a small part of what occurs. My interpretation of the literature on fine grained analysis would be, rather, to say that it shows the *multiplicity* of communication. That is, it has made us recognize that in any occasion of face-to-face interaction there are a great many different things going on all at the same time. One thing that I think is lacking in Gearing's written discussion is any well developed notion of differentiable levels or aspects of what he calls "messaging." Gearing tends to talk about "knowledge" and "skill" as if it is a kind of substance that flows around, that this flow is facilitated or inhibited by the patterning of encounters and by the organization within given transactions. One should on the contrary think in terms of many different *kinds* of messaging. For example, two individuals who know each other well in having a conversation may at one level engage in a pattern-enacting interaction (I venture to use Gearing's terms), but at the same time and at another level engage in a pattern-forming transaction. That is, A's and B's conversation may have a behavioral organization that has been repeated many times; yet at the same time something new emerges from it (A acquires information or ideas he did not have before, or jointly some new agreement is reached about something). It seems to me that this is happening all the time. From the point of view of the organization of the conversation *qua* an interactional event, different aspects of the behavior "take care" of different aspects of the encounter. Thus participation in an "F-formation" functions to define who is and who is not a participant and functions to define the boundaries of the event and facilitates the maintenance of the "interaction membrane"; the particular arrangement the participants are in helps to maintain the definition of the phase (greeting phase, topic phase); other aspects of behavior, such as face orientation and direction of gaze take care of address and turn-taking; then within a given utterance exchange axis (my new term of what, in 1970, I called interactional axis) still further aspects of behavior deal with the moment-to-moment maintenance and change of the system of exchange of the participants involved. Thus, while it may, from one point of view, be correct to speak of massive redundancy, from another point of view I think one should be impressed by the high degree of differentiation in messaging that occurs.

Second, I should like to comment on the use of "face formation," or F-formation as I prefer now to call it. At the time Gearing et al. were writing Working Paper 6 my paper on this had not yet been published. (This paper is now in press as a chapter in *Studies in the Behavior of Face-to-Face Interaction*, to be published in 1977 by Peter de Ridder Press, for the Career Research Center for Language and Semiotics, Indiana University in the series *Studies in Semiotics*.) Gearing et al. say that F-formations are patterns of signalling, principally nonverbal and *principally* proxemic (my emphasis) — implying that they can be other things. An F-formation arises whenever two or more individuals so locate and orient themselves with respect to one another that the frontal region of each torso faces inwards to a small space which each individual may be said to share with each other individual, but which is not easily accessible to others who may be nearby. My actual definition is in terms of the overlapping of transactional segments to create a joint transactional segment or "O-space," but to give this would involve giving the concept of transactional segment and what I have just presented is adequate for this discussion. One may speak of a F-formation system as arising when people enter into this spatial orientational arrangement and cooperate to sustain it. It is a behavioral unit. However, it is a unit of behavior at the interactional level of organizational level or organization for it refers to a particular system of behavioral relations. It lasts as long as these relations may last, notwithstanding changes in participants. Now the point about this system is that it refers only to a system of spatial orientation relations. A group of individuals may enter into an F-formation system and they may or may not talk or exchange gestures. Likewise, individuals may engage in utterance exchanges, gesture exchanges, glances, and yet not enter into an F-formation system. Now the F-formation system may function as a means of creating the circumstances in which utterance exchanges of a sustained sort may occur. Indeed I believe we enter into them because they make sustained utterance exchanges easy, but they are not defined or identified in terms of anything else but spatial orientational relations of a rather restricted sort. It is my belief that for the purposes of systematically describing the organization of occasions of face-to-face interaction, we must separately deal with the different systems of behavioral relationships that can be observed. The F-formation system is one such system. Thus Gearing's implication that somehow F-formations involve more than spacing and orientation is incorrect according to my usage. Furthermore, a basketball game, a classrooom, a church service are offered by Gearing as possible varieties of F-formations. This is not correct. Such complex occasions may contain facing formations, but they do not constitute them. Though we may be able to specify a system of spatial orientational relations that encompasses all these, this still would not be a facing formation.

COMMENT *by Norman A. McQuown*

I am impressed by the very sizeable convergence of views (mine and those of Gearing) represented in this paper. Indeed, I could find very little wherein I differed with him. Either we are both right, or more likely, both, to more or less the same extent, are wrong.

In one respect, repetitive in the paper, I find I cannot take the same, (to me, somewhat paranoid) point of view: namely, that blocking necessarily has harmful effects on society as a whole. Some blocking may be beneficial and result in more efficacious application of individual talent; some blocking may be an artifact of poorly designed transmission systems and may call for conscious redesign. Poorly designed transmission systems would include, of course, informal, traditional ones. Formally — and, presumably, innovatively — designed systems have no monopoly on inefficiency or inefficacy. Finally, only some blocking may be the result of individual aberration, excessively narrow focus and short vision, removable by corrective measures such as the deliberate widening of focus and extension of vision. This point of view, of course, may be taken by Gearing to confirm his.

In another respect, I find the broad theory lacking in specificity with respect to the constitution of dyadic groupings — the cross-referencing double dyad is only one, albeit an interesting one, of a number of conceivable and likely more complex constellations of dyads that are actually functional in everyday life. I would submit that no such *a priori* restriction should be entertained until after some preliminary intensive microanalytic work in a variety of $(n + 1)$ constellations had empirically shown some to be more prevalent than others. There is, as yet, no natural history of such groupings that would help to answer the question. I do not see how it is profitable arbitrarily to shortcut the preliminary exploratory phase (McQuown 1971a; Scheflen 1966). Why restrict theoretical reality to an entity that falls so far short of self-evident practical reality? Let us not fall into "the rats-in-the-maze" trap!

Finally, I find that the instrument for discovering what is really going on in such groupings, repeatedly asserted to be a microanalysis of behavior, is poorly specified. I miss, likewise, any reference to the considerable body of preliminary theory with respect to the potential valences of particular microanalytic bits of behavior for the marking of shifts of stance within a group and of shifts of reference without the group (McQuown 1971b, G. Bateson et al. 1971).

The paper, I think, would be strengthened by a softening of the "I bleed for society" posture and a reinforcing of the "I work for society" stance with fuller specification of precisely how.

I think that a full application of Gearing's suggested apparatus to the testing of the general theory would reveal reality to be much more complex, more full of available options, and considerably less grim than the present article leads one to feel. All systems have deviance — tolerating provisions. Excessive straitness leads to breakdown in communication. Optionality is built into all efficiently functioning systems. It is the characteristic that permits change without rupture and the characteristic that permits taking maximal advantage of individual variation in effecting that change (Labov 1973; Hale 1973).

SECTION THREE

Commentaries, Principally on Micro Versus Macro Levels of Analysis

COMMENT *by John J. Gumperz*

> John Gumperz expressed a preference for a telephone conversation
> with the editor as the most convenient way to respond to our request
> that he comment upon Working Paper 6 by Gearing et al. The follow-
> ing remarks are a version of that recorded conversation, which Dr.
> Gumperz himself kindly consented to edit for this volume.

I had some difficulty in reading through the manuscript. I had to read it
several times because it seems to be couched in such general terms, and I
had a little trouble finding out exactly what issues the manuscript deals
with. As I understand it, the paper is an attempt to see education as part of
the flow of information in the cultural system and to suggest ways of
looking at the constraints to the flow of information within that system.
That is a very general notion, and it leaves a number of questions open.
For example, there is the problem of what we are dealing with. Are we
dealing simply with learning, or are we dealing with education in general?
If we are talking about some kind of transfer of information, are we
dealing with the kind of information that is transferred in a single session
or, rather, in a single encounter, as the word is used, or are we also dealing
with the cumulative transfer of information and learning that requires
different kinds of mechanisms, somewhat different kinds of theories? It
was not clear from reading the general theoretical account which of these
issues are being dealt with. I have some other problems about the notion
of agenda. A contrast is drawn between open agenda and stable agenda. I
do not know what, in any kind of interaction theory that I know of, open
agenda would mean. Does it mean that one subscribes to a kind of a
tabula rasa theory of mind? Can we simply think that there is any situation
where any one approaches any kind of information without some kind of

cultural predisposition, preconceptions? Certainly, if that is what is claimed, there is plenty of evidence from psycholinguistics to contradict that. There is, for example, the whole history of innateness versus behavioral approaches to language and also cognitive development that would have to be dealt with. But, maybe I misunderstand what is meant here.

Another problem relates to the notion of stable agenda. These stable agendas are supposed to relate to various kinds of social categories. But the only kind of social categories that I see mentioned are gross categories, the kind of social indicators that are usually used in surveys (but that are not exactly interactional categories): sex, class, ethnic identity, and so on. I think one of the findings of recent work in interaction is that these gross categories are useful in studies of large-scale systems. When we study person-to-person interaction, however, social categories are communicated rather than given. The kind of social categories that are symbolized in everyday interaction are much finer and more specific. This is exactly the problem that people like Goffman and, more specifically, Aaron Cicourel, in his recent book, *Cognitive sociology* (1973), deal with — the whole problem of status and role and how they are communicated. I do not know what is meant here, what are the authors thinking of — is it correlation between these categories and some kind of a behavioral effect or is something else meant?

I might cite the findings of sociolinguistics during the last ten years, for example, concerning attempts to correlate educational success with gross categories of dialect deviance or ethnic identity. The initial finding was that members of minority groups and speakers of minority dialects were behind members of the majority group on all measures of educational success. They performed less well on all kinds of intelligence and achievement tests. A great deal of work, therefore, has gone into trying to examine the relationship between minority language patterns and educational success. It has been found (in a number of studies, including some at Berkeley) that, while there is a correlation with such gross social categories, this does not mean that speaking a minority dialects impedes reading in standard English as such. There is no correlation between dialect pronunciation and knowledge of minority dialects and a child's ability to read. To the extent that there is a correlation between social categories and educational success, the relationship is one among three factors: (1) reading, (2) language, and (3) the interactional characteristics of the classroom situation (Piestrup n.d.). When you have the kind of classroom interaction that is open in the sense that the teacher is responsive to student suggestions, when what is being done in the classroom is adaptive to student initiative, there tends to be no correlation between dialect deviance and educational success as measured by reading tests. If you have a rigid situation where the teacher controls the interaction closely, where she follows a set strategy and is not responsive, there does arise a correlation between dialect deviance and educational success. I do not know how to fit this type of data into the notion of open and stable agenda. I do not know whether the distinction between responsive and rigid strategies would fit into the notions of open agenda or stable agenda being dealt with here.

Another problem is that I am not sure what is meant by microbehavior. Are the authors dealing with actual ongoing interaction or with the results of interaction? Frederick Barth and a number of other writings were cited. There has been insufficient attention paid to the distinction between small group or interaction studies, which try to specify how social factors constrain each individual's action, and large-scale studies, which really deal with social systems and see these systems in Weberian terms as the result of a number of interactions. I think the two types of study require a different method of analysis. Another important point that is not referred to here is that most of the work in linguistic anthropology during the last ten to fifteen years shows that we simply do not as yet have adequate methods and techniques for observing interaction validly. For studies of interaction, we do not have available the kind of methods that we have in more limited types of linguistic study. Linguistic anthropologists can go into any society, study a strange language, come up with a phonemic analysis of that language, and then be 80 to 90 percent sure that his analysis will be validated by another linguistic anthropologist. That is not true for studies of interaction. A great deal of mention is made in the literature of the work of Bernstein (1964). His notion of restricted and elaborated code is widely cited. Yet these notions have never been defined linguistically. Nobody has ever examined whether one investigator's identification of an instance of an elaborated code is the same as that of another, a fact that has been established by the critiques that have been made of some of Bernstein's detailed studies. We don't know what elaborated or restricted codes are. I think the same thing is true of the notion of cognitive style. Cognitive styles are arrived at through language, because we always observe either speech or nonverbal communicative behavior, yet the methods for studying these types of behavior are not at all clear. There is a methodological problem here, one that a linguistic anthropologist would see in studying interaction but which is not apparent from the surface reading of the existing literature. In literature reviews, there is too much acceptance of findings at face value, too little questioning of what these findings mean. Some of the most frequently cited findings may turn out to be reversed once more valid methods are developed. I think this is probably most of what I wanted to say as a general comment. Now I do not know if this is useful or not.

Sangree: Yes, it sounds very helpful. It seems to me that you think actual data gathering and data analysis is going to provide some problems, not just with this theory but with any kind of theory.

Gumperz: I am not saying that any other kind of theory will not have these problems.

Sangree: I am particularly intrigued by your very clear statement of certain problems of methodology. In particular, I am referring to the problem of being able to define these different kinds of agenda that are very crucial to being able to develop this theory.

Gumperz: Yes, I think — I really wonder whether the notion of open agenda should not be clarified. I was not quite sure about the notion of property involved there. I recall Erving Goffman's "free goods," which I think is related. In other words, there are certain kinds of information that are "free goods" and certain kinds of information that are clearly not. But, if that is what is meant, then things are a little bit clearer. In that case, I think open agenda is kind of a misnomer. At least, it ought to be specified what is meant by it; because then my assumption that the *tabula rasa* theory of human perception was adopted is wrong. But I had no way of finding that out. I am trying to guess at what is meant here.

Sangree: Right. That is helpful, I am sure, to the people who are working on this, because if they do not have comments from people about what comes to mind when the manuscript is read from different perspectives, then they could not carry on. Do you have any particular comments about their notion of cultural premises? Did this help in clarifying your ideas of agenda or trying to grasp what they meant?

Gumperz: Well, here I would want to point out that there are a number of definitions of culture. There are two major kinds of definition of culture at the moment. There is Kluckhohn's definition of culture, which is pretty much the one that is followed here: the designs for living, customs, beliefs, values, and so on. And then there is Goodenough's definition of culture which is much more narrow and states that culture is what you have to learn to interact in a society. Being a linguistic anthropologist, I happen to be prejudiced in favor of the Goodenough definition, basically because it is studiable through language; and because, as a matter of fact, I can find ways of looking at interaction in conversations and find out what the cultural premises are. I think some of the recent developments in linguistic semantics and ordinary language philosophy for example demonstrate that understanding verbal acts and understanding speech acts really is a matter not only of sharing grammatical knowledge, but also of sharing certain kinds of unstated social presuppositions. It is possible to study conversations, especially conversations as seen in terms of interaction dyads, or turns of speaking by examining the logic of the sequencing of the questions and answers, and by checking one's interpretation through interview techniques, i.e., trying to get interpretations of particular conversational sequences and trying to find out what these interpretations imply in terms of social presupposition. It is possible to get a great deal of cultural information in this way.

The notion of culture that I like and that I think is most useful in the study of interaction, is the notion that culture is what I have to know in order to interpret and produce sentences. That is a limited notion, but I find it very useful for interaction studies. Obviously, if one wants to draw conclusions, to generalize from these interaction studies, one has to look at other kinds of phenomena. Analytically at least, I like to separate these kinds of things. I like to look at studies of interaction and of premises that are symbolized through interaction, separately from the study of such macrophenomena as the overall effect of certain kinds of conditions, certain kinds of socioecological constraints on interaction patterns.

Sangree: Is this a fair statement to make? There may be a point at which viewing culture as information flow, as seems to be done in this theory, will have to be curtailed somewhat, or at least analytically pieced down.

Gumperz: I would say it would have to be broken down, that these two approaches would have to be separated. I think this implies different methods, different kinds of data-gathering techniques.

Sangree: I wonder if you had a few more words to say about that.

Gumperz: If we are looking at culture and interaction, we can then simply work from transcripts of conversation; we can then work with detailed small-scale studies, very intensive studies of interaction sequences. If we are looking at the macrophenomena, obviously we have to then work with statistical data of various kinds, and possibly with data on social networks and things of that sort.

Sangree: And you foresee difficulty; there seems to be a world between them.

Gumperz: I feel that the gap between these two kinds of study has not been bridged. And I think that is one of the questions for future research — how is this gap to be bridged?

COMMENT *by Ray C. Rist*

In any attempt to devise a set of propositions that are interrelated in such a way as to lead toward theory-building, there is an inevitable tension between the *scope* and the *specificity*. It is no less the case in the present instance. While on the one hand, the authors are seeking the scope of a cross-cultural theory of education, they offer little in the way of precise statements that would make their theory operational for empirical verification. Given that scope and precision exist in a reciprocal relation to one another, it is beside the point to fault the authors for having opted for scope as the major consideration of the theory. Nevertheless, it is important to note that with this choice, the theory gives only vague clues as to how it might be evaluated. One of the more apparent difficulties, then, is how to find negative evidence. The authors suggest that, if such evidence could be found, then they would have to limit their theory to only select cultural systems. But again, no readily available evaluation methods are suggested, and one is left hesitant to proclaim the virtues of the theory as a theory.

There are several other aspects of this attempt at theory construction that deserve mention. The parsimony of the theory is one of its most appealing attributes. There are relatively few elements in the theory and thus relatively few assumptions. Consequently, the fewer the untested assumptions, the more powerful the theory if those assumptions turn out to be essentially correct. Further, the propositions that are presented are systematically interrelated. They do not stand alone. The case for a certain model of causality is built step by step through the theory. This is of critical importance, because, if methods can be found to evaluate the theory empirically, it should be apparent almost from the first analysis that the validity of the theory is due to the interrelatedness of its parts.

The title of this theory is somewhat misleading. When one writes of "education," the instinctive image is that of a formal, often bureaucratic endeavor occurring in special locations called schools. Yet, this is not a theory of schooling. It is a theory of information transfer. Consequently, the issues addressed in this theory are not ones that focus on the structural issues of how and who is allowed to partake of "education," but rather, they are more related to the sociopsychological dynamics found in face-to-face interaction. What happens in schools becomes only one possible subset of all the situations with which such interaction occurs. I used the term "possible" advisedly, for there is considerable debate as to whether education in the way in which it is used in this theory does occur in schools.

The fact that this theory does not address itself directly to the processes of schooling, which is a compulsory activity for millions of children and young people throughout the world, is one of its major omissions. (But this is one of the consequences of the theory's scope.) By offering no means by which to link the theory to specific institutional arrangements, the theory is unable to suggest what the interactions might be between two individuals or between groups of individuals within various institutional settings. Though the authors note that although they derive much from the analysis of Goffman, they have not followed him in his attempts to make an interconnection between the individual and those institutions that impinge upon him, as was his aim in *Asylums* (1961a).

Another important point is that, given the emphasis on the transmission of information as the basis for what is described as education, I am unconvinced that the almost offhanded dismissal of the mass media from their theoretical focus is valid. The authors limit their investigation to "events where two or more persons come into recurrent face-to-face interchange." For them this rules out the impact of the media. It is understandable that they do this. They have at once a very broad and a very narrow definition of the phenomena they are studying:

Where two or more persons come into face-to-face exchange, and where any two or more of those same persons do so recurrently over some duration, they are engaged in an encounter; the educational system of any society (or smaller group or wider social network) is the totality of all such regularly occurring encounters.

By restricting themselves to face-to-face encounters that are recurrent, the authors have built into their theory the assumption that education has as one of its basic components some pattern of reciprocity. Thus, education becomes both functional and normative to the established order (cf. Gouldner 1959).[1] The impact of the media had to be eliminated from this theory, for it is essentially its Achilles heel. Glaringly absent from the media as a tool of information transfer is the face-to-face interaction, and more fundamentally, any norm of reciprocity. One leaves the television or radio when one is ready. One does not have to go through any sort of disengagement technique to break off the interaction other than to flick the switch. One uses it as one wishes and when one wishes. There is no need for the taking of the role of the other so as to be sensitive to their needs, their emotions, or their investment in the interaction. The media allows one to depersonalize the absorbing of information.

At this point, the essentially liberal and humane thrust of the theory becomes apparent. The authors rule out the media because they do not want to have to grapple with what is to them inhumane and noninteractive. The "boob tube" makes it all so easy, so quick and so noncommittal — opposites of a recurring face-to-face exchange, which is the core of the theory. Ironically, though the authors would likely espouse the traditional values inherent in the transmission of Western thought (and notions in the academy of teachers that they teach willing students who are there because they want to be), the reality does not fit. Children in the United States, the most advanced of the industrial countries and the first to move into the post-industrial age, now watch television more than they engage in any other single activity except sleep. Tens of millions of American children are in front of sets watching "Sesame Street," "The Electric Company," "Zoom" and hundreds of other programs that do not even pretend to be educational.

[1] Though it would take us afield, it is worth noting that, with the norm of reciprocity so close to the center of this theory, it would be worthwhile to explore how the theory allows for education as an agent of social change. I suspect it would not easily do so. By placing the stress on interaction, one could talk only about change as it happened piecemeal and nonsystematically.

The single nation that spends more on education than does any other nation, is the one where one finds decreasing opportunities and circumstances for this theory to be applicable. Granted, face-to-face interaction does occur, but I seriously doubt that it is any longer the primary source of information for children or adults. To ignore this fundamental transition in how information is exchanged (in the United States, at least) is to narrow the theory to a point of diminishing returns. For example, based on this theory we would ignore the impact of the US Senate Watergate hearings in the summer of 1973 — a dramatic instance of information transmission where there were no patterns of reciprocity. This is tantamount to missing the mark of what is entailed in education. McLuhan may not be completely correct in his prophecy of a "global village," but the US as a "national village" is already a reality.

The authors of the theory made the following statement: "It should additionally be mentioned that, in the course of doing education work, parties also generate an additional kind of social identity — smart and dumb — in the variety of ways that may be phrased and perceived."

I find this a profoundly important statement, and yet there is totally absent any elaboration of how such labelling comes to occur. To continually stress that the theory deals with the dynamics of face-to-face interaction in the transmission of information, and to suggest that in that interaction there are differential evaluations of participants that generate "an additional kind of social identity," and then not to detail that process, considerably weakens the applicability of the theory. For I would suggest that the imputation of a new social identity of one who is "dumb" and, therefore, cannot learn, directly influences the options one has for future participation in the learning process. So we come to the point where it may not be the actual ability the person possesses that influences his likelihood of further learning encounters, but the perceptions of others as to his worthiness to do so. The consequence of this is that we need not only a theory of education, but a theory of how it is that some persons come to be perceived as able and worthy to learn and others do not. Further, we need to know what the consequences are for both groups as a result of these designations. Finally, it is necessary to encompass who is deemed as the proper evaluator of others and how it is that they came to occupy such positions of evaluation. What this critique ultimately implies is that there is a need for more attention to the social context in which that face-to-face interaction occurs. When that interaction is between persons of unequal power and authority to decide the outcome of their interaction, I suspect much of what is thought of as education is ultimately a screening process, a process whereby potential is only one of a number of factors that decide the outcome for the child, with social contingencies being of great importance. As one brief example, in my own observations, I have found several instances where children who came to school with a strong odor of urine were segregated as untouchables from the remainder of the class. Here the social contingency of body odor superceded any other attribute the child might have possessed and resulted in an isolation that precluded any face-to-face interacting with a teacher or peers.

In summary, I am encouraged with this attempt at developing a theoretical model that will allow for the cross-cultural examination of learning. It is imperative that it become a comparative examination. However, I am most disappointed in the lack of attention paid to the systematic issues of who is to participate; when they are to do so; what the consequences are from differential evaluation of that participation; and how it comes to pass that, in interaction, there are differentials of power, authority, and legitimacy for the construction of a particular reality that is seen as true while alternative realities are viewed as untrue. Learning never occurs in a vacuum; interaction is never in a vacuum; therefore, I think it necessary to be cognizant of the context in which face-to-face meetings occur. Otherwise, one must opt for the erroneous assumption that there is a uniformity in the social world that allows us to ignore it. And I hardly think we are safe in doing so.

COMMENT *by Carol Talbert*

> Upon invitation, Carol Talbert held a telephone conversation with the editor relating her own research among black school children and their black teachers to Working Paper 6. The conversation was recorded on tape, transcribed, and edited.

Gearing's paper is relevant to research conducted in 1970, which analyzed classroom dynamics and linguistic usage (Helen Gouldner 1971). It was found that the capacity of first grade, poverty area black children to switch from black English phonology to standard English phonology in appropriate settings was an attribute that was selectively distributed in the population of the children in the classroom. The measure of standard English usage was the r usage, the expression of underlying r (W. Labov 1968). Suprasegmental indices further validated shifts in style. It should not be difficult for any black child to learn standard English. All the students did convert some of their black English speech patterns to standard English usage. Ability should diffuse randomly throughout the population of black speakers. But it was blocked in this case. It was not random but systematically distributed. In other words, certain children in the class who were the most favored children — "teacher's pets" — learned standard English. The restraints that reduced randomness should be investigated.

Tape recordings were made of classroom proceedings. By this method, interesting facts about the teacher's linguistic usage were discovered. A teacher who was herself black used black English phonology and switched to standard English phonology at predictable times. Pupils able to do the same were rated by her as potentially successful. That is to say, the teacher was requested to rate the children in terms of their potential success or lack of success in school and a close correlation was found between a child's ability to switch to standard English and a teacher's high rating of the child. The child who could use standard English phonology in particular contexts 100 percent of the time was at the top of the teacher's list. The child who switched to standard English intermittently and in a rather unpredictable fashion was not designated as potentially successful.

There was a baseline of black English grammar that all black speakers shared. All black children learned to speak black English; all the children tested used black English grammar in certain situations, e.g., talking to each other, group discussions, singing, laughing, telling jokes or "kooky" stories — they were all competent black English speakers. All the children were competent black English speakers and used this language form in their interaction with each other and with teachers in informal settings. None of them spoke standard English all the time.

In Gearing's terms, "any item of information or skill can move from adult to child, or child to child automatically." However, in this situation blockage occurred: some children became adept at standard English and others did not. The usual measures of intellectual capacity or socioeconomic status were not used to make distinctions among children. All these children were from an extremely impoverished neighborhood. They had had no intelligence or achievement testing at this point. The teacher could not use these results to measure child potential. The question was, "Why is it that some of these children learned to use standard English when appropriate and others did not?" This is the question Gearing's model asks. But we do not know the answer.

The teacher used standard English in situations in which she was addressing the class as a whole, in which she was being instrumental or "teacher." When she was mother, talking one-to-one with a child, or admonishing a child, she used black English. When talking with each other the children used black English all the time. When responding to the teacher during recitation in the classroom, they used standard English with varying degrees of competency. They used standard English when reading aloud, as did the teacher (Talbert 1973).

It seemed there were two separate agendas found in our data. One agenda was a dyad of people speaking their natural language, black English; these were open agendas. There was little confusion, and information flowed quickly. Initiation and responses were congruent with cultural norms, e.g., black children usually do not initiate conversations

Table 1.   Ethnography of black English and standard English speech events: determination of code usage

Code	Usage	Sender		Receiver		Channel		Setting		Message form
BAE	←	AD	+	CH	+	V	+	1–1	+	IC
BAE	←	CH	+	CH	+	V	+	PG	+	GR, SG, JK, IC
BAE	←	CH	+	AD	+	V	+	1–1	+	IC
SAE	←	AD	+	GRP	+	V	+	CL	+	DIR
SAE	←	CH	+	AD	+	V	+	CL	+	RDG
SAE	←	GRP	+	GRP	+	V	+	PG	+	RDG

Key:
BAE = Black American English
SAE = Standard American English
AD = Adult
CH = Child
V = Verbal
PG = Peer group
1–1 = one-to-one conversation

CL = Class
DIR = Giving directions
SG = Singing
JK = Telling jokes, spooky stories
IC = Informal conversation
RDG = Reading

with adults; this is an expression of one of the salient characteristics of intergenerational respect behavior in black culture.

In the second type of agenda, the troublesome agenda, involved the use of standard English. On the one hand, a speaker — the teacher — used standard English, and in some situations, a child responded in black English, which the teacher defined as an error — a wrong answer.

Gearing discussed classes of persons and classes of information that were systematically absent. He indicated that the absence of information was related to perceived categories of people. This was a major concern in our research. What did the teacher perceive in her class of kindergarteners that caused her to react to different children in a different fashion? They all shared the same ethnic identity, though, importantly, as a teacher, she was of a higher social class than they. The teacher reacted positively or did not have troublesome agendas with some of the children, and it was hypothesized that these are the ones that she perceived as being upwardly mobile. There was no investigation of factors in the home that produced children who have had more exposure to standard English speech or to behavior that was more "white-like." The teacher in some unconscious fashion appeared to react to the perception of some of the children as being socially mobile. There were others she appeared to perceive as not being mobile, as being truly impoverished children who would remain that way. In interviews with teachers and principals, there was a prevalent attitude that "some of our children will make it, and the rest of them will not."

Did the teacher perceive her competence with standard English to be similar to having property? A particular technological skill or information, namely, the ability to interact using standard grammar and the ability to read using standard grammar, is the property that produced success on the part of some of her pupils. As Gearing points out, possession of it serves as a mark or standard with all the privileges it entails.

The fact that the teacher and the students were all nonwhite members of a racist society was a cultural premise not consciously allowed for and not consciously expressed by the teacher or the students. The child cannot alter his ethnic status and become white. On the other hand, social class mobility is possible.

Where mobility and sharing were problematic, troublesome agendas regularly emerged. As the teacher was not sure who would succeed, she chose those who were most "white-like" and most similar to her. She selected those to be most positive within her interaction. This was a situation in which mobility and sharing of understanding were indeed problematic for some children, and troublesome agendas would be predicted. In the classroom interaction study it was found that four or five "teacher's pets" emerged. Some children — those that were not able to code shift — became peripheral to the learning situation altogether. All positive features of the interactions went to the few potentially successful pupils. Where the teacher used standard English and the child was not able to repeat it, the teacher defined this as an error — the teacher did not listen to the child, and generally pushed the child out of the learning situation (Talbert 1970). As Gearing pointed out, finally the child quits playing the game at all. This did not occur with all the children of the classroom, only the ones who were least favored by the teacher — the peripheral children.

Patterns of initiation and response discussed by Gearing evoke a consideration of early learning and open agendas. All black children became competent black English speakers in their families. Oftentimes the children in the classroom looked on their black teacher as black mother, and she would respond to them as a black mother would — in black grammar. In these interactions communication did not break down. These were open agendas, and the communication was understood by both.

Gearing discussed cultural premises. Where troublesome agendas prevail he said that cultural premises are not exchanged or shared. This applies to certain assumptions about relationships between people, largely unverbalized by the teacher, which had an impact on her reactions to the children. The unspoken assumption was related to social stratification and racism in this society, i.e., some of these black children will make it, and some of them will not. There is an implicit conflict and contradiction between the cultural premise that our society is racist and the premise that the teacher is democratic and gives everyone an equal chance to succeed. The teacher was herself black, which added to the paradox of the situation. How could she, as an oppressed black person, oppress others because of the behavior she herself exhibited? She was a black English speaker, yet she penalized children for being black English speakers. To an extent, she was not aware that she was a black English speaker. She did not teach the children black English; she did not tell them that, if they learned to be nonblack in certain situations, they would more readily succeed. She talked about "good English" and "talking right" even though on a familial level she preferred to use black English — the language of life, the language she used to punish and to love.

Black English grammar learned in the home — an open agenda — was predictable, organized, systematic, or as Gearing would say, "is a settled pattern of initiation and response and is some pattern of control." The concept of black English fits into this, as would standard English. Standard English was a skill in which the children were not necessarily competent when they came to school and which they learned selectively. A cultural premise in a sense is equivalent to a speaker's grammar. Black English was not a barrier to initiating communication with others who also spoke it. A troublesome agenda could be predicted in movements across the two grammars.

Gearing noted that an educational system was a series of reenactments of the wider social system. Our research indicated the teacher indirectly communicated to the children that they would be more successful if they would suppress their own language and use standard English. Unconsciously, language became a moral issue, that is, "It is good to speak standard English; it is bad to speak black English." In this way, the first grade teacher reenacted the wider social system. She acted as a filter, as the one who selected and identified the garbage collectors, welfare recipients, and the college graduates.

During our observations, none of the children who were in the back of the room or in the lower sections of the class were ever moved up to the "stars" table. Some of the children moved back, down, and became peripheral, but no child ever moved up. Once the pupils were put into a category, usually in kindergarten, there was a lock-step progression until they finally dropped out or achieved some success in the school context. In Gearing's words, "the parties declare war, with the contenders aligned in such a way that the sectors of society at or near the center of power are assured of winning." The powerful in this society were assured of winning by teachers who filtered out those children who do not share the knowledge and value system of white society. These data fit into Gearing's thesis that educational systems serve as brakes against social change.

Sangree: Could I ask you to elaborate a couple of points? The child coming from the home already has skill in black English.
Talbert: Right, all the children that I tested had a base of black English. They all were very competent.
Sangree: Some do and some do not speak easily in standard English?

Talbert: Yes, given the appropriate situation — reading from a book, writing — all the children endeavored to use standard English phones. But their competence in this matter was very, very different, ranging from 10 to 100 percent.

Sangree: Was there some way of noting whether these children, from their home experience, are more or less set by that competence they display when they first come to school? Was some kind of microanalysis directed at catching whether teachers actually discouraged some children from becoming competent in standard English? If so, for what reasons? Was it just because they already were not? Or was it because they had some other kind of background or behavioral characteristic that the teacher intended to make sure, not deliberately, that they did not become more competent in standard English?

Talbert: One thing is fairly certain; it was not by sex. I think that is important because one of the assumptions is that black girls make it and black boys do not.

Sangree: But you did not see this in your —

Talbert: No, no, statistically not at all. There were girls on the bottom, and there were boys on the top. I did have a feeling that boys that acted like girls got to the top. Ray Rist had all kinds of ideas that were not empirically demonstrated (that the lowest children were dirtier, smelled of urine, etc.). I also took into account the jobs that parents had: who was on welfare, who was not, who said there was a father in the home, who did not, and I found that little statistical relationship existed. A welfare woman living by herself, or a welfare woman who is the sole family support, oftentimes will have a very clean house and be very conscientious about her child, showing him off, displayed excessive rigidity about his doing his lessons and getting his numbers —

Sangree: Did the teacher, in spite of all that care toward the education of the child, still discriminate against that child in converting into standard English in the appropriate situations?

Talbert: I found that there is a certain kind of child who is rewarded almost from the beginning. Jules Henry, before he became ill, was on this trail. He said that these are the children who come to school feeling competent, feeling egalitarian to the teacher; they could talk up to her; they could speak out; they could interrupt — all actions that violate norms of black culture. What you have are favorite children who are treated like adults. The teachers act seductively toward them; they make little remarks to them; and they make jokes, that is adult to adult — not child to adult — behavior in the black community. Children who act in child to adult fashion and are not aggressive, who never initiate interaction, always tend to be in the background. It is the aggressive, bold, little girls who are not intimidated by a female teacher. I think it is especially important that little boys learn how to handle a female teacher, too. You know, they usually are dressed nicely. It is never a really dirty kid who is the favorite kid.

Sangree: It must be a combination of factors, behavioral and —

Talbert: It is not anything like SES; all these kids were poor. This was a 90 percent poverty district, which makes it good. I think that teachers must have reacted to those youngsters' abilities to use standard English early on. I did not do linguistic analyses of new kindergarteners coming in; I just did the first graders. I did an analysis of Headstart children from the same neighborhood, and none of them were code-shifting. But I don't know if code-shifting is something that only occurs when a child begins to go to school and is presented with written information. I think a lot of black kids who have middle class parents or ones that are oriented toward the middle class are exposed to adults who code switch. This is a competency they have to learn. They would be laughed at if they code-switched improperly in informal situations. All this is unspoken; even the teacher does not know when she talks in black English. This is all unconscious, because the teacher is communicating different things to the child. When she acts like a mother praising, or getting angry, listening intently, or being very personable, she talks in black English. I have a tape of a teacher talking to one student, and her *r* usage goes from 80 to 30 percent. In fact, going from "shut your mouth" to "what is this?" which is really not even standard English — hypercorrecting. But she is certainly much more likeable when she speaks black English. She can communicate that to the kids: she can love and eat and enjoy people in black English, but she has to be uptight and rigid in standard English.

SECTION FOUR

On an Inductive Method

COMMENT *by Madeleine Mathiot and Paul Garvin et al.*

Madeleine Mathiot and Paul Garvin graciously consented to conduct a seminar on March 21, 1974, to address the general theory of cultural transmission as presented by Gearing and his associates in Working Paper 6. More specifically, they were willing to consider in that seminar the following questions:

In an analysis of interaction, the anthropologist who desires to conduct his inquiry in an inductive fashion is in rather a predicament. In order to begin observation leading to analysis, there must be some conceptualization of the units — both analytic units and behavioral units — and their interrelations. But what if the anthropologist desires to have these units come from the data itself, i.e., what if he does not desire to impose an arbitrary framework on the data if he is to work inductively? From your field and academic experience, can you detail the sequence of identification of the analytic and behavioral units in your work?

Can you specify what might be the general aspects of such units, thus enabling the start towards their use cross-culturally?

Can you comment on the verbal or nonverbal types of units? Is Goldschmidt's emphasis (1972) on verbal aspects of encounter analysis an emphasis the fieldworker can be comfortable with?

We have received the following comment from Norman McQuown: "Finally, I find that the instrument for discovering what is really going on in such groupings, repeatedly asserted to be a microanalysis of behavior, is very poorly specified. I miss, likewise, any reference to the not inconsiderable body of preliminary theory with respect to the potential valences of particular microanalytic bits of behavior for the marking of shifts of stance within a group and of shifts of reference without the group." McQuown's comment points directly at the underdeveloped aspect of Working Paper 6. The theory authors take an inductive posture; therefore, they must bear the burden of outlining the beginnings of their inductive procedure and its logical relation to the general propositions. Can you give us your views on McQuown's comment?

The Center for the Study of Man, the students present,[1] and Gearing and his associates are extremely grateful to Mathiot and Garvin for their generosity in giving their attention to these questions and an entire afternoon of their mid-term vacation for the seminar. The following pages contain passages of direct transcriptions from the two-and-one-half hour tape of the proceedings and summaries of the discussions that took place that afternoon. The direct transcriptions are as correct as we could make them. The summary of discussions taken from the tape were made by L. Sangree and F. Gearing. They take full responsibility for any errors of omission or any misinterpretation contained in this summary — with apologies in advance to Mathiot and Garvin.

Mathiot: In connection with face-to-face interaction, it seems to me that the point of central interest is how many structures or how many systems are being postulated.

I recently tried to make a list of potential number of systems by taking into account those that have been mentioned or isolated by various people. I looked at the various channels of communication. Preceding this, you ask yourself how many media are involved in the communicative process? For example, the voice is one medium, and another is the body. Then ask yourself how many channels you would have per medium. With the voice as a medium, if we start with the traditional distinctions we can distinguish a liguistic channel and a paralinguistic channel. Taking the body as a medium, we can distinguish between the kinesic channel and the proxemic channel.

If this seems to be more or less a good point of departure, we can look at each one of these channels and ask ourselves what kind of units there are.

With the linguistic channel and the proxemic channel (providing you conceive of the last one in terms of Kendon's work rather than Hall's), I think you definitely could talk about behavioral and analytical units, whereas in the kinesic channel and in the paralinguistic channel, the kinds of units are still not obvious. Consider for the moment behavioral units, which are the correct units to get at the analytic units that will surely be the center of discussion here. We can look at the linguistic channel and ask ourselves how many units we are aware of at the moment. There are the usual morphemes in the grammatical dimension and lexical units in the lexical dimension. To that I would add discourse units such as speech acts for conversation and what I have called informational statements for narrative — conversation and narrative being two types of discourse. And then there is a third type of discourse which you can call expository prose. Paul has done a study of that, but I do not remember what he calls his units. Do you call them predication types?

[1] The following individuals were present at the seminar on March 21, 1974, held in Hayes Hall, State University of New York at Buffalo: Thomas Carroll, Dr. Paul Garvin, Dr. Frederick Gearing, Karen Gordon, Pat Hurlich, Dr. Madeleine Mathiot, Leta Richter, Lucinda Sangree, Allen Smith, Moya Smith, Dr. Allan Tindall.

Garvin: Yes, predications.

Mathiot: Predications. Each one of these types of discourse would have a basic kind of unit to which I would give a different name. I would prefer to reserve the term "speech act" for use in conversational dialogue, the term "informational statement" for narrative, and the term "predications" for expository prose. Then we can look at face formation systems and ask ourselves what the units are. Face formation systems constitute an aspect of proxemics because they deal with the way in which people structure their environment — spatial and social. It seems to me that the work of Kendon fits these perfectly. What he calls a face formation system can be regarded as either another name for, or another aspect of, proxemics. I think Kendon does have his units, which he calls the *O* shapes. In the linguistic channel and proxemic channel, there are very clear-cut units we could consider behavioral units versus analytic units. In the case of speech acts, the distinction is very clear: an utterance occurs when a person begins to talk and ends when talking ceases, it is a *behavioral unit*; whereas a speech act is defined in terms of a particular cultural function or meaning — a request for information as opposed to a request for an action; this is an *analytic unit*.

The moment you work with conversation, you will see that speech acts are not coterminous with utterances. An utterance may contain more than one speech act, or it may contain less than one speech act. For this reason, it is a nice area in which to look at the difference between analytic and behavioral units. In other cases, such as morphemic and lexical units, the matter might become a little bit too technical.

In Kendon's face formation system, I have the feeling that his *O* shape is an analytic unit. As I understand it, it is the structure, uh — what is the word I want?

Garvin: The distinction is that the *O* shape has a function.

Mathiot: The function is to sustain interaction.

Garvin: Therefore, you say it is an analytic unit.

Mathiot: Although he didn't call it that, I thought it was an analytic unit. In the paralinguistic channel, for instance, though many dimensions have been isolated and many potential units have been isolated, I still don't think it is clear what units are.

Garvin: The classical Trager-Smith notion is that there are really no units in paralanguage because it differs from intonations by not having that kind of a structure. One can disagree with that, but that has clearly led to a suspension of the search for paralinguistic units. What they have is kind of an underlying property that covers a whole raft of linguistic units, such as rasp or unction, overloudness or oversoftness. These are really features that accompany certain linguistic stretches. Trager and Smith have never attempted to look at paralinguistic phenomena in terms of units because in their frame of reference that is counter to the conception of it. And I do not think that many people besides Trager and Smith have even talked about paralinguistics.

I want to talk very briefly about the basic notions of behavioral units versus analytic units. In our frame of reference behavioral units are units that are delimited in the behavior itself. That is to say, where, by simple observation, one can note breaks. And one could obviously say that anytime a behavior has a clear-cut beginning and an ending, it constitutes a behavioral unit. For instance, anything in phonology that is bounded by juncture, that is to say a phonological breaking point, is by definition a behavioral unit. Analytic units, on the other hand, are developed by analysis on the basis of some theoretical and methodological frame of reference. One could say then that behavioral units are input into the analysis, and analytic units are the outcome from the analysis.

In linguistics, it is necessary to distinguish between two basic kinds of behavioral units: spontaneous versus elicited. There are behavioral units that are self-delimited in spontaneous speech and behavioral units that are delimited because when you elicit data, you get limited chunks. You could have a comparable behavioral unit in nonverbal communication. You could ask an informant, for instance, to show you the gesture for "come here," and when he does, you have elicited a behavioral unit. An obvious point is that one has in linguistics the two possibilities of observing and eliciting. Most fieldwork in the anthropological tradition in linguistics is done by elicitation. One can argue about why and how, but the only point relevant to behavioral units is that every time you elicit you get delimited stretches that by definition constitute behavioral units.

Another question is, what kind of analytic units are sought? In order to talk about how behavioral units are maximally useful for the co-consideration of certain kind of analytic units, one must have some previous idea of the analytic units that one is aiming at.

Mathiot: And that will affect the choice of the behavioral unit that is most appropriate.

Garvin: In thinking through the problem of discovery procedure in linguistics, I have come up with the notion of the reference model. In order for the analysis to proceed, you have to make a number of fairly specific assumptions, which are nonetheless, only assumptions that serve as the frame of reference for the analysis. They do not have the status of assumptions that you must necessarily hold to be true. This is important because during the analysis, it may turn out that some of the features of the reference model are just not present in a given set of data. Also, the reference model indicates the likely kinds of analytic units that you can hunt for, the things Madeleine mentioned, morphemes and lexical units and so forth. These are all in some ways part of the reference model and I am not going to go into details of what kind of reference model is used in linguistics. The point is that the reference model is different from the theoretical model that represents your notion of the nature of the object. The theoretical model is very vague in my case and in Madeleine's. Language has some general properties, and since languages differ widely, you cannot make too many specific assumptions about the details. In order to be able to analyze you have to, however, make detailed assumptions and you put those in the reference model, as opposed to the true universal assumptions that you put into your theoretical model. This is really a two-model conception. One model is the theoretical notions that you have about the properties of language, which are necessarily very broad, and the other is a specific reference model that you construct.

Mathiot: And change all the time.

Garvin: And modify as you go along. The reference model is type specific, that is to say, for different types of languages, you would have different reference models.

One more general point. I think that one of the universals that applies to language applies to all of these different channels of communication. All are systems of signs and, therefore, must in some way manifest a form-function covariance. Unless each item of behavior can be assigned some function, it does not play a part in the system. Every gesture, every movement in a face formation system, or every distance in a proxemic system should in some way have meaning, cultural function, or whatever you wish to call it. I suspect that the basic tool in linguistics for establishing units is form-meaning covariance.

The problem of finding behavioral units per se is not very difficult. One has only to observe and note where things have some conspicuous break. There will be a lot of smooth movements and then suddenly an abrupt movement; one can assume it is a behavioral unit, between two abrupt movements. Conversely, if there are a lot of abrupt movements, followed by a smooth movement or anything along those lines, this will allow you to say: well, there is an observable boundary. The key question in mapping any kind of analytic units into or out of this is whether or not one can use some kind of form-function covariance or form-meaning covariance to get at this.

Summary of Discussion

There followed here a discussion between Gearing, Mathiot, and Garvin about whether an individual can usefully pay attention to only one analytic system in studying human communication. There was agreement that the grammar of a language can be considered as a system quite aside from any other aspect of that language, and the grammars of various languages can be compared to one another. The units one is considering in such a case fall within the grammatical structure or system. The major point was not whether the system one is studying is part of the larger whole, for indeed it is and it is only separable in an analytical sense.

Mathiot summed up the discussion by observing that the major question is whether what one is calling a system is isolatable, i.e., whether it has its own units in the sense that phonology is isolatable from the whole system of language as a particular type of structure that one can study independently of morphology, depending of course upon one's theoretical frame of reference. Proxemics is probably isolatable; kinesics probably is not.

Garvin distinguished between the kind of research focused primarily on emitting of behavior and research focused on the perception of the recipient. In their research he and Mathiot both rely on questioning informants about their own individual perception of messages. Even in the study of gestures one could use informants, e.g., by showing them silent movies and asking them to tell you what was happening. Garvin's criticism of Kendon, for example, is that Kendon tells you what is happening. Kendon did not ask individuals of the society to give their interpretations of the data, the films or video tapes he recorded.

There followed a discussion between Gearing and Garvin about the fact that the signaling that is going on among the individuals whom Kendon studied is in large measure tacit, not explicit, signaling. Therefore, if an informant, or informants, are shown the videotapes and asked to interpret them they will have to make an analysis of tacit behavior comparable to that made by the social scientist. Garvin said this is important, and that it is comparable to his spending hours with informants going over linguistic data so that he doesn't only rely on his own interpretation of the data. Gearing questioned the usefulness of using an informant, since what Kendon was after was an analysis of an observed signal that would permit a high accuracy in predicting what the counter signal would be. The interpretation placed on that is of necessity Kendon's — arising from his notions of human social behavior. Garvin maintained that no matter what kind of analysis is being made, the local informant's interpretation should be obtained and considered. Otherwise, said Garvin, how do you know it isn't Kendon's culture that is being analyzed and not that of the participants he is observing?

Garvin and Tindall discussed Garvin's notion that one observes and notes certain forms of behaviors, then seeks information from informants about what is going on in a sequence of communication, and thereby documents the covariance of form (behavior) and meaning (meaning to the members of that particular culture). Tindall asked whether it would be a useful approach to observe a behavior, then observe the next behavior, and finally draw from a series of observations the sequences of behaviors that occurs regardless of what any informants would or would not say about it. What Kendon has mapped out, said Tindall, is a predictable system of rules. And the reason he knows that it *means* something is because every time this happens, that happens. According to Tindall, Kendon has said after making observations of a sequence of behaviors — now, I think I know how this works.

Gearing pointed out that from here there are two ways to go. One way is to go to the informants and see how they read it insofar as they can verbalize it. Those are very interesting data. The other way is to make predictions and to test them by looking at sequences of behaviors, seeing the degree of regularity that unfolds in naturally occurring events.

But Garvin noted that even if you can predict that every time one person does such and such an act, then the other makes a certain gesture, it may be difficult to determine what this means in that cultural context. Meaning is, says Garvin, something we linguists assume to exist in a person's head and we have no direct access to it. One way to get clues as to that meaning is to ask informants to tell us their perceptions of the meanings of certain acts. We have to get access to meaning indirectly by translation or explanation. Microanalysts, he said, cannot know how finely drawn their analysis should be — how much detail they should attend to — unless they get information from informants about both the larger structure in which the observed actions take place *and* the psychological reality of detailed bits of observed behavior.

A discussion of meaning *versus* function followed. Mathiot said that one can make the distinction between eliciting statements about meaning from an informant — e.g., what is that meaning of a raised eyebrow in a given culture — and, on the other hand, an abstraction about function made by the social scientist after consideration of a number of such meaning statements — e.g., what is the role or function of gestures in communication in this given culture.

At Gearing's request Garvin and Mathiot proceeded to describe a hypothetical discovery procedure, imagining that Kendon's videotapes were the data. The procedure they outlined included the following major points: The theoretical model contains the assumption that each proxemic configuration is in some way culturally significant. They are nonrandom and are not meaningless. They are not just body motion without some symbolic value. The exact symbolic value is not yet known. In the reference model the social scientist might then make the assumption that the O shape serves conversation, or correlates with conversation. In other words, the researcher is speaking of the total proxemic system (or as Mathiot would prefer to call it, following Kendon, the face formation system) in a given culture. According to the reference model being constructed, one would expect to find various typical patterns that are characteristic of certain types of events. e.g., a party, a fight, etc. Each face formation configuration presumably is related to some denotable cultural event that has a name in the culture. One would go by folk taxonomy, seeing if there is an event that people can name. The *O* formation would be one unit, the battle formation would be another, a line of people looking at Niagara Falls would be another. Kendon, says Garvin, claims that the *O* shape maps into a conversation event. Accepting this as part of the reference model and carrying on with the building of the reference model, which rests on the assumption of form-function covariance, one would say that the *O* shape serves conversation. Therefore, the researcher would look at conversation and see whether in the development of the *O* shape there are any correspondences, e.g., whenever there is a change in interlocuter, is there anything that happens in the *O* shape.

The maximal unit is the entire conversation with the corresponding *O* shape — that is, from beginning to end. Then you want to break it up. One would try to find the culturally given elements of the events. One would use informants, perhaps showing them a film sequence and then asking them what is happening. Whatever the identifiable segments in the conversation are, one would try to relate those to something in the face formation pattern.

Gearing posed a question about the difficulty of simultaneously using discontinuity and informant awareness as boundary markers for behavioral units. He asked if there is not a problem of possible informant nonawareness of such discontinuities. Mathiot pointed out that in linguistic analysis the informant is not aware of morphemes — important behavioral units to the linguist. Garvin responded that certainly it depends upon the nature of the system, that in the case of the face formation system there may be discontinuities of behavior that don't correspond to discontinuities of cultural events to *meanings*.

Smith raised the question as to whether it makes sense to say that all analytic units have behavioral boundaries? All behavioral units are not analytic units, but perhaps all analytic units should be drawn to correspond with those boundaries.

Garvin observed that that is what Chomsky calls an empirical question. That is, you cannot theoretically assume that either all behavioral units necessarily correspond to analytic units or conversely. That is what the analysis should reveal. What is the relation between the two? It may be that this is the kind of behavior in which all boundaries of analytic units turn out to be also boundaries of behavioral units, but not conversely. It may well be, for instance, that the discontinuities of behavior that serve as boundaries of behavioral units are not all analytically significant. One may have an analytic unit within which there is a discontinuity of behavior that does not serve as a boundary between subdivisions of this unit but is inherently part of it. Smith asked whether, by the way you define the analytic task working with an informant, all of what Garvin is calling analytic units would always have behavioral boundaries, by definition.

At this point we return to the transcription of the recorded conversation.

Garvin: It is conceivable that the informant will say that now something has happened in the conversation, for example, that the speakers switched topics — and that's an important analytic event, if you will. If you assume that the analytic units are based on the configurations of the event as they relate to the face formation, and nothing happened in the face formation that corresponds to the shift of topic — that's conceivable.

Gearing: It is not conceivable to me that nothing happens that is not part of a set of behavioral units that go together to make up the whole system.

Garvin: I'm just inventing something to answer his question. If you can't conceive of it, then okay. But your real task is to put all these micro bits in their proper place. Because if you don't put them in their proper place you have something like an ant heap without any way of slicing it up, or interpreting it, or anything else; there is just a lot of milling around. You have billions of these little frames. He [Kendon] has 12,173 frames, and each of them then becomes a discrete piece within which you can observe billions of bodies, postures, shapes, God knows what — and you are lost. I'm saying that you have to zero in on the bit from the frame of reference of the event to which it corresponds. Then you have the conversation as an event, and you have subdivisions of this, and you will look for correlations in the face formation (behavior) with the subdivisions in the conversation simply on the grounds that you know what the conversation divisions are from the way in which people interpret conversation. They are less aware of the movements, so you are trying to get at the form through the meaning. And then you will see what it reveals. If it turns out that conspicuous divisions correspond to conspicuous movement, that inconspicuous divisions (correspond) to inconspicuous movement, then you will be very happy and say that that is a very nicely forming correlation. Your analysis therefore is considered "good," because you are confirming one of the basic assumptions that this is a communication system. Therefore, the neater the forming correlation, the happier you will be. If it turns out to be very messy, then you go back to the drawing board. You may have to revise your whole reference model or what have you: but let's regard that as a beginning. Now that you have put me on the spot, that's how I would go about it.

Gearing: All right, one other thing. There's no such thing as an analytic unit that you or I just pull out of the air.

Mathiot: No.

Gearing: They don't fit in this paradigm?

Garvin: Well, that's the Birdwhistell heresy of assuming analytic units on the basis of what we have in linguistics.

Gearing: All right, but it's not the Birdwhistell heresy; it's the social science heresy.

Garvin: Yet, but that's only because they like to admire people.

Richter: What was your question, Fred?

Gearing: All analytic units by this are culturally real. That means that the analyst — the observer — does not sit down and say, that's going to be a unit event.

Garvin: I am against the "Aha" method, which is the procedure wherein the analyst looks at the data and says "Aha, this is what *this* is." Then he looks at it some more and says, "Aha, and this is what *that* is." I'm opposed to that. And that, I think, is 90 percent of social science methodology.

Richter: I would agree with what you said, except my interest happens to be with young children, and I don't know how you work with them to avoid the "Aha" method.

Garvin: We got into that problem with two sets of informants, one was aphasics and the other was young children. What we decided was that in order to get at the meaning of their behavior, one asks their nearest verbal relative — that is, for the aphasic, it was the wife; for the children, it was the mothers or the people taking care of them.

Gearing: They don't know.

Garvin: They know more than you do. They know what it means to them, and they are closer to the child than you are. I am not saying that you should take it at face value. If it is not the parent, then maybe it is the older siblings; in other words, you pick as nearly as you can the informant who can interpret the behavior.

Richter: Could you ask another child?

Mathiot: Yes.

Garvin: You can always ask, but the point is, at certain ages, they don't answer.

Richter: It would depend on how small they are, I guess.

Garvin: Obviously you can ask ten-year-olds lots of things you can't ask five-year-olds.

Gearing: Also, that child is talking to you, and you are an adult.

Richter: Yes, that's true.

Garvin: I think the big problem that people have with children's languages is that they have no empirical control over what the children mean. I think the only way one can approximate such empirical control is through some of their elders.

Sangree: It is 4 o'clock. I feel that Madeleine and Paul have covered what we asked in the letter. We thank them very much.

SECTION FIVE

On Formalization

COMMENT *by Woodrow W. Clark, Jr.*

The study of education from an anthropological perspective has a well-established history. Anthropologists engaged in fieldwork have been fascinated by the formal and informal educational mechanisms for enculturation within any society. The results of such studies are long, descriptive narratives from every corner of the globe. Only recently have anthropologists turned their attention to modern, complex technological societies. As these descriptive studies now become widely discussed by social researchers, a definite need has arisen for a general theory of cultural transmission or enculturation that covers the entire scope of anthropology.

This paper attempts to comment on Gearing's general cultural theory in light of other social science disciplines as well as within the philosophical tenets of science. The result will be a presentation of Gearing's general cultural theory of education reformulated into a paradigmatic model. From this reformulation, a clearer and more precise investigation of the general theory can be made.

Philosophy of Science

Volumes have been written discussing the functions and roles of social science research in societal studies (Koestler 1967). Aside from the issues of "scientism" (Hayek 1942, 1944), our purpose will be to make three points about the scientific study of society.

First, philosophical issues and traditions have had and continue to have a significant influence on social science research. Essentially, there are two major traditions within Western philosophical history. One is the empiricist view in which behavior can be isolated or separated from the thinking or the mental processes of human beings. The empiricists see the body, i.e., behavior, as distinct from the mind, i.e., mental processes. A direct result of this view is the behavioralist paradigm within the social science disciplines, most notably psychology. The assumption is made that a baby is born without a mind. The child learns only from its environment and is thus subject to conditioning.

The opposite Western philosophical tradition is that of mentalism, where researchers see a baby born with certain innate abilities. The child is distinctly human because of its linguistic competence (Chomsky 1965, 1968). The transformational linguists have been instrumental in proving that human beings must be studied and understood in terms of their mental processes. Man's uniqueness from other species rests in his ability to create and innovate.

The position taken by the general cultural theory is a blending of the body and mind positions. One cannot be isolated from the other. This integrative approach approximates what Chomsky has called Cartesian linguistics (from Descartes) and is similar to many Eastern philosophies. Gearing's combination of these philosophical traditions is a departure in and of itself from the normal social science approach to theory building.

Second, whatever philosophical position is taken, a paradigm can be formulated (Kuhn 1962). A paradigm is a "universally recognized scientific achievement that for a time provide[s] model problems and solutions to a community of practitioners" (Kuhn 1962). Paradigms are, therefore, points of departure for further articulation and specification.

The general theory discussed below is a paradigm.[1] It has a set of propositions and testable rules that will allow researchers to study and analyze educational issues. The paradigm itself, as indicated earlier, may be transferable to other areas of anthropological research or to the entire social science community. Paradigms do just that; they establish a format for investigation.

Third, paradigms, as general theories, must do four things. First, they must provide descriptive data from which analysis can be made. Second, they must provide explanations of the data. Third, they must allow for predictability. Finally, paradigms must be vulnerable to change. In fact, Kuhn's major hypothesis (1962) is that paradigmatic revolutions must occur in order that knowledge be advanced. The notion of change is part of what a paradigm must do. Gearing's general cultural theory takes these factors of a paradigm into account.

---

[1] The terms "general theory" and "paradigm" will be used interchangeably.

The Paradigm

Essentially, the general cultural theory of education, according to Gearing et al., states: "A theory of education must predict that items of identified categories of information and identified categories of skill will or will not regularly pass between members of identified categories of persons." The theory "must explain how that regularly occurs."

Gearing continues: "A general theory must be able to so predict and explain for any human society. A general cultural theory of education proceeds to such prediction and explanation by employing analytic categories (a) whose contents are solely cultural things, (b) categories which are ascriptions of meaning established and (c) categories which are daily re-established among the actors themselves in the course of their everyday lives" (Gearing 1973: 2–3).

Social organization

↓   ↓   ↓

Educational system

↑   ↑   ↑

Body of knowledge and skill

The basics of a paradigm are present. The paradigm allows for descriptive data, explanatory analysis, and prediction within the context of change.

Gearing et al. then defines the parameters of the general theory. Briefly, they see a limited, yet fundamental, kind of educational phenomena when two or more people come into face-to-face exchange, especially over a period of time. An educational system is the totality of (1) personal encounters and (2) the regularity of such encounters.

Four additional pivotal elements of analysis within the paradigm are:

1. Turns, where people within an encounter take turns, as in speaking; this is a universal behavior but with culturally relative implications.

2. Turn-taking, a pattern that forms a public dyad so that the participants have an "eye to each other" and to any other audience present or remote.

3. Transaction, the same pattern of turn-taking but the relationship between parties changes (a) in part consciously, (b) in part through verbal and nonverbal channels, and (c) in part, by generating a multiplicity of changes in the parties' relationships.

4. Agendas, which are educational in that they pattern reciprocal behavior based on past experience and future relationships.

The Propositions

At this point, a departure or reorganization of the Gearing's working paper on the general cultural theory will be made. Rather than consider the eight propositions in the paradigm as propositions, they will be reformulated below as testable rules with possible universal application. For our purposes, there are five propositions to be considered. Detailed discussion of each can be found within Gearing's working paper.

Proposition 1   The capacity of people to know is unlimited, but people are limited in their ability to act.

Proposition 2   Images shape thought in such a way as to define the "differences that make a difference"; therefore, images filter thought.

Proposition 3   The flow of information and skill should be random, but are frequently hampered by barriers.

Proposition 4   The identification and mapping of restraints (barriers) to the flow of information and skill is most important, but one must also understand the barrier's processes: (a) which are generated, and (b) through which they do their work.

Proposition 5   The end product is the attested conceptualization of the process.

The Rules

The essence of a general theory is to provide rules that must be subject to analysis, change, and revision. The goal is to find universal rules. Linguists have been able to discover rules for grammar and then further reduce them into logical notation. Mathematical systems, then applied, allow for further elaboration of the paradigm. At some later point, the same could be done with the following eight rules (i.e., Gearing's eight propositions); the notational form is from recent linguistic phonological formulation. The slash mark (/) shows the independent variable; the line (———) defines the environment as the dependent variable; and the arrow (———➤) indicates the resultant behavior. The discussion of each can be found in the Gearing text.

Rule 1.0.   Distribution Rule

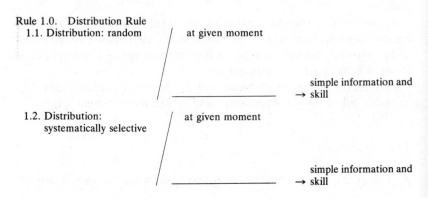

1.2a. Regular / at given moment

simple information and
→ skill

1.2b. Not regular / at given moment

simple information and
→ skill

1.3. Distribution: classes of / at given moment
items

simple information and
→ skill

1.3a. Systematically to / at given moment
member of a cat-
egory

simple information and
→ skill

1.3b. Unsystematically / at given moment
absent in other cat-
egories

simple information and
→ skill

Rule 2.1.   Encounter Rule: social identity
  2.1.1. Encounters: within / parties together in
  categories of social / identified classes of
  identity / encounter: handle
  more than one class of
  simple information and
  skill

→ agendas

  2.1.1a. Information = / parties together in
  property / identified classes of
  encounter: handle
  more than one class of
  simple information and
  skill

→ open agendas

  2.1.1b. Information = not / parties together in
  property / identified classes of
  encounter: handle
  more than one class of
  simple information and
  skill

→ open agendas

2.1.2. Encounters: across
    categories of social
    identity
parties together in
identified classes of
encounter: handle
more than one class of
simple information and
skill

        → agendas

2.1.2a. Information =
    property
parties together in
identified classes of
encounter: handle
more than one class of
simple information and
skill

        agenda types which in
        common filter informa-
        → tion and skill

2.1.2b. Information = not
    property
parties together in
identified classes of
encounter: handle
more than one class of
simple information and
skill

        → open agendas

Rule 2.2.   Encounter Rule: Mobility

2.2.1. Encounters: mobility
    will not occur between
    involved categories
encounters across
categories where infor-
mation = propertylike

        → agendas

2.2.1a. Information ex-
    change:
    privileged or pre-
    scribed
encounters across
categories where infor-
mation = propertylike

        → stable agendas

2.2.1b. Information ex-
    change: prob-
    lematic
encounters across
categories where infor-
mation = propertylike

        → absent

2.2.2. Encounters: mobility
    is problematic
encounters across
categories where infor-
mation = propertylike

        → agendas

2.2.2a. Information ex-
    change
    privileged or pre-
    scribed
encounters across
categories where infor-
mation = propertylike

        → absent

2.2.2b. Information ex-
change: prob-
lematic

encounters across
categories where infor-
mation = propertylike

—————————— → troublesome agendas

Rule 3.1.   Pattern Rule
3.1.1. Patterns: settled
pattern of tacit initia-
tion and response

encounter

—————————— → stable agenda

3.1.2. Patterns: enacted
pattern of tacit initia-
tion and response

encounter

—————————— → troublesome agendas

3.1.3. Patterns: discrepancies
appear

encounter

—————————— → pattern itself defines
agenda

Rule 3.2.   Pattern Rule
3.2.1. Patterns: asymmetrical
form where one party
initiates and the other
responds

bureaucratically
organized centers:
stable agendas across
hierarchical levels of
organization

—————————— → liminality interludes

Rule 4.0.   Distribution Rule
4.1. Distribution: simple
information and skill

stable agendas

—————————— → systematically flowed

4.2. Distribution: simple
information and skill

troublesome agendas

—————————— → unsystematically
blocked

Rule 5.0.   Items Rule
 5.1. Items: complex informa-   / stable agendas
      tion and skill is selective
      and regular

                                    ───────────────────   successful communica-
                                                         → tion

 5.2. Items: complex informa-   / troublesome agendas
      tion and skill is ca-
      priciously introduced

                                    ───────────────────   abortive communica-
                                                         → tion

Rule 6.0.   Cultural premise Rule
 6.1. Cultural premises: / same cultural premise
      exchanged   communicated to
                                      another

                                    ─────────────────── → stable agenda

 6.2. Cultural premises: not   / same cultural premise
      exchanged   communicated to
                                      another

                                    ─────────────────── → troublesome agenda

Rule 7.0.   Role learning Rule
 7.1. Roles: enactments and   / open, stable, and
      elaborations   troublesome agendas

                                    ─────────────────── → role learning is in force

 7.1a. Roles: invidious   / open and stable
       distinctions   agendas

                                    ───────────────────   role learning is covert
                                                         → or absent

 7.1b. Roles: invidious   / troublesome agenda
       distinctions

                                    ───────────────────   role learning is dis-
                                                            played in behaviors of
                                                         → those involved

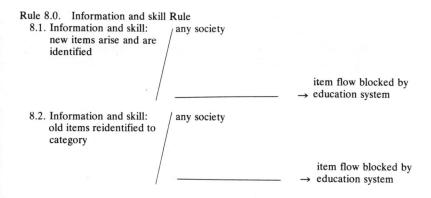

Rule 8.0. Information and skill Rule

Conclusion

This paper has formulated the general cultural theory of education into a paradigmatic framework. Kuhn (1962) argues that progress and scientific discoveries are not accomplished through rigid theories and paradigm. Instead, science is the predominance of one paradigm over another. Paradigms are frameworks from which other theories, models, and hypothesis can be drawn.

The general theory is a paradigm. Each hypothesis and theory is outlined in a sequence of rule formulations. Each rule is a specific, complete, and testable proposition. The general theory as a paradigm thus satisfies the three of the criteria of a paradigm: (1) gathering of descriptive data; (2) providing explanatory formulations and concepts; and (3) providing the means for predictions of future events. Further research will undoubtedly bring about modifications and changes, and perhaps a paradigmatic revolution will provide a totally different mode of analysis.

The second accomplishment of this paper has been to set up the basic elements from which the paradigm can be formalized into logical and mathematical notation. Assuming that one of the goals in theoretical and paradigmation formulation is to present a coherent, simple, and logical set of suppositions (Chomsky 1968), the presentation of the general theory in the above format is a concrete step in that direction. The next step is to reduce the rules into logical notation (the basic symbols used to construct the rules are a form of logical notation). The accomplishments of generative semantics, and particularly phonology, provide the model for further work.

Finally, the general theory, seen as a paradigm, suggests fertile territory for further research. The dissemination, discussion, and possible acceptance of the paradigm will spark research throughout anthropological and educational circles. I have just concluded some research on learning environments outside the schools. The use of the general theory as a paradigmatic framework for guiding the research and reporting the findings has been very productive.

SECTION SIX

Commentaries, Principally on Inter- and Intra-psychic Analysis

COMMENT *by Craig Jackson Calhoun*

Theories are generally posed between two continuing efforts in science and philosophy — to explain information that has been gathered and to suggest new ways of discovering information. One may judge their success by their usefulness in either or both of these endeavors. It should further be noted that the word "theory" is not synonymous with "hypothesis" and that theories are by definition writ large. They are complex explanatory systems. They create intentional views of the world or of a segment of it. Thus, one looks through the theory to discern the operations of the world. In the case of the present general theory of education, two particular questions related to the possibility and utility of such a world view seem important. First, to what extent can the theory stand alone as an explanatory system, as opposed to being dependent on external explanation of included phenomena? Does the theory provide sufficient means for the understanding of that which it takes to be its topic? Second, do the pre-positions that define the concerns of the theory denote a content sufficient to correspond to the stated conceptual topic?[1]

---

[1] The general question for theories of how to define a minimum of *a priori* postulates while including a maximum of explanatory territory is relevant here. It may be seen as the distance one travels in the empirical world before returning tautologically to the initial postulates. Jacob Needleman (1963: 32–39) has discussed this issue far better than I can. He views theories as composed of a circle of explanation taking as its radius the diameter of a smaller circle of presuppositions. If one draws a narrow inner circle, one defines a narrow circle of explanation, and the usefulness of the theory must be judged all the more by the quality of its definition, and perhaps by the reasonableness or sense of inevitability of its terms. As Weiss (1958: 193) indicated: "A conclusion which repeats the premise conforms neatly to the requirements of the most stringent logic. What is wrong with the circular argument is that it is often uninformative, coming back to its beginning too quickly. But if the circle is all inclusive, if it encompasses all there is, it does all that a philosophic system demands."

In the present endeavor, we are concerned with an attempt to formulate a general cultural theory of education. This paper will attempt to present some relevant observations with regard to the two questions just posed. It should first be noted that the author continues to be impressed with Gearing's efforts to keep his theory open to the process of comment, revision, and consideration by his colleagues. Further, I respect the effort to formulate some sort of unified whole out of the scattered relevant works in the sociocultural study of education. I would suggest, however, that empirical knowledge and paradigmatic development are at such a stage that we would better serve the goal of systematization by attempting to formulate a conceptual framework without the added completeness implied by a theory.

It seems to me that the present theory rests on four preestablished positions. It is these pre-positions that establish the realm of information at which we will look, and from which we can argue that this information constitutes what is rather impressionistically called education. At the outset of this paper, a folk image of education is presented. It is then argued that we can better substitute another image. The four prepositions on which this image rests are, briefly stated:

1.   All simple information will flow randomly throughout a population unless blocked.[2]

2.   The study of education is the study of this blockage.

3.   Education systems are the sum of face-to-face encounters.

4.   By examining salient encounters, one can gain the necessary phenomena for analysis.

There are several problems associated with defining education in these terms. The first condition is based on the assumption of a very broad statistical sample of enough diversity to wash out any single correlative factor. It assumes also that blockage is the only determinant of flow.

The first assumption would seem to be rather a statistical fluke, i.e., in a large and complex sample, so many factors are intertwined that an isolated one will seldom show up at any given time. This does not mean in fact, that, distribution is random or that the various single factors are ineffective. In relation to the second assumption, one may object that it is

---

What we must ask, then, is what the theory explains, what it takes for granted in order to explain it, and whether we are willing to accept that premise. In the last case, we ask especially whether the specific premise conforms to the stated demands of the topic. In this case, are we willing to accept the theory's premises as the definition of education?

[2] The terms "randomly," "freely," and "completely" are all used by Gearing to describe the flow of information. These three are not synonymous. It seems reasonable to assume that randomness is the concept referred to. Freedom is the opposite, I suspect, of Gearing's idea of restrained flow. Completion is perhaps the extreme of what might happen in unrestrained flow. Even without blockage, however, it seems that not all possible connections and/or transactions would be made.

untrue that only blockage is a determinate factor. I would argue, for example, that intention, as both a sociocultural and as an individual conception, is effective in determining the flow of information. It may be returned that this only constitutes a special case of blockage, but I think that is a skewed perception. Cultures determine interaction not only by rules that forbid certain transactions, but by establishing predispositions to others. It would seem that one reason Gearing finds education systems to prevent social change (or tending in that direction, to the extent that their conservatism is successful) is because he has defined them as the blockages to the flow of information. By not including the aspect of intention, i.e., the nurturance of certain flows, he has obscured the situation in two ways. First he has failed to remember that individuals are the ultimate unit of social action, and that as individual actors, they have intentions that must theoretically be taken into account. This has been amply argued elsewhere by Homans (1950, 1952) and by one of Gearing's favorite sources, Barth (1966: 2). Second, on another level from individual decision, it should be noted that cultures act not only to minimize the likelihood of certain encounters, but to maximize the likelihood of others. Further, cultural configurations influence not only the occurrence, but also, the content of encounters. An individual coming into contact with another through his church may not act to restrict certain information, but may so order priorities that it is never foremost in any particular encounter. Further, without the notion of intention, one is left to wonder why individuals tend to communicate at all? It may thus be argued that the very notion of blockage implies intention. As a further note, one must question the implicit assumption that all adults and children have the same capactiy for education (information storage) at all times in their lives. One may suggest that capacities must differ among persons and vary with age in the same individual.

The third and fourth pre-positions present problems as well. It seems that these positions represent an attempt to incorporate a clear behavioral base into the theory. It would seem, however, that the theory is not fully oriented in this direction. For example, the theory takes as a central point the idea that individuals operate in social situations, reflecting agendas that have personal as well as cultural characteristics. To the extent that these agendas are personal, one may suggest that dealing with them is an attempt to get inside the head of the subject, rather than simply to record his behavior. In addition, one must ask how the theory will take account of cultural transmissions through such media as books, television, radio, and films. These do not involve face-to-face encounters. To an extent, one may solve the problem by suggesting that an individual will treat these media as implicitly involving encounters and will imagine a turn-taking situation. This, however, would represent another psychological assumption with no clear base in behavioral evidence. It would be inadequate, as well, in that the differences in these non-face-to-face forms of communication are relevant to education themselves.

The particular formulation of the course of encounters has an internal problem associated with it as well. The enactment of cultural premises does not constitute their transmission. Yet the premises that individuals hold and enact do change over time, and one must ask how. The present theory argues that, when common premises are not enacted, communication becomes difficult and frequently is terminated either in the suspension of the encounter or its routinization into pro forma conversation. One may suggest that there are broad options in the range of cultural premises that individuals may enact in any given encounter and that it may be possible to effect the communication of a would-be conflictual premise while basing the exchange on a common one. Compatibility is always partial, so the questions become ones of extent and choice. It would seem well worth the theoreticians' time to explore further this aspect of the communicative process and to try to incorporate it more directly into the theory. The issue should also be raised of how the theory proposes to handle information that may be known but not enacted. Two particular cases of this seem relevant. First, the theory would seem unable to identify the particular state of educational processes at any given point in time. Not only would this require a further and extra theoretical step, but this step itself could be argued to violate the theory's presumption that one can gain the necessary phenomena for analysis merely by the examination of salient encounters. In order to assess the state of educational progress at any given time, one would need a procedure to evaluate the change in the total information content of individuals. Although such a procedure would be external to the encounter analysis process,[3] it would seem to be necessary to test whether or not the theory's description actually accounted for any exchange. Second, it seems likely that there are social situations in which a person may gain a considerable amount of knowledge of a sort that would normally be forbidden to him to enact in the same encounters from which he gains it. For example, a poor man in a highly class-oriented society may very well learn a great deal of the most salient cultural premises and behavioral characteristics of the wealthy with whom he comes in contact. He may also be forbidden to enact this knowledge in exchanges with its socially approved possessors. In this case, it would seem that analysis of encounters, especially with primary

---

[3] It could be argued that the analysis of encounters — with a different focus — could constitute a sufficient methodology for evaluation. This argument would rest on a strong behavioral bias suggesting that only actual behavior may be counted as knowledge gained. In addition, one would have to argue that behavior in encounters would represent an adequate base of relevant behavior. One would also have to analyze a tremendous number of encounters — theoretically, all — in order to have evidence of all such displays of knowledge. The second objection on the point of behavioral knowledge display in the body of this critique is also relevant to this problem specifically.

reference to the concept of agendas, may very well fail to account for what in fact, is, learned.[4] This raises a third point. If an outside analyst may come to understand the agendas of the individual actors and the extent of their communication from the analysis of salient encounters, may not another observer do the same? It would seem clear that he may, can, and does. People constantly act as social scientists, discerning and sometimes even achieving a surprising degree of systematization of the processes that go on about them. If they did not, they could not survive socially. The processes that Sullivan described as consensual validation (1940:43 ff.) are, in fact, a large part of this continuing operation. In order to deal effectively with life one must come to understand the premises of our culture and our fellows, which form a system. We learn of these premises, as Gearing has suggested, in face-to-face encounters, but also through contemplation and through the observation of others. The rebuttal of the theorist to this argument will be tested within them and will not achieve a significant meaning to the individual unless they are reinforced. This is partially true, but it would seem that, especially to the extent that the information concerned is objective rather than either subjective or a premise to thought, it could very well be gained from a distance and held in isolation.

Perhaps the most important system of educational blockage seems to have been left out of the present theory. This is the determination of what persons will have encounters with what others. To be in any way complete in its stated intentions, the general theory of education[5] would have to

---

[4] Again, the procedures of evaluation of what is learned are in doubt. Is an actual change in observable behavior required? To what extent does the theory rest its case on the early postulate that all information will flow freely and randomly unless blocked? If this is the case, one may (must) assume that the individual will succeed in gaining all information presented either intentionally or inadvertently in every encounter. This would seem to be an unlikely premise to take on either faith or simple reasonableness.

[5] One could argue, I suppose, that by stipulating that the theory is "cultural," Gearing has absolved himself from the necessity to deal with such plainly "social" factors as the frequency of interaction. Whether or not one were justified in drawing such a strong line between society and culture in the abstract, one must ask whether in this particular case it is possible to thus proceed with valid explanation. I suggest that it is not. One must take the likelihood of occurrence of interaction into account, and further, one should note that troubled agendas will probably be seen to arise in encounters between members of social categories that have (or have had) a low frequency of interaction. A simple schematic diagram may make this clear.

Definition of the situation

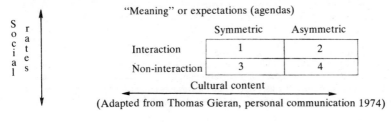

(Adapted from Thomas Gieran, personal communication 1974)

account for this blockage, which is more effective than any troubled or closed agenda. In the first place, it becomes important to map out topographically the patterns and frequencies of association for the population under study.[6] If two people do not come in contact with each other, no information will flow between them. On a larger level, if two categories of people do not come in contact, information will not flow according to the theory, and one will not even have encounters to microanalyze. It is also important that one attempt to learn the frequency of the sort of encounters one analyzes in the population as a whole, as well as the parameters that are salient in the sorting of their frequencies. In addition, it would be interesting to attempt to gauge the changes in frequency and their meaning. For example, one may postulate that troublesome agendas are likely to occur more often when two groups with differing cultural premises have frequent contact. If one looks only at the agendas and only at one point in time, it is true that one sees blockages. It is possible, though, that this would be a skewed and shortsighted perception. The blockages — that is, the troublesome agendas — may be the result of the two groups coming into contact with each other when before they did not, or they may result from an increase in frequency coupled with a move away from pro forma interaction. In some situations, one might argue that troublesome agendas may exist as an intermediate state between closed and open agenda situation. For example, if one looks at black and white interactions in the United States, one sees a move from encounters that were representative of stable agendas, closed to information flow on a great many fronts, to encounters representative of troublesome agendas as more frequent attempts are made to remove the stable blockages. Encounters also become more frequent. Although the data are not all in yet, one may effectively argue that the social process is one of increasing integration. This would be contrary to the results one would gain from the postulated data gathering analytic methods of the present theory. Troublesome agendas, then, may be on one level the key to a view of change, as opposed to conservation, in the theory.

Finally, there are some minor problems associated with the use of the concept of liminality in the theory. Gearing draws entirely on Turner's

---

The four boxes of course, are not absolute, but rather, are intersections of continua. The symmetric-asymmetric frame follows upon Weber and would seem as well to represent much of the Gearing stance. Symmetric definitions would correspond to both open and closed agendas. Asymmetric has to do with dissonant definitions that Gearing has called troublesome agendas. Another dimension is introduced with the vertical sorting on frequency of interaction. Not only is it important to know whether or how often particular types of encounters occur, but it is interesting to attempt to gauge the changes in frequency.

[6] This is the task that Peter Blau has set out in his conceptual framework of social structure. Very simply, he argues that social structure may best be seen as the combination of parameters that influence the association of individuals and groups (Blau presentation in 1974 to Columbia University Sociology Department Seminar on Social Theory).

discussion (1969) of liminality and communitas in *The ritual process*. As the title of that book indicated, the thrust is toward an analysis of ritually significant events, not any or all occasions on which actions are taken that are distinct from the formal ideological construction of the situation. In his usage, Gearing carries a confusion that Barbara Myerhoff (1971) and others have attempted to correct. I would argue along with Myerhoff for a conception based upon perception (whether of an actor by himself or others) for both liminality and communitas. Liminality is not synonymous with collective behavior, or with rebellion. It also does not mean a simple and permanent dropping out of a system. The word is drawn from the Latin root, *limen*, meaning "threshold," and refers to the assumption or perception of being *between* two categories or positions or worlds. If one has an experience of mystical union during this movement in and out of structural positions, then that is communitas. As van Gennep (1960: 2) in his fourfold conception of the stages of liminality (the source of Turner's [1969: 94, 95] term, "the rites of passage"), has indicated, the individual leaves and is reincorporated into a structure conceptually as he moves from one status to another. When this becomes a "new world," that is a matter of perception. In the tribal and other small-scale areas, van Gennep notes that it is clear that the individual does not leave the social field, but rather, he leaves a particular situation in it. Liminality-oriented rituals are more likely to accent the hierarchical aspects of a system than anything else. In fact, if they are a check on hierarchy, as Gearing suggests, it is because they sometimes include the experience of communitas. Communitas acts as a check by meshing in a temporary experience of altered perception members of various social categories. It would seem that this concept might indeed have some relevance for a general cultural theory of education. First, it can (as Gearing suggests and I have tried to specify further) act as a check on runaway hierarchical patterning of interaction. Second the experience of altered perception that may or may not coincide with liminality would seem to provide for encounters of significant dimensions for analysis. In particular, where encounters between certain persons are usually characterized by stable uncommunicative or troublesome agendas, they may be made in the very fullest sense open during an experience of communitas.

In sum, then, I feel that the general cultural theory of education proposed in Working Paper 6 is in many respects confused or conceptually weak and in need of revision; in other respects, it is fraught with perils that dictate caution and serious thought in the process of development. It is also, in a great many respects, full of potential. Some of its potential will almost undoubtedly be realized in causing anthropologists to think seriously about a subject they are all too often willing to treat casually or as a peripheral issue. In addition, it will bring about an integrated view, however rough, and this can only help to further the definition of a field of study and make its practitioners aware of the large body of relevant but only occasionally systematic material they may draw upon. Whether the theory will ever succeeed in becoming truly general, or in having the seminal impact or ability to instigate research and conceptualization that its authors hope, will remain to be seen in the rather distant future. We may hope that the nth or n-hundredth working paper will allow us to speak with the sort of theoretical confidence we should like to have in the field of education.

COMMENT *by Ward Goodenough*

I like the idea of looking at information and skills as flowing, except as blocked, in that it is distinctly more productive for educational theory than the usual view of things to which it is presented as a counter. But, as the theory itself says, there is no flow without encounters. The mere frequency of encounters is, therefore, a factor that must be plugged into the theory. Some minimal level of encounter frequency, even in open agenda relationships, is necessary for information and skills to pass from one to another in those relationships.

The theory mentions information and skills, but, in reality, it addresses itself only to information and the learning of cultural themes without coming to grips, it seems to me, with what is involved in the acquisition of skill (as in learning to play the piano, to play chess, to speak a foreign language or to do arithmetic). Encounters are necessary for skill acquisition, but they are more necessary for some skills than for others. A real difference exists in becoming skillful in speaking a language and becoming skillful in handling an axe. There are skills in handling encounters and skills that do not pertain to managing encounters at all. Clearly, the extent to which encounters are necessary to learning is relevant to understanding individual variation in what is learned. The sharing problem, or as I would prefer to state it, the variance problem comes in here.

This brings me to my major criticism of the theory: its assumption of flow of information and skills unless impeded, as if there would be indeed a mental sharing. I prefer to assume that each individual orders his experience for himself, including what he experiences in word and deed in encounters with others. He keeps reordering his experience until he comes up with principles and themes he can attribute to others that permit him to do his business with those others without too much difficulty. In other words, information and skills do *not* flow; they have to be reconstituted anew in each person in what are never perfect replicas. The three types of agendas presented in Gearing's theory thus serve to limit in varying degrees the experience that is to be ordered, from which ordering information (and skills, to some extent) is reconstituted with varying degrees of replication and social effectiveness.

As I see it, then, the heart of the theory consists of the three types of agendas and their implications for learning, whether one sees the problem as blockages to otherwise free flow or as limitations on the kind and extent of experience to be ordered so that knowledge can be reconstituted.

That I find myself preferring the word "knowledge" to "information" is also significant and something that Gearing must take into account. Knowledge involves, among other things, understandings as to how experience is categorized; whereas information involves knowing how categories are distributed with respect to one another. I think something also needs to be sorted out here.

I find the three types of agendas a helpful way of looking at things, recognizing that they are a set of broad categories. Two questions immediately come to mind in relation to them. First, what are the sources or causes of troublesome agendas? Once they come into existence, the failure of communication that they produce guarantees, under some conditions, that the next encounter between the parties concerned will also have a troublesome agenda, but that does not explain how a troublesome agenda arose in the first place. Indeed, for unacculturated outsiders coming into a strange society, all encounters have troublesome agendas at first. But the parties to the encounters, if they are motivated to get them not to be troublesome, work to transform future agendas so that communication can more readily and easily occur. So motivation and perception of future encounters as desirable or undesirable enter in. The second question is, why do different persons learn differently when all things in the theory are equal? Even a cultural theory of education must somehow take account of human limitations and individual differences in those limitations.

COMMENT *by Jean Carter Lave**

Gearing's broad overview of education starts with a well-placed focus on the importance of intracultural variability in the distribution of a culture's inventory of knowledge and skills. He suggests that we have all along had a folk view to explain the differences in who knows what. Diversity in individual knowledge and skill has been treated primarily as a function of the complexity of the human mind and a function of our inability inten-

* Research among the Vai of Liberia was made possible through a grant from the Office of Education (OEG-O-72-4628.) The paper has benefited greatly from Michael Cole's thoughtful reading and advice.

tionally to produce desired educational results in the face of that complexity.

Gearing suggests an alternative orientation, one which he feels should replace the other: most items of information and skill are quite simple in terms of the mental and motor operations involved in acquiring them. Any item of simple information or skill can move from any normal adult or child to any other without effort. If the move does not occur, it is because the parties involved jointly raise barriers. If simple information is blocked, so is complex information, even more so.

The theory is meant to hold for "events where two or more persons come into recurrent face-to-face interchange." Gearing feels that the theory, if adequate, should be able to predict which kinds of people will block information exchange on a regular basis and how the blocking occurs. It should apply across cultures and to groups within a culture.

Gearing has outlined an extraordinarily ambitious field of inquiry and is certainly to be commended for the breadth of his interest and the wide range of his speculations. My own work lies within a small part of the general overview. Therefore, rather than attempt a critique of the whole, I will confine this discussion to the area in which I can bring direct experience to bear. In particular, I want to discuss the concepts of simple and complex information inventories, in relation to my work on culture-specific teaching and learning techniques among tailors and their apprentices in Liberia.

My general position contrasts somewhat with that of Gearing. He feels that we should supplant the old "people's heads operate differently" model with the view that "social barriers through interaction mechanisms" account for differences in the distribution of information within a culture. Rather than viewing these two orientations as mutually exclusive, a modified position seems to fit the known facts better. Even within sets of homogeneous people, where simple and complex information transfers are demonstrably taking place, differences in educational experiences will lead to differences in the distribution of knowledge and skill. Put another way, social interaction barriers undoubtedly account for some of the variance in the knowledge and skill inventories of individuals, but differences in exposure to educational experiences, e.g., schooling, literacy, apprenticeship training, will lead to important differences in the knowledge exchanged between otherwise identical people. It may well be that Gearing would agree with the general principle that both are relevant. Even if he accepts the contributions of both sources of variance, however, we still might disagree about the importance of social interaction, in contrast with other kinds of experiences, as factors that influence the distribution of knowledge and skill in a population.

It may be that in different cultures the importance of one or the other does differ. Certainly Gearing's background in investigating educational interactions in the United States schools, where social heterogeneity and social barriers to learning are salient, should influence his theoretical perspective. In the same way my experience working within an occupationally specialized subgroup in a homogeneous tribal group in Liberia should lead me to place emphasis on variation that remains after the major social divisors mentioned by Gearing (age, sex, social strata) have mostly been controlled. That is, while our theoretical learnings certainly enter into our differences as regards emphasis and interpretation, it also seems to me that differences between cultures may cause social barriers of the type he describes to be more important in some cultures and less important in others.

I begin with a short description of the Liberian work to provide concrete examples for the discussion that follows. Then I will deal specifically with the problems concerning the application of Gearing's formulation of the nature of knowledge — a set of discrete named items and relations, ranging from simple to complex, for which the interaction patterns of dyads have differential implications.

The Vai of Liberia have been practicing tailoring for several hundred years. New tailors are taught their trade in an apprenticeship system that is itself probably quite old, if not unchanged, over the years. The traditional methods have been modified in the last fifty years as the treadle sewing machine has become ubiquitous and as clothing styles have changed. But the methods of training apprentices have at least two generations of consistency, based on master tailors' statements about the similarity of their apprenticeship to that of their apprentices, and almost certainly stretch much further back in time. As for changing styles, there is good reason to believe that this has been a constant problem for tailors for a long, long time. In addition, very few Vai master tailors have had non-Vai training in tailoring or non-Vai schooling of any kind. Thus, it seems reasonable to assume that a study of Vai tailors and their apprentices, in their capacities as teachers and learners, will capture specifically Vai methods of teaching and learning tailoring.

Preliminary ethnographic work suggests that the Vai tailors and apprentices treat apprenticeship training as a formal educational enterprise. Masters see themselves as actively responsible for the training, both technical and moral, that the apprentices receive, and the apprentices see themselves as pupils. Apprentices are not selected into or out of tailoring by any obvious principles that would make the beginning apprentices different as a group from other children of their age and sex. Only males are apprentices; they begin their training between the ages of seven and ten, and the training period lasts from four to seven years.

The training includes an inventory of knowledge and skills about which there is high agreement. I attempted to discover if the inventory is transmitted to the apprentice in a regular way or according to any kind of general principles. Both the beginning and the ending steps in the training process are well-defined, but the vast majority of skills, kinds of garments, etc., appear to be taught in no generally agreed upon order. The novice first learns to make buttonholes, how to hem and press garments, and how to care for and use the sewing machine. At the end, the near-master learns to make a "guinea suit" — a complicated trousers and jacket combination. There is one general principle that applies to learning to tailor all types of garments, and that is, that the apprentice learns how to sew each garment before learning how to cut out that garment. Each pattern piece is sketched directly on the cloth, using only the customer's measurements as a guide. The process of drawing the garment pieces in correct proportions is a complicated one and appears to involve a more fundamental understanding of the relations underlying construction than does sewing the pieces together.

Almost anyone who wants to become a tailor can learn the trade. The reasons given for the few failures seem to rest more on lack of motivation than on lack of ability. But on the basis of my limited experience working with Vai tailors, I believe the training process itself affects the processes by which simple and complex information and skill are transmitted and received, as well as the transmission of cognitive processes and information.

Gearing suggests that it is useful to distinguish between simple knowledge/skill and complex knowledge/skill. "A theory of education ... must predict that identified categories of information and skill [that is, the categories "simple" and "complex"] will or will not regularly pass between identified categories of persons and must explain how that regularly occurs." He emphasizes the notion that the distinction is not hard and fast in any given case. In this, I think he is clearly correct. In going over the Liberian data, I find it is difficult to classify the knowledge and skills of the tailors and apprentices one way or the other. Is being able to name the parts of a pair of trousers simple or complex information? Asked to do this task, apprentices and masters may name the same parts but in different ways: apprentices do so with far less organization in the way they name things than do the masters. Is making a buttonhole a simple or complex skill? It seems that it depends on whether one classifies the task as a single operation or as a complex sequence of movements involving complicated hand-eye coordination and several steps (getting thread, threading needle, knotting thread, cutting slit, etc.). In more general terms, one might also want to ask whether the processes involved in learning tailoring, such as problem solving, remembering, and using logic, are simple or complex? Or are they possibly both?

The determination of whether the processes are simple or complex is not inherent in the activity itself, but rather, it depends on the goals of the analysis. It does seem that the simple/complex distinction, whether applied to the content of what is learned or to the processes by which learning occurs, needs further attention if it is to be used operationally in analyzing actual educational encounters. Also, it is possible that Gearing may want to consider other information classification dimensions that might also affect transmission patterns (e.g., learning versus learning to learn: small versus large categories of items to be learned).

The overview conveys the impression that the culture-specific body of knowledge consists of discrete items of information. Two qualifications might usefully be added to this characterization.

First, the notion of "items" of information suggests that the stuff to be transmitted comes in discrete bits. It seems more likely that much of what is to be learned in a culture is of a continuous nature or that it involves connotative and affective aspects that are not learned at some point in time but which come into existence through some gradual process of growth.

Secondly, it seems that the processes by which people learn are culture-specific (in addition to the learned content). The culture-specific nature of learning and teaching processes stems from the fact that, although people in all cultures are capable of utilizing the same set of teaching and learning devices, in each culture, some devices are more salient than are others. The high-frequency teaching and learning techniques may become salient through accidents of history and tradition, and also because different kinds of culture-specific content-to-be-learned can best be attacked using one teaching or learning process rather than another.

On the basis of these two considerations, it might be useful to extend the concept of "cultural inventory of items of information" to include both information that doesn't come in discrete bits and learning and teaching processes as well as content.

At this point, it might be worth referring back to Gearing's reasons for making the simple/complex distinction. It is important to the overview because different educational agendas have different implications for simple and complex information. In general, constraints on information diffusion deriving from the type of agenda in force, which, in turn, depends on differences in the social characteristics of dyads, affect complex information more than they affect simple information. Thus, if one wishes to predict the spread of a given item of information, one needs to be able to classify it along the simple/complex dimension. Yet, from the work of experimental anthropologists (e.g., Cole et al. 1971), it seems that whether or not people will learn simple information depends not only on encounter, and hence, the agenda characteristics, but also on what kinds of complex knowledge the learner has. For example, children who have been to school appear to solve problems by seeking a general solution rule, more often than do children who have not been to school.

The school children seem to learn to see a new problem as an instance of a class of problems they are already familiar with. They have learned to learn differently than have the other children. Thus, one would expect to find different kinds of relations between simple and complex information arising from other sources in addition to the agenda differences explored by Gearing.

For example, it has been suggested that a training process, a task-oriented, informal learning situation, should not produce learning to learn. Since emphasis is on learning a task, it is claimed that the generalized principles behind the task will not be learned. Hence, in a new situation calling for similar solution principles, the apprentice will treat the task as an entirely new and unfamiliar one.

But in applying this to the Vai tailors, all of this presupposes too simple a view of what might be involved in at least some of the skills or knowledge mastered by apprentices and almost certainly in other tasks as well. The tailors construct garments on the basis of a few measurements of the customer, and customers come in quite different sizes and shapes. Given a single measurement, tailors can produce the measurements of hypothetical customers and also meet the requirements to shape a garment to a nonstandard figure. This is what might be called a "native variable." Another such complex task is that of making garments with different finished shapes and detailing. These tailors have two basic pattern shapes — a trousers shape and a bodice/shirt shape — and they think of all variations in terms of operations on the basic shapes. They can do many variations; every master tailor claims to be able to construct any garment in the Sears Roebuck catalogue with no construction details except the picture in the book. A third example is that two levels of considerations must both be taken into account in cutting out a garment: the necessities, in laying out the garment, of taking into account both construction requirements (seam allowances, facings, and darts) and customer requirements, in terms of size and style.

I suspect that, where native variables exist, learning to learn may occur regardless of the task-oriented framework of the learning process. This hypothesis will soon be tested through a series of graded experiments. For a given skill, demonstrated competence in tailoring will be followed with problems involving the same kinds of skills/knowledge, but in ways that look less and less like tailoring tasks. The experiments are intended to explore the boundaries of generalization of the learning-to-learn produced in the course of learning to be a tailor.

At this point, I am exploring the boundaries of my current knowledge and thinking about the informal, task-oriented learning situation, the specific cultural teaching and learning styles of the Vai tailor, and Gearing's approach to the study of educational encounters. All three strike me as complicated and exciting issues about which we are just beginning to figure out the right questions (never mind the answers). Given the great scope of Gearing's project, it would be especially inappropriate to reproach him for sins of omission, and this is definitely not my intention here. Rather, I hope to have made some suggestions for filling in the broad outlines as I am sure Gearing will do in the near future. I shall certainly look forward to his further elaborations with great interest.

COMMENT *by Thomas R. Williams*

This commentary begins with some observations concerning the development of theory for research on the process of socialization. Then, the discussion turns to comment on two theoretical points made by Gearing et al. that appear to require attention. The commentary concludes with some suggestions for advancing socialization theory.

As a discipline, anthropology has been characterized by a singular focus on the concept of culture. Until recently, this discipline also was marked by a limited theoretical understanding of the culture concept. It was not until 1952, with the publication of Kroeber and Kluckhohn's theoretical review of the culture concept, that anthropologists began to have a fundamental understanding of the basic nature of the concept central to much of their descriptive and analytic study. The definition of culture formulated by Kroeber and Kluckhohn states:

Culture consists of patterns, explicit and implicit, of and for behavior *acquired* and *transmitted* by symbols, constituting the distinctive achievement of human groups, including their embodiments in artifacts; the essential core of culture consists of traditional (i.e., historically derived and selected) ideas and especially their attached values; culture systems may, on the one hand, be considered as products of action, and on the other, as conditioning elements of further action (Kroeber and Kluckhohn 1952: 181, emphasis added).

Kroeber and Kluckhohn's definition has been helpful to anthropologists concerned with the study of the ways human individuals become aware of, incorporate, and act according to culture. First, this definition gave support to research being conducted on cultural transmission. And by beginning their definition with the concepts "acquired and transmitted" Kroeber and Kluckhohn made it clear that they believed that culture must be transmitted between human generations in some nongenetic way.

A definitional legitimization was important to studies that had been conducted on the processes of cultural transmission and acquisition by some anthropologists for a period of nearly thirty years, since it finally provided a recognized place in anthropology for such research. Prior to that, many anthropologists had reservations, often expressed in polemical terms (cf. Williams 1974a), concerning the place of studies of child rearing in contemporary anthropology. Margaret Mead has noted (1972: x) that in 1922 Franz Boas said that he had come to realize that the study of the diffusion of culture traits was finished, since it had been demonstrated that cultures could borrow from each other and that each culture did not have to go through a specific evolutionary sequence. Boas said it was now time for anthropologists to conduct research on the related questions of (1) which aspects of individual behavior were biologically given and (2) which aspects of behavior were due to having been born into one culture rather than another.

During the next two decades, Mead and some other anthropologists and their students devoted attention to the questions posed by Boas. Such research tended to be excluded from a recognized place in the discipline of anthropology by more traditionally oriented colleagues even though Mead's early works (1928a, 1928b, 1930a, 1930b, 1932, 1935, 1937) were exemplars of precise description and analysis of the processes of cultural transmission and acquisition. Mead and others associated with her in the initial research efforts to cope with Boas' questions were subjected to criticism for their persistent concern with study of cultural transmission and acquisition in different settings. During much of the 1930's and 1940's, such criticism often focused on the use by Mead and others of psychoanalytic theories concerning human learning and individual behavior. Such criticism missed the essential point of studies in the early culture and personality tradition in anthropology. For the first time, systematic descriptions and analyses of cultural transmission and acquisition were being conducted by scholars specially trained for anthropological research in field locations and prepared by knowledge of human evolution and culture history to place data in a time perspective (or transtemporal) and a comparative (or transcultural) framework.

In the decade following the close of World War II, it became increasingly more acceptable for young anthropologists to establish professional careers on the basis of ethnographic and theoretical studies of the processes of cultural transmission and acquisition. Although such activities continued to draw condemnations from some established anthropologists, and the phrase "child-rearing studies" was still employed as a pejorative sobriquet for allegedly vague, soft-headed, or useless research, it had become possible regularly to conduct research on these topics.

Three events occurring in the 1950's brought research on cultural transmission and acquisition fully into the mainstream of modern anthropology. The first event was Kroeber and Kluckhohn's (1952) conceptual emphasis discussed above. Then Whiting and Child (1953) published a theoretical work based on a detailed comparison of data of cultural transmission and acquisition in seventy-five societies. This study finally made it clear that this type of research was a vital part of anthropological efforts to understand the nature of culture and the ways that culture affects individual behavior.

In the time between 1955 and 1958, increasingly larger sums of money became available for basic research in all areas of anthropology, including study of cultural transmission and acquisition. For the first time, it became possible for anthropologists concerned with these studies to secure adequate support for basic field research. Thus, in the late 1950's, John Whiting, in association with Bernice Whiting, I. L. Child, W. W. Lambert, and a team of Harvard graduate students, undertook a study of cultural transmission and acquisition in six cultures (Whiting et al. 1966; LeVine and LeVine 1966; Minturn and Hitchcock 1966; Romney and Romney 1966; Fischer and Fischer 1966; Nydegger and Nydegger 1966; Maretzki and Maretzki 1966). This large-scale research effort, the first of its type in this area of study was possible only because large amounts of money had become available to support such fieldwork primarily because it had attained legitimate status in the discipline.

A general acceptance of this type of research and the availability of research funds, led during the 1960's to growing numbers of research projects in still unknown or incompletely described cultures. At the beginning of the 1970's, this area of anthropological research was an active and integral part of the discipline. Yet, there are some major problems and contradictions in this burgeoning research effort that increased support has not solved. For instance, until the publication of a brief account of the field methods used by Whiting et al. (1966) in their studies of six cultures, there were few ways for anthropologists to become knowlegeable about the research methods and the formal design of research projects that would follow from the experience of prior research efforts (Hilger 1960). Anthropologists seeking to join the effort to understand the nature of cultural transmission and acquisition often have been forced to repeat the methodological errors of their predecessors due to a general lack of formal accounts of research methods and research design. Some anthropologists have had an opportunity to conduct their graduate studies with scholars, such as Mead, Kluckhohn, John Whiting, and others. Through the oral tradition in graduate seminars, tutorials, and conferences, these experienced researchers regularly advance the methodological and design sophistication of their students.

For the most part, this area of anthropological research continues to be characterized by a generally unsystematic approach to methods and research design. It is accurate at present to say that graduate students and young anthropologists with such interests usually are forced to rediscover the methods and research designs used by others. Thus, Kluckhohn's innovative accounts (1939, 1941, 1947) of his successful research methods and designs in the study of Navaho cultural transmission and acqusition tend to be ignored, and then rediscovered, as students and younger scholars conduct their research.

It is logically inconsistent and contradictory to the general aim of advancing scientific knowledge to engage in research without a fundamental comprehension of, and sophistication in, contemporary research methods and design. Yet, this appears to be the norm in such studies of cultural transmission and acquisition.

A second major logical contradiction in contemporary efforts to comprehend cultural transmission and acquisition is more serious than the failure to have developed an accessible literature on research methodology. Until recently, there has been little formal theory for study of cultural transmission and acquisition. Despite long-term research efforts, now extending over a half century, it was not until the closing years of the last decade that formal efforts were made to publish statements of theory concerning cultural transmission and acquisition. The first steps toward building such formal theory were taken in 1960 by Henry, with publication of a theoretical design for study of classroom education. In 1963, Mead presented her discussion of the conceptual distinctions between enculturation and socialization. In 1969, LeVine published a brief statement concerning his theoretical ideas on the nature and consequences of the processes of cultural transmission and acquisition. This work offered some definitions first published by LeVine in 1963, and subsequently elaborated upon in a text discussion (Le Vine 1973).

In 1972, I published a text account (Williams 1972a) and a chapter (Williams 1972b) setting forth a theory and conceptual scheme for research on the origin, development, and present nature of the socialization process. My theoretical work does not deal with the consequences for the individual of having been subjected to the processes of cultural transmission and acquisition, as, for instance, in the works written or edited by Scribner and Cole (1973), Cohen (1971), Shimahara (1970), Freeman (1970), Mayer (1970), Danziger (1970), Greenberg (1970), Goslin (1969), Clausen (1968), Brim (1968), Burton (1968), Greenstein (1968), and Whiting (1968).[1] These discussions tend to be reviews and critiques of specific research and directions of research of a type offered earlier by Child (1954). Hence, they do not constitute major efforts to present a theory for understanding these processes.

It is possible to explain the fact that until recently research on cultural transmission and acquisition proceeded with only limited formal statements of theory, by noting, as Mead (1972: x) has, that formal courses on the subject were taught long before any theoretical publications were available to students. A number of scholars have developed and taught

[1] See also: Elkin (1960); Elkin and Handel (1972); McNeil (1969).

theories of cultural transmission and acquisition, but did not publish them, thus limiting the dissemination of their theories to a very few scholars and their associates. This has worked to the obvious disadvantage of others and has been a factor in severely limiting development of formal theory.

The preparation and publication of the theoretical statement by Gearing and his associates is a welcome sign that we are reaching the close of a long period in which theoretical statements on this subject were limited in form and restricted to a few scholars and their associates.

I want to begin my comments on the theory by Gearing et al. by noting that my remarks are offered without reservations about the conceptual ability, personal dedication to the mastery of demanding and difficult tasks, or the willingness of Gearing et al. to be subject to searching criticisms of their concepts and theory. I also want to avoid any feeling on the part of readers of this commentary that I am like the mythical *salathund*, a species of dog who ate salad only when they saw other dogs eating salad. I also have tried to cope with the same theoretical problems faced by Gearing et al. (Williams 1972a, 1972b).

My comments will be concerned with two general points. First, I do not believe that Gearing has carefully drawn or followed out the basic theoretical distinctions between the concepts of cultural transmission, cultural acquisition, and the consequences for individuals of having been socialized. Secondly, the theory statement fails to take account of demonstrated relationships between features of human biology and features of culture known to be involved in socialization.

The theoretical dimensions of the first problem might be outlined by noting that, in a discussion of the concepts of socialization and enculturation, Mead (1963) found it necessary to distinguish between these concepts on the basis of their quite different theoretical frames of reference. Mead defined socialization as a concept referring to the process of transmitting and acquiring human culture. She noted that the concept of enculturation referred to the process of transmitting and acquiring a local culture (e.g., Navaho, Iban, Arunta). Thus, for Mead, human infants and children are socialized in a human culture, while Navaho, Iban, or Arunta infants and children are enculturated in the context of one particular culture, with all of its historical uniqueness and specificity.

Acceptance of Mead's conceptual distinctions requires an acknowledgement that there is a profound theoretical difference between these concepts with reference to their empirical nature and levels of abstraction. Following Mead's ideas, it has become possible to describe the details of a process of enculturation without any further specifications or qualifications concerning the historical background, uniqueness, or local complexity of a culture. Data of cultural transmission and acquisition (e.g., enculturation) in local cultures comprise the base level for further conceptual abstraction in comparative studies of cultural transmission and acquisition (e.g., socialization) in human culture. Following Mead's definitions, one cannot directly record the process of socialization, since this concept specifically refers to a collection of abstract statements of empirical reference, that is, to statements about many very different processes of enculturation. Another way to state this important theoretical point is to say that it is possible, by following Mead's conceptual distinctions, to describe and analyze the process of socialization through abstracting from a large number of discrete processes of enculturation features common to all such processes. This means that specific statements about Navaho, Iban, and Arunta enculturation must be taken as referring to the human process of socialization. Statements concerning details of different enculturation processes comprise the empirical data from which general statements about the socialization process would be drawn. Hence, we will no longer take as equally applicable statements concerning Navaho cultural transmission and acquisition and the human process of socialization. This is not to say that the Navaho, Iban, or Arunta are not human in any sense of the term. Rather, following Mead, it is to say that statements about the human processes of cultural transmission and acquisition must be abstracted from the historically particular and unique empirical data of local processes of enculturation.

In my opinion, Gearing must deal directly with the same type of theoretical problem, since failure to do so severely limits the heuristic precision and general utility of the theory statement. Specifically, it is not clear that Gearing has decided whether his theory is to focus on: (1) the process of cultural transmission; (2) the process of cultural acquisition; or (3) the consequences for an individual of having been subject to processes of cultural transmission and acquisition.

In my theoretical discussions, I have noted some of the problems that derive from discussion that shifts between these concepts and levels, as well as the types of teleological and circular reasoning that have been used (Williams 1972a: 1–4, 99–101). It appears to me that the Gearing theory is focused upon the process of cultural transmission, since the statement essentially consists of abstract statements of empirical reference concerning the ways culture appears to be shared between human generations.

But Gearing does not appear to have faced up to the problem of whether or not to define his theory statement in such a manner so as also to incorporate abstract statements of empirical reference concerning the process of cultural acquisition or the consequences for particular individuals of having been enculturated. Such statements occur, or are implied, in the Gearing theory statement with a frequency that indicates to me an uncertainty in this important task of conceptualization and theory construction.

I have concluded that the processes of cultural transmission and acquisition are conceptual reciprocals. Thus, the phrase "cultural transmission" directly implies the process of acquiring culture, while the phrase "acquisition of culture" directly implies the process of cultural transmission. And the term "socialization" implies no dichotomy between these two processes. I have also concluded that while the phrases "cultural transmission" and "acquisition of culture" are conceptual reciprocals, the concept "acquisition of culture" carries with it an important corollary theoretical meaning, that of the "consequences" for individuals of having acquired culture. The understanding of the consequences for an individual of the acquisition of culture requires, I think, knowledge of the precise ways in which personality characteristics and patterns leading to individual acts are produced in the course of socialization, that is, as a consequence of the processes of cultural transmission and acquisition. Figure 1 (Williams 1974a) notes the levels of conceptual abstraction and ordering in my organization of the major features of the socialization process.

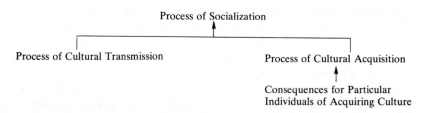

Figure 1. A conceptual arrangement of socialization process features.

In my theoretical statements, I have tried to focus upon and examine the nature of the socialization process, that is, to understand the origin, development, and present form and functions of the reciprocal processes of cultural transmission and acquisition. In this work, I have tried to hold constant the problems involved in defining and understanding the consequences for individuals of having been socialized. The study of the consequences of socialization is a separate and well-established area of research, known by a variety of current designations depending on the academic discipline involved (e.g., psychological anthropology, social psychology, developmental psychology, etc.). It seems clear that it is necessary to hold as a constant the topic and area of investigation of the specific consequences for an individual of having been socialized, since considering these data requires a basic shift in the conceptual orientations used, from a macroproblem (or molar theoretical orientation to a micro-problem or molecular) orientation. Another way to state the required conceptual shift would be to note that it would involve a basic change from a nomothetic (the general processual whole) to an idiographic (explication of individual cases) conceptual orientation.

I believe it is clear that Gearing and his associates have not concerned themselves with the theoretical problems involved in fully specifying their conceptual focus. Thus, Gearing introduces the theory statement by clear dismissal of the folk culture idea that "education" is not to be understood by examining the varying conditions of what is contained in the "heads" of some people and not contained in the "heads" of others, but through application of a cybernetic model to the problems of "education." In this cybernetic model, cultural information and skills are diffused randomly throughout a society if there are no restraints to impede flow of such cultural information and skills. If restraints are present, there is a systematic or selective distribution of cultural information and skills in a society. In Gearing's theory, it follows that the principal empirical task is to identify and to map the various restraints that reduce or impede a truly random distribution of cultural information/skills.

Gearing cites Bateson's theoretical development of the concept of cybernetics, (Bateson 1972; Bateson and Reusch 1968) as a principal basis of their understanding and use of cybernetic concepts. Their essential conceptual problem — clearly stating a focus on the study of (1) a process of cultural transmission, (2) a process of cultural acquisition, or (3) the consequences for an individual of having been socialized — becomes acute with such a declaration. This is because it is clear that Bateson's theoretical development of cybernetic concepts, in his long-term efforts to understand socialization, not only incorporates consideration of both the processes of cultural transmission and cultural acquisition as conceptual reciprocals, but has as well a primary focus upon an understanding of the consequences for individuals of having been socialized. Thus, if one reads the works in which Bateson developed this theoretical focus (Bateson 1935, 1936, 1941, 1942a, 1942b, 1944, 1972), it becomes apparent that he means to concern himself theoretically with two problems: (1) the qualitative structure of behavioral contexts, rather than the intensity of behavioral interactions; and (2) the consequences for particular individuals of having been socialized (Bateson 1972: 155). Bateson is not generally concerned with study of the origin, development, or major features or functions of the processes of cultural transmission or cultural acquisition. Bateson is concerned with development of research methods, such as cybernetics, for understanding the qualitative structure of behavioral contexts and the consequences of socialization for individuals.

Thus, Bateson's cybernetic ideas, applied to his understanding of the nature of culture, essentially are focused on trying to explain and master the conceptual and theoretical details of what it means for individuals to be socialized in terms of individual actions and life careers.

It may be asked what the effects are of Gearing not recognizing that the theory lacks a clear statement of a conceptual focus? As I see it, the major consequence is a strong uncertainty as to whether, having discarded a folk culture image of "education" and then having accepted as valid a cybernetic model for socialization (Mead's term, as used here), he conceives of "education" as including the three processes mentioned above.

My second point of general concern involves the fact that there is no reference to, or concern with, the demonstrated relationships between culture and human biology. I do not believe that it is possible now to propose a socialization theory, whether of a limited or a general form, without reference to the complex ways human biology and culture are known to be interrelated (Chapple 1970). I believe it is not helpful to formulate theory concerning essential processual features of culture, e.g., "... behavior acquired and transmitted by symbols ..." (Kroeber and Kluckhohn 1952: 181) without attending to the specific ways such features are related to specific aspects of human biology. My conviction can be stated in a more succinct form: The most important theoretical questions in contemporary anthropology involve specification of the ways features of culture and human biology are interrelated and function together.

I am concerned that Gearing has not acknowledged that he is concerned with features of culture (process of transmission? process of acquisition? consequences of socialization process?) that demonstrably have their empirical bases in human biology. I am not suggesting that, in considering "education," Gearing should reduce the theory to a micro-level (or a minimally irreducible level) of analysis of individual biology, such as the interactions of specific $mRNA$ molecules. I am proposing that, in developing a theory of socialization, it is vital to consider the ways significant features of culture are related to significant features of human biology. I believe that general culture theory (cf. Kaplan and Manners 1972) has advanced beyond the point where it is possible to argue that culture exists as a separate domain of nature, without reference to the forms of functions of other phenomena, including human biology.

Data of human evolution now indicate that culture and human biology evolved over a period of approximately three to five million years before the present, in a mutually dependent or cybernetic interaction process so that major changes in human biology led to major changes in culture, while significant changes in culture led to major changes in human biology (cf. Bajema 1971, 1972, 1973). This means that any contemporary theory of human behavior must, at the least, attend to the known evolutionary interrelations between human biology and culture.

Another way to state this point would be to note that among all life forms only *Homo sapiens* and the hominid precursors of *Homo sapiens* appear to have had an evolutionary heritage in which culture, a new and

160   Section Six: On Inter- and Intra-psychic Analysis

powerful phenomenon, came to be a directive force for, and at the same time, to be directed by, other powerful phenomena of biology. Our closest contemporary primate relative, the chimpanzee, does not possess such an evolutionary heritage, that is, a history of a cybernetic process between biology and culture extending over at least three million years. Hence, contemporary chimpanzees, who are structurally very similar to humans (Kohne 1970; Goodman 1971; Wilson and Sarich 1969; Sarich 1970) generally do not behave like humans, since they lack the total evolutionary heritage of millions of years of cybernetic interaction that has occurred between a human biology and culture. I think that it is very interesting to try to train chimpanzees to talk, solve puzzles of various types, read sentences comprised of abstract symbols, or to communicate with humans about their thoughts by the use of a symbolic typewriter keyboard. But the apparent similarity of some *Homo sapiens* behavior forms and the behavior forms of contemporary chimpanzees (or any other primate) should be treated with great care. Although it has been pointed out (King 1971; Washburn 1972a, 1972b) that many behavior forms once thought unique to humans (e.g. tool use, complex cooperative social acts such as hunting game) are, in fact, found among various kinds of free-ranging primates (and some other mammals as well), this does not at all mean that it logically follows that the precursors of modern chimpanzees, or other primates, have ever experienced a biology-culture cybernetic interaction process. In other words, it is quite likely that the apparently similar behavior forms noted today among humans and chimpanzees (or other primates) are the result of some parallel and convergent biological evolutionary processes operative over millions of years of chimpanzee evolution, and not because contemporary chimpanzees have an evolutionary heritage that includes a long-term cybernetic interaction process between evolving chimpanzee biology and a developing system of culture. In this context, it should be noted that I would be fascinated to learn of the "thoughts" of chimpanzees or other primates. And, I do not want to place myself in the position of a late nineteenth-century president of an association for the advancement of science, who, on retiring from his office predicted that little would be learned about science in the future, since the main outline of all that was to be known was already well described. Perhaps current and future studies of chimpanzees and other modern primates will inform us in ways that are profoundly revealing of basic insights into the nature of a human life. I am very doubtful this will be the case and continue to believe that the proper study of humans is the study of humankind.

The question is, then, how do these points bear upon a critique of the theory offered by Gearing. To propose a general theory of education or socialization requires explicit attention to the ways that education involves specific features of human biology. At the risk of appearing immodest by proposing that colleagues should attend to my work discussing such relationships, I would note that I have tried to suggest details of some of the ways that four features of human biology (species characteristic behavior, reflexes, drives, and capacities) possibly are related to the processes comprising socialization (Williams 1972a: 22–41). Based on some earlier theoretical work (Williams 1959), I also have noted a broad outline of the cybernetic development of the structural-functional features of human biology and culture that appear to be crucial to socialization (Williams 1972a: 6–21; 1972b). I have also tried to review major theories and recent research in the ways culture may be acquired in socialization (Williams 1972a: 42–66, 67–102).

My theoretical and field research (Williams 1969) have led me to conclude, with Gearing, that past portrayals of socialization have been too dependent on a folk culture conception of adult humans actively doing something, e.g., "rewarding" and "punishing", to infants, children, and adolescents in order to "teach" culture to what has been assumed to be reluctant and naturally stubborn members of the next adult generation. Unlike Gearing I have come to believe also that a substantial part of culture in most human societies actually is transmitted through operant conditioning. This can be seen in the ways infants, children, and adolescents teach themselves through regular use of species characteristic reflective (or reflexive) and symbolic behavior forms, various human capacities, including cognition, and a variety of motor functions. I have concluded that socialization does not occur primarily in repeated interpersonal contacts between infants, children, adolescents, and adults. Rather, socialization takes place to a large extent inside the "heads" and in the acting out motor behavior of maturing individuals. I am not at all certain whether my use of terms such as "substantial" can be put in quantitative terms. My present belief is that more than 50 percent but less than 75 percent of socialization consists of what might be termed self-socialization but I cannot really quantify my belief at present, since I have not developed specific methods of making precise empirical measures of features of socialization.

I have come to this theoretical position through examination of the empirical evidence of the structural and functional features of enculturation in a sample of 128 cultures. I must note that, although I have used the phrase "most human societies," my 128-culture sample is less than 5 percent of all cultures. Hence, conclusions drawn from such a limited sample must be treated with care. But in asking the question, "How is it that culture usually comes to be used regularly by human infants, children and adolescents?" I have had to cope, through the available literature, with the specific issue of how that which is outside the heads of young humans, e.g., culture, regularly comes to be inside their heads as adults.

My way of seeking an answer to this question has been to begin with an identification of the specific four features of human biology that I believe can serve as organic bridgeheads to culture. They are, the biological features through which an infant born bereft of culture comes to take on and ordinarily use culture as the central aspect of all personal behavior. This theoretical position is quite different from the one taken by Gearing et al. In their theory, Gearing et al. have looked to the social interactions between individuals as the locus where education (socialization) occurs. Culture is seen as contained, not in the heads (central nervous system) of adults as some type of entity with a reality and existence, but as something manifest in the complex interaction process that occurs when any two or more human individuals meet.

Gearing has constructed a theory that seeks to describe and predict ways that cultural information and skills may move in the absence of restraints from any physically normal adult or child to another virtually automatically and without specification of how such movement of cultural information and skills occur in terms of known interrelations between features of culture and human biology. Gearing probably is correct when he notes that in socialization research one should not worry about describing the contents and varying conditions of adult heads, since the available empirical evidence tends to show that the contents of adult heads are cultural in any case. Furthermore, there is less direct transmission of culture from adult heads to the heads of infants, children and adolescents than has been claimed in the past. I believe education occurs to a significant extent inside the heads of young humans through their operant use of particular features of human biology that enables each physically normal individual to be socialized. This may be termed a "human see, human do" theory of socialization, characterized by an emphasis on the notion that infants, children, and adolescents note cultural behavior forms that are usual and are said to be expected in a culture. They then "teach themselves" such behavior forms without generally experiencing such forms directly, either through specific instruction or in situations of social interaction.

I would be prepared, after my study of the Gearing theory, to also entertain hypothesis that my "human see, human do" approach to socialization must incorporate data of social interaction. It is obvious that infants, children, and adolescents as they mature participate in a variety of social interaction situations. I have no doubt that human young do acquire cultural information and skills in situations of social interaction. Certainly, there are specific types of cultural information and skills that can be obtained only in, and through, being a direct participant in a situation of social interaction. However, it is my belief, based on study of data from a sample of 128 cultures and my own field research on enculturation, that cultural information and skills usually are transmitted and acquired by an individual child repeatedly rehearsing through a physical acting out, or in a cognitive fashion, the patterned ways that would be followed if he were an adult. Thus, I would not take the position that cultural transmission and acquisition occurs infrequently in situations of social interaction. The empirical evidence is to the contrary.

One may ask, "But what then is the source of the cultural information and skills used inside the heads of human young as they proceed to socialize themselves?" It is clear that such cultural information and skills are not transmitted genetically. How, then, do maturing individuals come to be possessed of cultural information and skills needed to socialize themselves? My response is that my data on enculturation informs me that human young intensively use the unique biological features that have emerged in the course of a human cybernetic evolutionary process to size up, seize upon, and make their own the specific features of the culturally patterned world into which they are born. For example, human infants come well prepared to see details of culturally patterned activities. New-born humans quickly exhibit high levels of visual acuity, sensitivity, and coordination, so that by the fifteenth to twentieth day after birth most infants discriminate among basic colors and follow and focus on complex movements. Hence, well before human infants are able to physically manipulate cultural reality through fine motor control, they are well prepared visually to apprehend and, thus, minimally to comprehend culturally meaningful stimuli carried to them by their vision-sense structures. Similarly, human infants are well prepared to deal with and to learn about details of their culturally patterned world through their hearing and tactile sense structures.

I believe that the aspect of comprehension just noted involves the use of the species characteristic forms of reflection and symbolling in complex and little understood ways. As a human infant gains cultural information and skills through operant use of its unique biological sensory structures, it is prepared by its biological-cultural, cybernetic, evolutionary heritage to comprehend such detail by virtue of its possession of a means to store, quickly retrieve, and reflect upon patterns of past events in a present context and thereby to anticipate in patterned ways the dimensions and possible details of future events. Such reflection quickly increases in scope and power as additional symbols and language become available to them. What has been comprehended in form and pattern increasingly becomes a "knowing," an "understanding," and a "minding" as individuals mature in the context of culture. There also is substantial evidence that maturing individuals come prepared biologically to engage in a "pattern search and recognition" kind of reflective activity, so that details that are perceived through sight, hearing, and tactile structures are being scanned and stored, and then later recalled, in highly patterned forms (Brown 1974). Available evidence from studies of autistic and culturally isolated infants and children (Williams 1972a: 103–123) also appear to confirm my belief that human infants, children, and adolescents come well prepared biologically to socialize (educate) themselves, providing there is a cultural context in which they regularly can use the unique biological structures that provide the means for them to teach themselves culture.

The theoretical position I have taken could be dismissed through an insistence on considering "education" as something that occurs only in the course of social interactions between humans, whether they are adults or children. My theoretical position requires that one be willing to assign social interactions between individuals to a much less vital role in "education" and to focus instead upon the ways infants, children, and adolescents operantly condition themselves through the use of their unique biological features to live in and be a part of a culture. Again, this theoretical position does not require that data of cultural transmission and acquisition in situations of social interaction be ignored or devalued. But it appears to me that there is relatively little interaction between humans in socialization in proportion to the large amount of cultural information and skills finally acquired. Infants, children, and adolescents actually spend limited amounts of time each day as participants in social dyads in which cultural information and skills could be exchanged between participants. In the 128 sample cultures, available data tends to confirm that human young, particularly infants and very young children, spend much of their time in solitary activities. I am concerned that Gearing may have unwittingly allowed the theory to be influenced by an American and European classroom model for education (Scribner and Cole 1973). In such a model, it is assumed that most of the remainder of the world educates their young by placing them regularly into dyadic situations that force them to interact and at least to be exposed to the possibility of a cultural information and skills exchange with others in their culture. The fact is that in most cultures, after an initial absolute dependency period, children are engaged in regular social interaction contact with others considerably less than has been assumed by socialization theorists. Much of the time, human offspring simply are left to shift for themselves, to play by themselves, to be alone, to wander about while being minimally supervised by and in the nominal care of a baby tender or nurse. Children's play groups are found in all cultures. In such groups, they have an opportunity for dyadic interaction with others who could transmit cultural information and skills to them. But, on the balance, in total chronological terms, outside of American and Western European cultures, children really are required to teach themselves culture operantly. A careful look at American culture in the years prior to schooling indicates that older infants and children also are left to themselves for very large amounts of time each day, time in which young children can still see and hear and comprehend and know details and patterns of culture. American children tend to be alone in their preschool years, and yet they acquire large amounts of culture during these periods (Barker and Wright 1951, 1955; Barker and Barker 1961).

What is the point of this illustration? It is, simply, that by constructing a theory that focuses primarily upon dyadic social interactions between individuals, one possessed, the other not possessed, of cultural information and skills, Gearing has chosen a theoretical model that does not reflect data of socialization. Once again, it is important to understand that I am not claiming that socialization proceeds without any social dyadic exchange of cultural information and skills. In the initial part of an infant's life, there obviously is a high level of such interaction between a newborn human and its mother, sometimes its father, and on occasion, parent surrogates. Obviously there are regular times of social interaction in which cultural information and skills actually are exchanged in all cultures. Yet, to focus an entire theoretical model, as Gearing has done, only upon the constructs of dyadic social interaction is to ignore data indicating that the socialization process does not proceed solely through social interaction.

If one takes the theoretical position I have adopted, then the "restraints" operating on and affecting "education" are not only social and economic (e.g., class, caste, clan, residence, and income) but are also basic biological restraints. I want to specify very clearly that I do not believe such biological restraints are in any way the special property of particular racial, social, or ethnic groups. To the contrary, I believe that such biological restraints are distributed randomly throughout the entire human population. I believe the available empirical evidence strongly supports this position.[2] Thus, without regard to their social, economic, or ethnic situations, some human infants, children, and adolescents with particular arrangements of reflexes, drives, and capacities cannot acquire or will incompletely acquire cultural information and skills that other children acquire well.

I would expect that one counter to my arguments on these theoretical points would be to note that it is possible to limit data and theory of education, or socialization, entirely to the conceptual abstraction level of the social interactions occurring between individuals. My response would be to note that human beings do not respond, react, or behave solely with reference to stimuli from social interaction situations; humans define and interpret stimuli in accordance with their operant use of particular features of human biology to enable them to acquire, retain, recall, and use particular culturally patterned information and skills. Such individual

---

[2]   Thus, I *do not* subscribe to, or follow the ideas advanced by Jensen, Shockley, and others concerning supposed links between race, ethnicity, and subcultural affiliation and human capacities for learning cognition.

166 Section Six: On Inter- and Intra-psychic Analysis

definitions and interpretations of culture are variable depending on the level and general sufficiency of individual functioning of the major biological features that are involved.

My feeling is that Gearing must revise the theory statement either to include the known relationships between features of human biology and culture or to explain exclusion of such material.

In concluding my commentary, I want to note that the state of socialization research at present is comparable to the time in the development of modern physics when it finally became possible to conceptualize nature in new and very different ways. We are now entering an era in the study of socialization when basic conceptions of human biology, culture, society, and their specific interrelationships are changing drastically. I believe that a variety of limited theories, and then a general theory, will emerge from current studies of the socialization process. I cannot predict the time when a general theory for socialization will be developed, but I remain confident that such a general theory will come into existence. My confidence has been bolstered by the theoretical concerns exhibited by Gearing.

It would be my suggestion that an effort be made by other scholars concerned with development of a general socialization theory to convene regularly symposia and to publish statements of theory with accompanying critiques. Such formal exchanges would promote rapid development of a general socialization theory, provide a means for conceptual innovation, and lead to the development of highly refined conceptual schemes. Such meetings and published exchanges of ideas finally will put an end to a period in the study of socialization that has been characterized by a lack of concern with research methodology, restricted circulation of limited theory and concepts, and a constant rediscovery of old methods, concepts, and theory. I also believe that publication of the Gearing theory statement and its accompanying critiques marks the end of one era and the beginning of another in socialization research.

PART THREE

A Reference Model for a Cultural
Theory of Education and Schooling

A Reference Model for a Cultural Theory of Education and Schooling

FREDERICK GEARING

INTRODUCTION AND ACKNOWLEDGEMENTS

It may serve well at this juncture to look back at the commentaries just concluded and to sketch in outline where we will be going.

Recurrently, through most of the commentaries in Part II, there run expressions of a puzzle. How do theories usually get made? How might they best be made? Science is a public enterprise, inherently collective, but there is the problem of determining at what point in the development of a theory the work — the results to date — becomes public. Some commentators applauded; others did not. And although we have acted out one answer, we would not even attempt to argue its merits.

One of the commentaries questioning the nature of theory development — that of Paul Garvin and Madeleine Mathiot — offered a specific suggestion as to the logical nature of such an effort. This suggestion has obvious merit and helps to clarify the theory development effort. Recognizing the inductive logic inherent in Working Paper 6 and in the current research shaped by those ideas, they proposed a two-dimensional inductive procedure. They recommended that one construct a reference model, gathering data and near-knowledge from existing literature and experience and drawing these into a synthesis. This reference model must frame a methodological stance, and in addition it might contain various logically related propositions that make no strong claim as to external reality, but which do clearly admit of empirical examination. Such a reference model operates to shape the framing of research questions and to assist in the pursuit of the answers. Second, Garvin and Mathiot suggested that one additionally and simultaneously needs a "theory." This contains whatever may exist of knowledge that is germane and seems certain. Such a theory is at its early stages necessarily a nearly empty receptical, as it were. It will come to hold in logical order new knowledge, gained through empirical research and guided by the reference model, as it becomes firmly established.

Their suggestion redefines, in effect, what Working Paper 6 is: a reference model, in very imperfect and primitive form. I find this advice persuasive. Therefore what follows in the remaining pages is such a reference model. One hopes it over time will help generate a theory, specifically the cultural theory of education and schooling that is sought.

A second theme that recurred in the commentaries was: What exactly is this imagined theory intended to explain? It is possible to answer with a measure of precision. Very generally, the theory will not explain "mental" — as opposed to behavioral — facts of any kind. (In Working Paper 6, the authors were trying explicitly to disengage themselves from such psychological concerns, but we only half succeeded. Some of the language used — the "flow of information" or of "knowledge" and several other phrasings — was at best misleading.) That is to say that the theory is intended to *explain* how it comes about that some members of certain definable categories of person within a community predictably will, and all members of other categories of person predictably will not, come competently to perform some complex task, for example, designing a bridge, or dancing in a ballet company, or effectively becoming a fire chief. The explanation of how such competencies predictably get distributed would entail the identification of those kinds of constraints that are interactional, and that are not mental and not motor, in nature.

Conversely, the theory does *not* explain how it happens that, given two members of one of those categories of "eligible" persons above, one individual does and the other does not come to know how. Such an explanation in addition would necessarily entail the identification of constraints that are mental and motor.

There follows a matter of unusual importance to education research. Questions such as which specific individuals will and which will not acquire competence to perform some complex task are the principal kind of question education research addresses. The theory now under consideration seeks to show conclusively that, in the pursuit of *this* kind of question, the researcher is methodologically in error if he or she sets out to take a population, to measure in some fashion successes and failures among its members, and to seek directly to explain that variation in terms of intelligence, motor abilities, attitudes, and so on. The theory should show that analysis of interactional constraints is necessary *and must precede* analysis in terms of mental and motor constraints. Later, in dealing with hidden curriculums, the specific nature of this claim will be treated. For example, while this cultural theory would not show that the results of Jensen are true or false, it suggests that his research strategies were fundamentally in error.

A third concern, often implicit but only occasionally made explicit in the commentaries, entails matters of personal values and public policy. Among the commentators, Herzog phrased this concern forcefully; he felt it deeply. In Working Paper 6, the authors argue that education and schooling are powerfully conservative forces. Some readers wondered whether that sentence ended with an implied cheer or with an expletive. In hindsight, it is evident that both were intended.

Lack of change, it should be especially noted, is itself adaptive in some very substantial part, as McQuown noted in his commentary. One needs only to recall some of the attributes of our own species, *Homo sapiens* — our restless curiosity, which is shared with primate relatives; our linguistic ability to name things and, thus, to hold them in mind, our ability to recombine in the imagination the things so named, to invent and fantasize, and so on. It is therefore especially noteworthy that members of this human species can *somehow* forego changing their behaviors enough to be predictable to each other, relate to each other, and therefore to form a community. The claim that education and schooling are powerfully conservative is reiterated in the pages that follow. To describe a community as a system of education and schooling is, I believe, to describe that community as exercising this remarkable capability of not changing.

Not changing also can be painfully maladaptive. Toward the end of these pages is a discussion of how the scientific understandings entailed in a cultural theory of education and schooling, even as it now appears, can be put to work in the interests of certain kinds of change.

Beyond the three aforementioned themes that recur in the commentaries, a wide variety of concerns were expressed — all of which were matters of conceptualization and method in the basic sense. The commentators sought greater clarity in three closely related matters:

1. Of all observable behaviors, which ones are to be selected out and deemed education, and which are deemed schooling?

2. As was noted in the introduction to this volume, the theory pivots on the idea of constraint, and it focuses specifically on those nonmental and nonmotor constraints that are jointly generated by persons in their interactions. Erickson's treatment of "stumbles" will prove most helpful.

3. There is the difficult question of whether patterns of constraint observable at microlevels of small group interaction and analogous patterns described at community-wide macrolevels replicate each other and how this happens, if it does.

These three matters, while not altogether new, have not been extensively explored, so clarity of concept and operation is both difficult and unusually important.

The effort to unfold in the following pages is possible because several persons have worked with me for several years; they are named as co-authors of Part I, the early formulation of the theory — Working

Paper 6. The late Allan Tindall was a professor in the department of anthropology (SUNY at Buffalo); his contribution was large and we miss him sorely. Thomas Carroll, Walter E. Precourt, Leta Richter, Allen Smith, and Sigrid Töpfer were then graduate students in anthropology. Wayne Hughes and Patricia Hurlich were graduate students in educational administration. All these former students are dispersed now; some of them have become professors and others are professionals. They are not listed as co-authors to the second formulation, principally because they are now remote and preoccupied with their own work, variously related but in no case following this collective formulation. Nevertheless, I cannot imagine that this reformulation could have occurred, let alone in the form it now has, without their good advice and help over the past years. Other students of anthropology more recently have become involved, and among them Eleanor Dougherty is to be noted for her intelligent critiques which grew out of her own empirical research still in progress.

I am indeed grateful to the anthropologists and other social scientists who took time from their busy lives to read the working paper, a frequently rough and always cryptic document. They gave it their careful thought, and provided the critiques printed in Part II. These critiques substantially shaped the reformulation that follows.

What is perhaps the greatest debt of all is owed to three other persons. Over a period of some twenty years now, Solon Kimball, formerly of Teachers College, Columbia, and now at the University of Florida, and George and Louise Spindler, at Stanford, have been quietly insisting that formal education is a part of a wider set of phenomena called cultural transmission; that anthropologists and other students of culture not only can, but must, concern themselves with all these phenomena, which are to be joined in some systematic, integrated way; that a culture does not exist because it was transmitted across the generations but in and through the process of transmission itself. It seems altogether improbable that without the work of these three persons there would exist today the substantial surge of work by anthropologists in the topical subfield now known as anthropology and education. This subfield encompasses efforts in curriculum development and teacher training at all levels (anthropology *in* education) and basic research efforts to increase the understanding of educational processes (anthropology *of* education), the latter of which is a major concern of this volume. The author takes this opportunity to acknowledge this debt and to thank these persons for their continuing pervasive influence.

The reference model that follows is derived from — and attempts selectively to synthesize — a varied body of literature and research in progress which may persuade the reader that a cultural theory of education and schooling is reachable and that it will be worth the effort. The treatment contains four parts: (1) a rather extended discussion of the entailed conceptualization and the problems of method; (2) a terse array of logically related propositions admitting of empirical examination; (3) certain peripheral remarks; and finally, (4) a discussion of application, specifically as it applies to schools.

1. A REFERENCE MODEL: BASIC CONCEPTUALIZATIONS

There follow discussions in two parts: general orienting considerations and a discussion of the basic conceptual tools of which there are two kinds, namely, "behavioral units" and "analytic dimensions." Each permit analytic description, respectively in terms of structure and function.

Two General Orientations

The reference model under examination is designed to lead toward a cultural theory of education and schooling. One is wise initially to back off from a great deal of received wisdom about what education and schooling is or is not and, with some measure of purposefully induced naivete, to take a fresh look at the maze one is about to reenter — a human community in the process of educating and schooling itself.

In any contemporary community, every man and woman and every boy and girl moves daily into and out of at least two contrasting worlds. One is a personalized world that consists of household and kindred, neighborhood, and club, and so on. Within any contemporary community of any size, there are many such localized personal worlds. These local worlds coexist and contrast, each with every other in that community, and between two such localized worlds, where contrasting ethnicity and contrasting economic class are both involved, there is usually marked contrast. Every man and woman and every boy and girl also moves daily into and out of a second and quite different kind of world, which consists of some segment of the international network of bureaucratically organized business and government. This world in part unfolds in the same geographic space and in part draws persons daily outside that space; this network reaches around the earth and is remarkably similar wherever it goes. Paul Bohannan has called all this the "two-story" cultural system of contemporary life.

The life career of a man or woman consists of movements through two or more of these worlds. More particularly, a life career unfolds as a person becomes a participant in first one, then the others, of the regularly occurring events that constitute life in these worlds. These life careers are not random: within any localized world, boys and men move through that world differently than do girls and women; men from some localized worlds frequently move into the upper echelons of the bureaucratically organized world, while men from other, ethnically contrasting localized worlds do not, and in either case, women move into these upper echelons differently and usually less frequently than do men.

Life in any of these worlds is made up of some series of regularly occurring events. Each regularly occurring event is itself a little system of education or schooling. Any person who is to become a participant in any recurring event enters first as a newcomer and later becomes an old hand. What transpires in between — the face-to-face interchanges that transform the newcomer into an old hand — may look like instruction, or may more resemble on-the-job training, or may simply be a matter of "getting the hang of it," but what transpires in whatever form, is, education or schooling. Those transformations, in the events that together constitute the life of each localized world and each sector of that wider world, are together the community's encompassing system of education and schooling.

In the contemporary world, in short, every person gets educated and schooled many times. As the events that constitute a person's world vary, so do the processes that transform this person from newcomer into old hand in one event and then another, in one of his worlds and then in another, throughout his or her life.

From all this, it would follow that, the contemporary world being what it is, one cannot adequately comprehend any one part of a system of education or schooling in a community unless one comprehends as well something of the variety of the other parts that coexist and may compete. For an obvious example, the behaviors that regularly occur in the places called schools and colleges are most imperfectly comprehensible unless one also comprehends, as coexisting parts of the encompassing system of education or schooling, the households and neighborhoods from which the students come daily, the jails and asylums into which, as the students and their instructors know, some may alternatively move, and the factories, enterprises, and government agencies into which most will someday move.

One reenters such a maze, seeking to understand the nature of those behaviors, called education and schooling, that unfold there. And to that purpose, the key organizing concept is the notion of interactional constraint. It will be wise, as before, to back off and again to put aside most received wisdom about how one goes about understanding anything. We should look briefly at the use of the admittedly strange and sometimes counterintuitive notion — constraint — first generally and then more specifically as it is applied in this attempt to understand the nature of education and schooling.

First, consider the concept of constraint as it is applied to other than human communities. Together with other ideas historically related, the notion takes as given a great sea of randomness broken here and there with the islands of order we know as the brute matter around us. Order is some persisting arrangement of parts, and by these ideas, it is in the nature of these islands of order themselves to degenerate into randomness. As brute matter degenerates, order is lost, but often some order is recaptured in new forms of order. Along the way come the forms of order we call life, the living organisms.

Life has been defined — Bateson has so phrased it — as a struggle against that degeneration into randomness; it is a losing battle, but the processes of mutation (in the service of randomization) and natural selection (in the service of capturing order) make the struggle interesting. Any species, and any member of that species, plus the organs and other parts that make up that organism, are temporary successes. Order, a persisting arrangement of parts, has in each instance been captured.

Given its ecological slot, a species has certain jobs it must do to survive, so for any surviving species, the biological variation among the members of the species is held within limits. The survival tasks constrain variation in the order; otherwise stated, *function constrains structure.*

With life forms, constraints always operate indirectly. With some species, for example, the system made up of lungs, and respiration has the job of getting oxygen in the right amount from the air into the blood. The system must get information and act on it to get the job done. But the information "too little oxygen" would also be too late, for the organism would be hurt already. So the system monitors instead the intake of carbon dioxide, which is itself innocuous but chemically linked to oxygen. For life forms generally, this is to say, *function constrains structure indirectly.*

Constraint is not a mere state of limitation; it is the operation of a self-correcting feedback system through which information flows. Information is news about difference, specifically, two classes of difference: "too much" or "too little", which are both opposed to "just right" (within limits of toleration), which is itself information-empty.

All the above seems standard. We turn now to the uses of the notions of constraint in studying human group behavior, and here one must pick and choose (for example, Bateson 1958) and improvise. Specifically, impressed and encouraged by that pair of new facts named in the introduction to this volume, I have elected to deal with one kind of constraint — constraints generated by persons in face-to-face interaction. That pair of facts were the remarkable synchronies to be seen between parties to face-to-face interaction and the multiplicity of simultaneous messaging in such interaction. The implication of those facts was the radical "jointness" of the actions that normally occur in such interaction and, conversely, the empirical reality and power of the interactional constraints that preclude other actions.

Humans are a biological species, subject to all the above. I move past that and directly to the fact that the jobs this species must do are done through an arrangement of parts called a community.

Any description of a community that is guided by the notion of interactional constraint is oriented by the two principles just named. First, function constrains structure. The behavioral variation in any human community is held within certain ultimate limits; species requisites (food, shelter, etc.) must be met. But all surviving communities, with all their contrasts, do this, so variation for any particular community is evidently held within drastically reduced limits. Any community is evidently so complex an array of interconnected parts that almost any behavioral variation beyond the narrow established limits would adversely affect its balance. Thus, it can reasonably be assumed that variation is limited by the jobs they do in fact do, *in the ways they do in fact usually do them*. This is merely a way of alluding to cultural persistence. Yet, insofar as the notion of interactional constraint guides description, the question addressed is not whether this is always so, but, when cultural persistence is in fact in evidence, how it comes about.

Second, function constrains structure indirectly. This means that by this kind of description, using this notion of interactional constraint, the community is seen to include among other things a job-doing system. This job-doing system is normally kept unchanging through constraints operating through some other system or set of systems not directly connected with the doing of those jobs. It appears that these latter systems include the one here in principal focus, namely, the system of education and schooling.

Behavioral Units and Analytic Dimensions: Structure and Function

To enter any complex maze for the purpose of understanding it requires looking and listening, selectively identifying some of the behaviors and not others as data, arranging various juxtapositionings of those data into classes and into classes of classes.

We now imagine reentering a maze made up of a community of people, entering with the notion of interactional constraint as the principal tool for analytically describing what we see. Out of the buzz of persons, places, acts, and objects "out there," only regularity can capture the eye and ear. In general, the kinds of regularity that pivotally must form the raw material of *this* kind of description of a community are those routinized interactions that unfold in face-to-face gatherings that reoccur. We shall call gatherings of that kind "events" and call those interactions "routines." Description of a community would be made up pivotally of certain features of the routines that unfold in an adequate qualitative sample of events. Note that no less than 99 percent of observable phenomena will have already been left behind.

It is self-evident that the observer must somehow cause this maze "to hold still," or to seem to, in order that observation of the regularities can proceed at all. The observer can accomplish this only by breaking the whole into parts, by acts of his or her imagination. The observer's initial act in creating such parts is irreduceably arbitrary: the whole of human-kind forms today a single interconnected system. Thus, to single out some part of all that, to call that part a community, and to then proceed to study that, is inherently arbitrary. But this is, for most purposes and certainly for the purposes before us, a necessary act. For our purposes, a commun-ity, so singled out, must include males and females of all ages, and these persons must interact in some regular fashion; it must be a cradle-to-grave (but not self-contained) system. And for our purpose, it is required that the identification of such a community be done explicitly; one defines the community by defining its membership.

The community, so selected, must itself be divided into some array of parts. The purpose is to examine patterns of such constraints as are generated in interaction. That fact dictates two formal rules: (1) the total community must be divided into behavioral units and so described as a structure, and (2) it must in addition be divided by analytic dimensions by which whole behavioral units are selected out and reaggregated accord-ing to function. There results a structural-functional description. Let us see what, in general, these rules mean.

Behavioral Units: Structure

Behavioral units are natural segments in streams of behavior. These are natural in the sense that the behaviors of the actors are discontinuous at the boundaries; typically, participants have names for the segments or can be caused to recognize them and offer descriptive phrasings for them.

In terms of behavioral units, a community is made up of events, which reoccur and thus are named or describable by germane actors. An event is a kind of coming together wherein there is a measure of regularity as to who gathers; where, when, and how often they gather; and what they do when they gather. Events in turn are made up of phases (Kendon 1975); any occasions of an event have, for obvious examples, beginning phases, and some series of middle phases, and ending phases. Any phase, in turn, is made up of some repertoire of routines, and any particular occurrence of a phase is made up of an unfolding of certain routines out of that repertoire, plus the transitions between routines. A routine is a pattern of interactive behavior that, once initiated, normally runs a predictable course. But any routine may be interrupted and temporarily supplanted by a repair interlude, which is marked at its outset by the occurrence of a stumble (Erickson, in Part II) and through the duration of the interlude by interactions that remove errors and thereby repair the routine. A stumble always involves a momentary break in a pattern of synchrony between parties; repair work is joint action by which interactional error gets corrected, and synchrony is thereby reestablished. Finally, any routine is initiated by a move and runs its predictable course through a series of moves.

The interactions that occur during repair interludes are called transactions. Persons who are transacting are negotiating and renegotiating, tacitly in a large degree, their respective parts in the moves of the routine in question. In contrast, the interactions that occur during the trouble-free unfolding of routines are called enactments. Persons who are enacting are performing adequately their respective parts in such moves.

A nesting series has been named, consisting of events, phases, routines, moves. Of these units, two — events and phases — are readily visible. This is because the behavioral discontinuities that mark their boundaries are not unusually difficult to see; the observer needs only to be looking for them with care and method, and they present themselves. Routines and moves, however, are not as readily evident. These become partially evident as surface description of the event becomes thick description; through the identification of other behavioral units, also not immediately evident; and through a multi-tiered mapping of the event in terms of four sets of such units, which simultaneously unfold.

Thickness is increased, and routines and moves are partially revealed: (1) by mapping segments established through shifting facing-formations (Kendon, Part II above, and in press) and other spatial orientations of parties each to every other, and segments within these segments; (2) by mapping segments in the stream of utterance (Mathiot, Part II and personal communication), as, for example, shifts as to who in the total group are the pivotal actors central to the verbal interaction, and shifts in topic; and (3) by mapping analogous segments in the stream of other action, as may be involved, for example, in some joint performance of a manual task. The boundaries of these three kinds of units tend to coincide, segments of one kind with segments of another kind, and all these tend to coincide with the boundaries of the units named earlier. Whether and exactly how these boundaries in fact coincide is an empirical question.

Thickness is further increased and routines and moves are further revealed by mapping a fourth set of behavioral units. The boundaries of such units, marked by behavioral discontinuities, are real but extremely difficult to identify; for example, the shifts in enactment by some pair of participants of one and then another interactional role relationship. These interactional roles are not the roles indicated in descriptions of large systems, such as communities or nations — that is, social class, race, and ethnicity. As jointly enacted in face-to-face interaction, roles tend strongly to replicate those of the larger systems, but in some variant pattern with the parties both ignoring some of those distinctions and generating elaborated sets of additional distinctions (but see Gumperz and Talbert, Part II). In general, interactional roles are more fluid and shifting than are large system roles. For example, what in a description of large system roles is a clear relationship of super- and subordination, can be enacted face-to-face as an alternating series of dancelike leading and following, largely tacit, with the superordinate party leading while the counterpart follows, then the reverse with the subordinate leading, and so on. Among all role relationships, such patterns of leading and following are unusually salient in this context.

Routines and moves are not fully revealed, however, until functional concepts are brought to bear, as follows later.

All the above — events, phases, routines, moves, and the other units named — are together a minimal list; in any investigation, other behavioral units, perhaps less central, would almost surely emerge. A mapping of all these behavioral units and their relationships describes the structure of any event. The pivotal elements in such structural description for current purposes are routines. Thus, structure is described in terms of the internal shape of any particular routine, i.e., the structure of moves and other units that are the routine; and in terms of the structure external to a routine, i.e., the co-occurrence of the several routines that together constitute a repertoire, the occurrence of a given repertoire within certain phases but not others, and other such structural facts.

All the above are segmentations of streams of behavior; each segment has a boundary at its onset, marked by behavioral discontinuities; each has a duration and a regular shape during that duration; and each has an end, again marked by behavioral discontinuities.

To identify and map these behavioral units, filmed or videotaped specimens of naturally occurring events are necessary at most junctures. All these segments can be identified and mapped on the basis of two kinds of behavior: (1) the speech behaviors and other behaviors of the actors as these unfold in recorded, naturally occurring occasions of an event; and (2) the testimony of actors as drawn out in well-conceived eliciting procedures. Segments thus identified through eliciting are reconfirmed by reexamination of behavior which unfolds in those recorded, naturally occurring occasions of events. Usually the observer starts somewhere in the middle range of the nesting series, maps upward to the event and its behavioral boundaries and perhaps beyond, then downward through the smaller segments and their respective boundaries.

Moves, routines, phases, and events, together with their constituent parts are all created *jointly* by no one party but necessarily by two or several among those who come regularly together and interact. Recall that new pair of facts that were named at the outset of this volume — the dancelike synchronies and the multiplicity of messaging that can be seen in such interaction. One deals, throughout, with interactional constraint.

Analytic Dimensions: Function

Analytic dimensions are brought to mind when one thinks of tasks getting done and of aspects of getting those tasks done, by thinking about function. Analytic dimensions are formed, that is, by functional concepts.

To describe a system of education and schooling is to describe a total community, to describe in principle each and every event which when combined constitute life in that community, but to describe it selectively. Specifically, among the many tasks getting done on some occasions of any event, the germane task getting done is this: unpracticed newcomers to that event are in the course of becoming practiced hands in that event. This is "education" or "schooling." Put summarily, in any event, a practiced old hand "knows how," and, in fact, does join in displays of many of the know-hows entailed in the event, typically in ways deemed appropriate by fellow old hands according to that old hand's interactional roles in the event and in ways deemed correct according to established modes of performing the tasks at hand. A newcomer at the outset does not "know how," but does join in displays of many of the entailed know-hows, often in ways deemed by old hands inappropriate and/or incorrect. As these errors are eliminated, the newcomer becomes an old hand. The interactive behaviors by which transitions of this kind are brought off are data, and all other behaviors are peripheral or irrelevant to the current purpose. Thus, in any description of education and schooling, the total community is selectively described in the act of getting this specific task done, of bringing off transformations of newcomers into old hands.

"Education" is an analytic dimension and not a behavioral unit; so is "schooling." These functional concepts, as defined here, sort events; every event is either one or the other. The criterion that identifies some events as schooling but not education is this: the manifest content of talk and other action prevailingly includes information deemed to be needed or useful principally in some other place at some other time, both somewhat removed. This criterion sorts events, not institutions as such. Schools, it is obvious, are places where events frequently occur in which there is schooling in this sense. A teachers' meeting is not, however, as a rule, such an event, and some classroom events also are not, though most are. Similarly, schooling in this narrow sense occurs frequently in mental hospitals and jails and in much lesser frequency in churches. There occur analogous schooling events in any community not of the Western tradition, as in many initiations in tribal societies.

Events that do not include schooling in this sense are education. These interactions may resemble on-the-job training; a novice on the ski slopes with more proficient friends is participating in such an event, as is a newcomer in a shop or office. The identifying criterion is here the reverse of the above: the manifest context of talk and other action prevailingly includes information deemed to be needed or useful in reoccurring occasions of the event itself.

Events are usefully sorted as either education or schooling in this manner if and only if the tasks done in the two classes of events are significantly different. Education events and schooling events do so contrast — among other things, only the latter are describable as hidden curriculums and manifest curriculums unfolding side-by-side — as will later be seen.

In an event of either kind, any newcomer transacts during repair interludes with the old hands in that event; otherwise he enacts. He transacts, that is, when there is trouble with the performance of some move or moves, and he enacts when the performance is trouble-free. At the outset, he transacts a lot and enacts commensurately less. As the newcomer moves toward becoming an old hand, he transacts less and enacts commensurately more. The research task is analytically to describe as precisely as possible what the entailed moves are; that is, to describe the patterns of display of the entailed know-hows that are being transacted and enacted. This requires a set of analytic dimensions in addition to the behavioral units discussed above and within both named classes of events — education events and schooling events.

Analytic dimensions are formed by functional concepts. The principal analytic dimensions entail two cross-cutting pairs of functional concepts. Together, these make up the overarching function, which is the transformation of newcomers into old hands. These four functional concepts are as follows: newcomers with old hands transact and enact "appropriate displays" and "correct displays" of know-hows entailed in the event. This means they transact and enact, respectively, the newcomer's interactional roles in the organized group and the newcomer's task performances as both are involved in bringing off the event at hand. By virtue of all this, they transact and enact "relationships of equivalence" or "nonequivalence." Additional subsidiary functional concepts will be named.

In the section dealing with behavioral units, it was said that routines are but incompletely and imprecisely revealed through the identification and mapping of the involved segments in the behavior stream. Why that is so, and the solution to that problem, will now be evident. During trouble-free enactments of routines, everything is of a piece. For example, the correctness and appropriateness of a display are being enacted in a manner that is indistinguishable to an observer. It is evident that one identifies features of the internal structure or a routine by observing not solely the enactments of the routine, but principally by noting breakdowns — stumbles — and by examining the interludes of consequent repair work. The nature of the repair reveals specifically what the trouble was. To pinpoint such trouble, one needs as tools the analytic distinctions provided by an array of functional concepts. For any newcomer to an event, transactions will be required with respect to the appropriateness of the displays. That is, at the outset the newcomer's displays of entailed know-hows will frequently be correct but inappropriate. Over time, this in some fashion gets fixed. Appropriateness is defined by the actors in terms of the roles assumed by the newcomer in the organized group that brings off the event in question. Conversely, transaction also will be required with respect to the correctness of entailed task performances. At the outset, displays by the newcomer will frequently be appropriate but incorrect according to established usage in the event; over time, this, too, gets fixed. Throughout a series of transactions, the focus of interaction typically shifts back and forth between these two functions. At one point, appropriateness of display is the troublesome dimension, thus being the foreground to correctness of display, which is not at that moment troublesome. Then the reverse occurs. All this becomes evident through observing the substantive nature and direction of the repair work. Having thereby identified features of the internal organization of a routine, one can then readily observe trouble-free enactments of a routine, watching those features as they unfold.

The first pair of functional concepts, as named, is the *appropriateness* and the *correctness* of displays of know-hows. One deals in the first instance, however, with stumbles and consequent repair interludes. Within this context of repair interludes, the concepts point to errors, that is, inappropriate and incorrect displays. The pair of concepts thus lift out of the stream of behavior those moves and small sets of moves in which errors have occurred, and they aggregate these in two classes as to the kind of error. In the context of trouble-free enactments, the two concepts identify two dimensions that are inherently a part of all moves and, thus, of all routines (and these, cumulatively, of all phases and all events).

The first class of errors — displays that are inappropriate according to interactional role — treat the propertylike nature of most know-hows. This kind of error can be more precisely identified with the use of a set of four subsidiary functional concepts by which moves and small sets of moves marked by inappropriate displays are sorted into four subclasses of inappropriateness. In the context of trouble-free enactments, these concepts lift out all moves and aggregate them as analytic classes of moves which together constitute routines. These subsidiary concepts are *open, paced, selective, and pro forma exchanges*.

It is frequently necessary to see into the internal organization of a routine at this level of increased detail, and to do this, stumbles need to be identified and consequent repair work mapped according to a logical scheme.[1]

The logical scheme is best described in two parts schematically. First, within the occurrences of some one event wherein old hands and newcomers come together in one or another of two identified classes of interchange and where they handle items from one or another of two identified classes of know-how, they transact toward contrasting kinds of patterned exchange, in their displays of know-hows, as follows in Figure 1.

	Item of know-how is propertylike *or*	Item of know-how is not propertylike
Interchanges where both parties identify themselves by the same category of interactional identity *or* Interchanges where the parties identify themselves by contrasting categories of interactional identity	Open exchanges	Open exchanges
	Other types of exchange in which displays of some know-hows regularly do not occur	Open exchanges

Figure 1.

The parties may transact toward a pattern of interchange, wherein on certain occasions they act as if they are alike in terms of the interactional identities salient to them at that moment. Their identities are identically defined by them according to categories of age, sex, and other attributes of identity as these categories are established in the particular event. And they may also transact toward a pattern of interchange wherein on occasions they act as if their interactional identities saliently contrast at that moment. Further, these persons may be dealing at any juncture with know-hows, germane to the event, which to them are or are not propertylike. Among all such know-hows, those that are observed to be displayable by any participant with any participant are not propertylike, but all other know-hows are.

A pattern of open exchange occurs with the permutations noted above. Trouble-free enactments of this pattern, unlike other types of exchange

---

[1]   Note that, in Working Paper 6, closely related ideas were treated as empirical propositions as to the co-occurrence of variables; here the terms are not variables but are redundant, reciprocally defining dimensions that together define the four patterns to be named. Note also that, for this reason and others, the term "exchange" (not "agenda") is here used; that two patterns of exchange (paced and selective) were earlier not distinguished; that the pattern of exchange earlier called "troublesome" is now called "pro forma."

to follow, are marked by the absence of any identifiable patterns of avoidance in the know-hows displayed. Conversely, where stumbles occur, the nature of the repair work suggests that the trouble — the interactional error — was that one or another party was holding back, that the matter-at-hand was not, but should have been, talked about or otherwise enacted. In the vernacular, there are to be no secrets.

Conversely, an old hand with a newcomer may transact toward a pattern of exchange wherein their displays of know-hows are selective, that is, where it is possible to observe that, among know-hows germane to the event, one or the other or both parties do not talk about or otherwise enact certain ones.

There are three basic forms of such limitation. Within the occurrence of some one event, where old hands and newcomers come together in interchanges across contrasting categories of identity, and where items of know-how are propertylike (as within the lower left cell, Figure 1), they may transact toward all of three patterns of constrained exchange: see Figure 2.

Where mobility between the saliently involved categories of identity is destined to occur	paced exchange
Where mobility between the saliently involved categories of identity is destined not to occur	selective exchange
Where the identities (the categories themselves or the role relationships) are problematic or the matter of mobility is problematic	pro forma exchange

Figure 2.

Between parties of contrasting interactional identity, it may be clear to the parties that the future identity of one, sooner or later in the normal course of events, will certainly change so as to become the current identity of the others, as, for example, when the salient contrasting identity attributes are contrasting categories of age. It also may be clear that, in another case, in the normal course of events, an analogous identity will certainly not so change, as, for example, when the salient contrasting attributes are a contrast in sex. Similarly, where other contrasting identity attributes are to the parties salient, as are, for example, some interactional variants of social class, race, ethnicity, levels of organization, smart-dumb, etc., analogous shifts in identity may be virtually automatic (as with categories of age) or virtually impossible (as with categories of sex) in the context of the event in question. These two classes of interchange stand in contrast, however, to a third, where the identities and/or the possibility of mobility between the identities are (is) to the parties chronically unclear or disputed. This may occur, for example, where events unfold within and are directly affected by a wider social context marked by long-term pluralism/assimilation dilemmas, but it can also occur in other situations, including within a family.

Where clarity reigns with regard to interactional identities and to mobility or its absence, old hands with newcomers can be observed to be transacting toward the joint exercise of regular patterns of avoidance in displays of certain know-hows by one or the other or both. Where such clarity reigns, two types of exchange unfold, respectively: paced exchange, where a future shift in identity seems certain to the parties and whereby certain displays that are inappropriate now will be appropriate later; and selective exchange, where it seems to them certain that no shift in identity will occur and whereby certain displays are not appropriate now or later. That is, where stumbles occur, repair work may show that some know-how, usually on the part of the newcomer, was inappropriate in terms of his or her interactional role in the organized group. In the vernacular, in trouble-free enactments, the parties are jointly sustaining some pattern of reciprocal censorship.

On the other hand, where these identities and/or mobility are (is) to the parties problematic, patterns of pro forma exchange are found. This is a pattern of parallel coexistence, a pattern of displays wherein each does "his thing." The displays thereby principally reiterate the contrasting identities of the parties. Here a stumble and consequent repair work may reveal that an otherwise most commonplace display was inappropriate in the sense that, by such display, one party inappropriately imitated the other, or perhaps a display violated the shaping "distance" between the two. In the vernacular, the parties reciprocally withdraw and, other than in their reiterations of their contrasting identities, they tune out each other.

Any old hand with any newcomer will transact an array of interactional identities and a commensurate array of patterns of exchange; through such transactions, displays will become appropriate. If the event were the services of a church, for example, at one moment, the two persons may deem themselves to be identically church members in contrast to others who are not. (Thus there is the pattern of open exchange with respect to displays of the know-hows at that moment.) At another moment, it may seem salient to them that one has a high office in the church hierarchy that organizes the event, the other is an heir apparent (thus paced exchange); at another moment, one is male, the other female (thus, selective exchange); and finally, it may seem to them at some moment that one is affluent, the other poor, and that this contrast is between them somehow problematic (thus there is the pattern pro forma exchange).

In principle *all* these can occur between any two parties in any series of occasions of an event. However, whenever an old hand is transacting with a newcomer patterns of pro forma exchange — that is, where joint displays of that kind occur in some nontrivial frequency and with decreasing stumbles and consequent repair work — these patterns of pro forma exchange tend to assimilate or transform other coexisting patterns, to create between the two persons a relationship which consists, in the extreme, of solely pro forma exchanges.

I have turned to the second pair of functional concepts, earlier named: *relationships of equivalence* and of *nonequivalence*. These concepts reaggregate moves previously lifted out of the stream of behavior, into two classes. A relationship of equivalence describes any two persons who jointly enact some mix of any and all moves that make up open exchanges, and paced exchanges and selective exchanges. A relationship of nonequivalence describes any two persons who jointly enact some mix of all those, plus moves that constitute pro forma exchanges, the last of which tend to prevail over the rest. It follows that an old hand may have established a relationship of equivalence with some newcomers and may enact with them one set of routines. The same old hand may have established a relationship of nonequivalence with other newcomers and enact with them a parallel, contrasting set of routines. This pair of concepts thus sorts whole routines into two analytic classes.

In the vernacular (and to the current theoretical purposes I am now speaking quite figuratively) the contrast between the two types of relationship is this: if in any event, an old hand and a newcomer are transacting toward the types of routines that together are members of one analytic class, a relationship of equivalence, each increasingly imagines that he or she knows or adequately knows about what the other knows, and that the other knows or knows about what he or she knows. But if an old hand and a newcomer are transacting toward the routines that form a relationship of nonequivalence, each increasingly imagines that he or she does not, will not, and perhaps cannot know what the other knows, and vice versa. By the time relationships of nonequivalence are well along in being transacted, the old hand is usually referring to the newcomer, and the newcomer is referring to the old hand, with words that connote that the other is by nature or experience permanently flawed: crazy, dumb, etc.

Recall that the overall task is analytically to describe a community in the act of educating and schooling itself. It is virtually self-evident that this last pair of concepts will reveal contrasts that are unusually salient in terms of function, and that a major fact to be revealed through a detailed examination of the internal organization of a set of routines is the type of relationship among the parties to those routines.

The preceding pages have dealt with stumbles and consequent repair work that reveal that a display was inappropriate, according to roles and typically in respect to the roles in the organized group being transacted with and for a newcomer. Through these analyses, the internal organization of routines is revealed, and the routines are aggregated, insofar as the appropriateness of displays are concerned. There remain the stumbles and the kinds of consequent repair work that reveal that some particular display was not inappropriate but was simply incorrect, as measured by established usages in the performance of tasks at hand in the event. And, as before, the observer looks principally at repair interludes, at stumbles, and at the direction of consequent repair work, and thereby identifies features of the internal organization of routines as these unfold of a piece in trouble-free interaction.

No well-considered analytic concepts can in this context be named; the direction of further development, however, seems evident in outline. It is clear, first, that when one begins to think about the correctness of displays, one stands at the threshold of the kinds of studies done by cognitive anthropologists and cognitive psychologists. It is also clear that, as long as one deals in logical consistency with interactional constraint as the overarching notion that is to guide analytic description, one may not step over that threshold, nor deal (in analytic seriousness) with "mental" constructs of any kind. It is clear, finally, that it is important, nevertheless, to keep an eye open for bridges that can be built, from what can be said here to work being done there. To those bridge building purposes, we can make three assumptions: (1) no two parties in interaction ever perceive identically what they are talking about or otherwise interacting about; this is to say, they are not "thinking alike"; (2) two parties, when interacting under some frequently occurring conditions, nevertheless act as if they were thinking alike as long as they possibly can; and (3) when they cannot, this is evident in their interactional behaviors (Lyons 1968; Wallace 1970). Those "frequently occurring conditions" are those established relationships of equivalence just discussed; acting "as if they were thinking alike" are those trouble-free enactments of routines; and conversely, the interactional behaviors by which they express the opposite are those stumbles and consequent repair work. A fourth assumption can more tenuously be made: when routines are unfolding trouble-free, "assimilation" in Piagetian terms is probably occurring, and when repair work is underway, probably "accommodation" is occurring. It should be noted, especially following the work of Thomas Carroll (1976), and following (and perhaps unwarrantedly extending the contribution of) Jean Lave in Part II, that these two Piagetian processes can be seen unfolding not only by examining the speech and nonverbal behavior of an individual subject, but in the above interactional behaviors as well.

There are several functional concepts that seem to require development in order to treat errors as to the correctness of displays in the context of a cultural theory of education and schooling: *simple* and *complex information*, and *digital* and *typological categories*. Each pair of concepts represents a continuum; the pairs together create a field upon which any interactional error as a complete whole can be located, relative to any other (see Figure 3).

	Digital	Typological
Simple	"2 + 2 = 4"	
		"Fishing is good".
	Two apples and two giraffes are four".	"That movie was like Mozart".
Complex		
		cultural premises

Figure 3.

A "complete" error is that whole interchange in a stream of behavior that gets corrected through repair work. In respect to simple and complex, very roughly, where the error or its corrected counterpart is a small behavioral unit (a single move, perhaps), the error is located toward the top of the field. Where sets of moves or larger behavior units get corrected, they are located downward in the field. Note this contrast: where with the verbal display "2+2=5," there occurs a stumble, and where through repair work, "2 + 2 = 4" comes to stand in its place, the utterances are probably tense, and error and its corrected counterpart are probably to be located toward the top on the field. But where an error is corrected to "Two apples and two giraffes are four entities," the repair work might entail going back over ideas of set and number, and the error and its corrected counterpart are then located toward the bottom of the field.

The contrast between digital and typological categories has been treated by E. Heider (n.d.). A class is digital in form when it is marked by a set of attributes such that an item has, or does not have, each attribute. And if all attributes are present, the item is a member of that class. A class is typologic in form where a prototypic example stands for the class, and items are more or less members of the class insofar as they approximate the prototype. A complete error or its complete counterpart usually is made up of some words that are digital and others that are typological. Two such errors or correct counterparts can be located, relative to one another, toward the left or right in the field according to their respective mixes. "Fishing is good on the lake these days" probably is located, as in "2 + 2 = 4," toward the top of the field, but, unlike the former, to the right. Analogously, "That movie was like Mozart" is located toward the lower right. And finally, what are usually called cultural premises by anthropologists — those unspoken assumptions that underlie and pattern behavior pervasively in any community — are located far into the lower right corner.

It should especially be noted that the observer certainly could not map displays by watching trouble-free enactments alone; possibly, with some development of the concepts named, displays can be mapped through examining errors and the nature of the interactional repair work.

In general, as newcomers move through the transition by which they become old hands, the frequency of stumbles decreases. It would appear that, in respect to those stumbles that occur when displays are incorrect, the rate of decrease is slower as one moves from left to right and from top to bottom in the above field, as the matters involved are "harder to get." It is also evident that transactions and consequent enactments with respect to this analytically separable dimension, the correctness of displays, are somehow controlled by patterns described by that other dimension, the appropriateness of displays. It is not at all uncommon, for example, for an objectively incorrect performance to be considered, according to role, an appropriate and "correct" performance; that is, in such instances, the inept performance is not accompanied by a stumble and consequent repair work, but is instead expected. I think of the behaviors of the "oddball" in a factory or classroom, for example.

A General Implication: "While"

I have named the basic behavioral units and analytic dimensions which seem necessary in an empirical study in pursuit of a cultural theory of education and schooling. At the outset of the volume, it was noted that the pair of new facts that have made the notion of interactional constraint empirically graspable have also made the efforts reported in this volume plausible. It will be well to pause at this juncture to make fully explicit one pivotal methodological implication of that pair of facts. The implication appears to apply wherever observers seek to identify and map behavioral units and to analyze them functionally for whatever descriptive or analytic purpose, including, most critically, that of the current purpose.

All observation of behavior is necessarily observation of classes of behavior; this is almost certainly prescribed by the nature of any human observer's nervous system. To set out to identify and map behavioral units as here described is to seek to identify *how the actors have already classified their behaving*, and then to observe and map in terms of those identified classes. This is, to anthropologists, the familiar problem of identifying emic categories, seen here in purely behavioral terms.

The methodological implication, phrased very generally, is this: the observer discovers the way some person has already classified behaviors principally by watching not that person alone, but by watching his or her counterpart as well. One deals with joint enactments. It necessarily follows that the principal analytic juxtaposition of one datum with another is therefore not before-and-after, but *while*. In face-to-face interaction, people do not principally act and react; they dance.

All the above-named segments in a stream of behavior are themselves classes of things. An event is an event because it reoccurs with some greater or lesser frequency. Similarly, any phase reoccurs, as does any routine or any move, and so on. And all these classes are jointly enacted. If the reader wishes to infer that the actors "perceive" those classes and that they "share" those perceptions, the reader may do so. I find it sufficient and less removed from the facts to say that in interaction, the actors jointly enact those classes most of the time through their observable dancelike behavior. When they occasionally act differently, this is enacted through observable stumbles followed by jointly enacted repair work.

Thus, the methodological implication, in more concrete terms, can be put as a question: A behavior having been noted, with what other behavior or behaviors is it to be juxtaposed? The evident answer, contained in that pair of facts named at the outset, is that actions are principally to be juxtaposed with other actions that occur simultaneously. While the speaker is talking and acting, moment-to-moment, what is the listener, or listeners, simultaneously doing? And while this message unfolds, what other messages simultaneously unfold?

This implication is easily recognized but may prove hard to follow. All participants in face-to-face talk tend strongly to focus their conscious attentions on the speaker, on his words, and on his other signals directly connected with those words, such as facial expressions and standardized gestures. All else is taken care of through subliminal awareness. We who are social scientists are forever engaged in face-to-face talk in our everyday life and that selective attention quite adequately gets one through the day. In some large measure, however, this has been carried over into scholarly work, at some cost now evident. In face-to-face talk, one person (by and large) talks at a time, thus (by force of habit or whatever), social scientists have tended to observe face-to-face talk much as a bleacher full of spectators watch a tennis match — following the ball. The principal analytic tools have been, fittingly, sequential in form, as cause and effect, stimulus and response, act and reinforcement. It does not seem accidental that these familiar terms are comfortable, that they even seem objectively "true."

The implication recommends, not before-and-after, but while, so it runs against deep habit. By that pair of facts, it was noted, a listener can, in many common contexts, stop a speaker in midsentence without even consciously intending to do so. Thus, difficult or not, this reorienting of description is revealed by the pair of new facts to be imperative. When one describes face-to-face talk in the better established, sequential manner, one may note an action by A and juxtapose this with an ensuing action by B. Yet, data now empirically revealed as crucial — actions having controlling power — have by that familiar mode already fallen by the way, namely, that while A was saying and doing what he said and did, what was B simultaneously saying and doing? Later, the reverse of that.

Sets of such paired, synchronized actions between speaker and listeners or between participants in some joint manual task or other body work, all unfold as sets and in some sequence, and thereby, they form patterns. The juxtaposition of one such set of synchronized actions with another set is appropriately before-and-after. Such a sequence may be particularly salient when mapping a pattern of leading-and-following; here one party joins another's dance. But even in the unfolding of these messagings, before-and-after is revealing only in a qualified sense. The redundancies in face-to-face messaging are typically so massive as often to permit participants or observers to recognize the whole message in the earliest occurring bit of it, though the message will usually continue to unfold "unnecessarily." More importantly, while that message unfolds another may simultaneously be unfolding, for example, a negotiation as to how long the speaker of the moment is to speak and who will speak next. This tacit negotiation may unfold through a pattern of making and breaking eye contact and other related behaviors between the speaker and a listener. These behaviors stand in qualitative contrast to analogous patterns enacted between the speaker and the other listeners, through all of which the parties arrive at a tacit agreement as to who will speak next. This message may further unfold through a pattern of ebb and flow in eye contacts and other behaviors by which the actual switch in speakers is brought off. All that *is* a message: (1) because the participants can later report, at a very general level, on what happened; and (2) because there follows a regular outcome, the switch in speaker does in fact normally occur. The juxtaposition of one set of data with other sets has now, of course, fully shifted back to while.

As was noted earlier, face-to-face talk is made up of actions unfolding within the confines of various preexisting limits and within the confines of many other limits established in the course of the interaction itself, and all these must necessarily go on simultaneously. These preexisting limits are real because they are usually honored; therefore, in face-to-face talk, whatever else is going on, these preexisting limits are normally being enacted. While that enactment continues, negotiation is underway as to which particular kind of talk is to be established. Once that is determined, its enactment continues while other limits are established. There are limits nesting within limits nesting within limits. All these are made up of behavioral units that function.

The sole point is, then, that in the kind of analytic description here at issue, behaviors are to be prevailingly juxtaposed with other behaviors that occur simultaneously. The observer recognizes how behaviors are already classified by watching not solely an actor but principally that actor's counterparts. Thereby, the observer identifies the behavioral units, maps them, and analyzes them in terms of functions being served.

Summary

The description of a community as a system of education and schooling "will be made up pivotally," as was said at the outset of this chapter, "of certain features of the routines that unfold in an adequate qualitative sample of events." It is now evident, by the terms here adopted, that the transformation of any newcomer to any event into an old hand in that event is the induction of that newcomer into the appropriate and correct displayings of know-hows that constitute participation in the routines that together are the occasions of that event. To conclude this description of the involved conceptual tools, I turn again to these pivotal structures-with-function — routines.

An event is, in the first instance, made up of old hands in interaction with one another. Some events, perhaps most events in the contemporary world, include old hands in established relations of equivalence with some fellow participants and in relations of non-equivalence with others. One imagines now such an event. All these old hands interact, and because the event is an event — it recurs — that interaction tends strongly to be routine. Any particular routine involves some parties centrally, others peripherally, and still others as spectators or not at all. Necessarily, some of those routines are made up solely of regular sequences of those open, paced, and selective — but not pro forma — exchanges just discussed. Of all participants in the event, the participants in these routines are persons of diverse interactional identities, but where only those patterns of exchange are in evidence, all are in relations of equivalence, each with every other. Often such an event is largely described as two sets or a very few sets of persons, each subgroup being made up of persons in such relations of equivalence with one another. In addition, in an event of this kind one imagining other routines, namely those that unfold across the groups, involve those pro forma exchanges just discussed; participants in such a routine enact relationships of nonequivalence across the subgroups.

If one wished to describe a community as a pool of know-hows *already* distributed to, and being selectively displayed by, its members according to their roles, one would surely have to describe such routines as enacted by old hands with each other, in some adequate sample of events. If, as here, one wishes to describe a community educating and schooling itself — that is, in the process of perpetually redistributing that pool of know-hows — one must describe the induction of newcomers into those same routines, variously according to their emerging roles. Wherever in the organization of an event, relationships of equivalence and of non-equivalence coexist, newcomers are inducted into both of these. If one is describing a community educating and schooling itself, this last fact is functionally most salient.

It should finally be noted that routines, in all their variety of organization, are inherently interactive. Because of the pair of new facts described in the introduction, a routine can be seen to exist insofar as all its participants jointly enact it; any participant can in some literal sense destroy it. Newcomers do momentarily destroy routines. But unless they simply leave, they typically join in the repair work and thereby help re-create the routines — even when, as is not uncommon where the routines embody relations of nonequivalence, they imagine that they protest. Think, for example, of the recalcitrant nature of Indian-white relations or of race or other such ethnic relations more generally.

Early in this discussion, it was noted that a cultural theory of education and schooling deals with those kinds of constraints generated in interaction, and that this fact dictated two formal rules, which bear repeating now: (1) to our purposes, the total community life must be divided into behavioral units and so described as a structure; (2) it must additionally be divided by analytic dimensions by which whole behavioral units are to be lifted out of the stream of behavior and aggregated into classes with an eye to jobs getting done, that is, by function. There results a structural-functional analytic description, in this instance, of that much of community life that is described as a system of education and schooling.

2. A REFERENCE MODEL: PROPOSITIONS

In this chapter, a series of logically related propositions will be listed and discussed. All derive through inference, sometimes through very tenuous inference, from published information or experience, which usually offers very incomplete data for these purposes. All the propositions, however, permit and invite empirical examination through analytic description of a community using the conceptual tools just reviewed. The intended purpose is to generate such empirical examination.

To describe a community as a system of education and schooling is to describe a total community — in principle each and every event that regularly occurs in that place — but to describe all this selectively. It will have become evident from the preceding chapter that, if a community is so described using the suggested conceptual tools, the description picks up a great deal of all that goes on. But what does *not* get described? It is well, before turning to a listing of propositions, to sketch in outline certain features of that wider context within which education and schooling unfolds and to which it variously relates.

Context

Impressed and encouraged by the pair of new facts cited at the outset of this volume, a mode of analytic description has been discussed in which the notion of interactional constraint is the prevailing mode of explanation. Others have said that function constrains structure indirectly. "This means," it was said earlier, "that ... the community is seen to include, among other things, a job-doing system, which system is normally kept unchanging through constraints operating through some other system or set of systems not directly connected with the doing of those jobs, [which] latter systems include education and schooling." Inclusively to describe "life" in a community, guided by the notion of interactional constraint, is to describe the whole, then to redescribe it and redescribe it again, as a set of systems performing some set of functions. The necessary number of such descriptions appears to be three.

Any human community operates in nature and in an environment of other human communities; the principal life-or-death jobs of the members are their collective handlings of those externals (for example, getting food, distributing it, and consuming it). Variations in how members behave are constrained by the doing of these jobs in the ways the community does in fact do them. Those limits of variation are revealed by description of a first subsystem that has no well-established label but which will be called here the work system. Anthropologists have dealt well with the interplay between this first system and the natural environs in studies of cultural ecology (following Julian Steward 1951). They have also dealt, though less extensively, with the analogous interplay with other communities.

This work system is not a thing; it is the total community selectively described. A set of functional concepts conceived by the observer would guide description of a community as a work system by establishing criteria by which some behavioral units are lifted out and sorted into classes, others not. This selective description of a community includes description of three aspects of the work system, three aspects of the doing of the work: (1) a directly visible surface structure that varies within limits, (2) an infrastructure that normally does not vary, and (3) a monitoring process that constrains the variation of the first in terms of the second. Behavioral units that constitute these aspects are lifted out and organized by functional concepts, and thereby the community is described, selectively, as a work system.

These three aspects of a work system are familiar to anthropologists, though they appear never to have been treated as conjoint aspects of a single system. The first aspect, the surface structure is usually called (following Firth 1964) the social organization, the *de facto* ways a community at some moment is getting its tasks done. This surface structure is at any moment some pragmatic compromise between a set of norms as to how a task normally and most appropriately gets done and the particular contingencies affecting the doing. This surface structure therefore varies, but within limits. The second aspect is the infrastructure — that set of norms that establishes the limits of the variation. The infrastructure has two dimensions, which are actually two sides of the same coin even though only one is a well-established field of inquiry. The well-established dimension is known (again following Firth, above, and British social anthropology generally) as social structure; it is a set of norms depicting how the community's pool of human resources is in principle sorted and deployed as personnel. The reverse side of the coin has been but sporadically treated: a set of norms depicting how the community's pool of know-how is selectively distributed among the members of the community. Anthropologists (following Wallace 1970) know this latter as equivalence structure, an engaging but little-elaborated idea which deals with the fact that persons who never "think alike" can nevertheless coordinate efforts as if they did — the organization of cognitive diversity. Of course, both of the two dimensions come explicitly into view when the familiar matters of division of labor are under discussion. These two dimensions of this infrastructure interpenetrate totally. This is made evident by a little noted but virtually self-evident fact that most of the know-how in everyday use in a community is propertylike. This is true in the sense that the display of almost any bit of know-how is appropriate for some persons, but not for others, and in the presence of some persons, but not others, all these persons being defined by members of the community according to age, sex, kinship, and so on. This is to say that virtually all displays of know-hows are role behaviors. This infrastructure addition-ally has a more abstract form, known to anthropologists as unstated cultural premises, or "unconscious canons of choice", to use Ruth Benedict's happy phrase (1934), which establishes firm outer limits of possible variation. I shall refer to this unnamed infrastructure, consisting of the social structure, the distributed know-how or equivalence structure, and cultural premises together, as the community's template for work. Finally, this selective description of a community, as a work system, includes a third aspect, a monitoring process, familiar to anthropologists (following Barth 1972) as transaction. It is the on-the-job process of role adjustment and role elaboration and the ensuing regulation of the acting out of roles so elaborated. Through this monitoring process variations are generated and — critically — those variations are normally kept within the preordained limits named.

These three aspects — surface structure, infrastructure, and monitor-ing process — operate as a single system. The stable infrastructure is the encapsulated long-term experience of the community as to how, through sorting persons and allocating to them know-hows (including knowing how to exercise authority or allocate rewards and penalties), the community can successfully get its work done. This is an averaged-out experience, in effect, a precipitate of many persons doing many different jobs many times; it is general. There follows a near-paradox: without that preserved experience serving as a template, persons would hardly be able to begin any coordinated action; but that experience would provide insufficient guidance for doing almost any particular job under the specific conditions that would prevail at any particular time. Thus, humans at work transact. They act as if they imagine that they are receiving three classes of information about their fellows — too little, or too much, as opposed to just right. With respect to the displays of specific kinds of know-hows by specific kinds of persons — that is, exertions of various efforts, exercises of differential authority, sharing of rewards, and so on — they monitor, and, as much by actions as by words, they negotiate adjustments and in general fine-tune their roles to the specific tasks at hand. Moreover, these variations are always kept within the limits established by that template in its more abstract form of cultural premises (unconscious canons of choice), principally because aberrations from that are normally unthinkable. Many groups of persons transacting in many such contexts generate the visible surface of the work system, the social organization of the community in its momentary form.

There remain two necessary redescriptions entailed in any description of a community, if informed by the notion interactional constraint.

This description of the work system surely raises a special mystery: why are transacted role elaborations not simply absorbed into the template itself? Why do communities not change cumulatively in this way? Perpetually to re-create unchanged the above-named infrastructure of the work system is the principal work of a second system — the system of education and schooling broadly conceived. To describe this system is to describe the community a second time, now in the process of distributing and redistributing those know-hows to those personnel, the right kinds of items to the right kinds of persons at the right times throughout their lifetimes, specifically throughout the duration of those interludes wherein inept newcomers to any event become practiced old hands in that event.

It was earlier said that "education and schooling" are functional concepts. Put in this wider context, this means on any occasion of any event, of the several functions being performed, some have to do with getting money to get food, getting food, distributing it, or consuming it. Analogously, some handle the problem of shelter or of war and peace. Among the several other functions simultaneously being performed in an event, specifically in interchanges between some old hand and some other who is in some sense a newcomer, some functions involve the distribution of kinds of know-how to kinds of persons. Insofar as one describes the earlier named functions, the work system is being described. Insofar as one describes the latter functions, the system of education and schooling is being described.

Describing communities as systems of education and schooling is, of course, the principal task envisaged in this volume; to these matters, I shall return.

The third and final subsystem is the system of ritual and play, which again redescribes the total community. I merely name it and note that it appears to re-recreate the template for work. It serves any community as a kind of back-up system in this regard.

Description shaped by the notion of interactional constraint thus describes a set of three large systems of constraint, in which one system, the work system, is being constrained by the other two, and whereby the social system as a whole tends perpetually to re-create itself. The result is that the behavioral variation among members of the community is kept within most narrow limits.

Finally, it is important to focus specifically on the work system and the system of education and schooling in order to note a critical contrast between these two descriptions: the work system is a description at the macro level; the system of education and schooling, at the micro level. This is to say, when one describes the work system, events are described in aggregate as interlocking sets of events; when one describes the system of education and schooling, events are described severally, one at a time. This is made evident by the contrast in analytic description of that monitoring process — transaction — in the two contexts. Persons transact; they are caused by recalcitrant particular circumstances to renegotiate some feature of the template for work. Moreover, when one describes the work system at the macro level, one describes transactions in aggregate. In principle, one describes effect — the results of such transactions. When one describes the system of education and schooling at the micro level, one describes the transaction itself from the inside, including the stumbles and the consequent repair work.

One persisting empirical question is whether patterns revealed by the macro descriptions are to be found replicated in microcosm in the micro descriptions, whether each single event contains within it all the major features of all other events in any given community.

It bears repeating that this attempt to get at the regularities of behavior at the micro level would be, in the author's judgment, idle, except for that pair of new facts that transforms constraint from a way-of-speaking into a visible, empirically investigatable form. One can see not only the fact that variation in behaviors is constrained, but in those dancelike behaviors, and particularly in the effective veto powers that listeners and spectators often have over what can be said or done, one can see the *constraining*, the controlling behaviors themselves in their waking reality. Transaction and analogous monitoring processes, by that pair of facts, are not something one knows happened because the results are evident; one can see it happening.

Propositions

A cultural theory of education and schooling, formed according to the modes of analytic description here offered, would fairly early in its development come to contain many, perhaps hundreds, of true propositions. Some would be true only of some one community; others, of all members of some class or type of communities; still others, of all communities. Ultimately, all these would come to be contained by a few propositions, parsimonious in number, precise in formulation, and universally applicable to all human communities, past and present, near and far.

These pages describe a reference model, whose purpose is to help guide research in its earliest stages. What follows are a few seemingly universal propositions. They are few, because a few will suffice. They seem universal, principally because they are little-elaborated in behavioral detail. They sketch a useful beginning. What will emerge from any research effort so guided, is generally this: any empirical examination of any of these propositions in any particular community will not be a test of the propositions as such, but rather, an elaboration of them in the culturally specific terms that describe that community. Then, as empirical examination proceeds comparatively in several communities, these elaborations will be reduced to the condensed elaborations that can well describe types of communities, and ultimately, to the further condensation that describes all communities precisely.

The propositions, this beginning, are ten in number.

PROPOSITION 1. OLD HANDS AND NEWCOMERS. In any selected event in any community, old hands interact with each other. This is not education and schooling per se; it is, however, the curriculum to which any newcomer who comes along will be exposed. What these old hands to an event enact with each other is already described if one has described the work system. This must be redescribed, at a micro level: the old hands who participate in any selected event are together enacting some established repertoire of routines; these routines are made up of arrays of moves in which the old hands correctly and appropriately display the know-hows involved in the event, and thereby enact, each with every other, one or another of the two kinds of relationship named, of equivalence or of nonequivalence. This, so phrased, is the curriculum which awaits a newcomer to the event.

When one or several newcomers join such an event, education or schooling, as the case may be, begins. The tendency is very strong for the old hands to teach the newcomers, not the reverse. There is, on the face of it, some mystery as to why this and not the reverse occurs. That mystery is addressed by a proposition, best phrased in two parts:

1a. Where any newcomer with any old hand are transacting toward a relation-ship of equivalence, they early transact, and then regularly enact a pattern of tacit leading-and-following wherein the old hand regularly leads. As that relationship of equivalence becomes increasingly well established, that single-directional pat-tern gives way to a more complex but still regular pattern of leading-and-following, varying in form according to the particular interactional role relation-ships that are emerging.

Leading-and-following, as here used, is not primarily acting and reac-ting sequentially; it involves simultaneous, joint behavior, a form of dance. One deals again with those matters of synchrony, as between speaker and listener, or as between persons jointly involved in some manual task or other bodily action. The analogy of ballroom dancing is apt. Who leads and who follows simultaneously is a matter of who joins whose dance. At the inception of any occasion of such dancing, the patterning is sequential, one party establishes a rhythm, another joins in; that having occurred, they dance together. Leading-and-following, as all other dimensions of such dancelike interactional behavior, is very largely tacit. The actors can later report at a very general level that, for example, they were influencing or being influenced, but the parties during the interaction are not consciously aware of most the behaviors involved or of the synchronies among those behaviors.

1b. Where a newcomer with an old hand are transacting toward a relationship of nonequivalence, they early transact and then regularly enact a pattern of tacit avoidance. As that relationship of nonequivalence becomes increasingly well established, that avoidance remains unchanged.

Avoidance, as used here, like leading-and-following, is not acting and reacting sequentially; rather, the parties behave simultaneously. And as in leading-and-following, avoidance is largely tacit. On the other hand, unlike leading-and-following, the behaviors are not synchronous. Avoid-ance is evident where two rhythms can be seen coexisting, side-by-side, with neither disrupting or otherwise interfering with the other.

In general, when the group organization in any event includes old hands in relationships of equivalence with some of their fellows, and of nonequivalence with others, newcomers get inducted into both kinds of relationship. And when this is so, learning occurs across relationships of equivalence, but across relationships of nonequivalence, each party "keeps what he has." Thus, certain old hands will teach certain newcom-ers (not the reverse), principally by virtue of such patterns of leading-and-following. Note that this also applies, perhaps with special interest, where a new supervisor joins an office or where a substitute teacher enters a classroom. But certain old hands will not teach certain newcomers, principally by virtue of the emerging relationships of nonequivalence and the entailed patterns of avoidance.

PROPOSITION 2. TWO KINDS OF ERROR. Education or schooling (as the case may be, according to the nature of the event) proceeds by the elimination of erroneous displays of know-hows entailed in the event. In some substantial part, this means the elimination of error in displays of know-hows that are altogether commonplace, as in behavioral expressions of deference or authority, as with manners generally, as with performances of a host of tasks that make minimal demands on cognitive or motor capacities.

Errors in displays of such commonplace know-hows are of two kinds: the first is inappropriate displays on the part of a newcomer, appropriateness being determined by the newcomer's interactional role relationships as they emerge; these generally give way to appropriate displays. There are also incorrect displays on the part of the newcomer, correctness being determined by the established modes of performing the tasks at hand; these generally give way to correct displays. Any display of any commonplace know-how simultaneously involves both dimensions of appropriateness and correctness.

The career of any newcomer who is becoming an old hand would entail that the following frequently occur. This second proposition is best phrased in two parts:

2a. Transaction proceeds until any display of a commonplace know-how by a newcomer is established as being appropriate *or* until such a display is, by this newcomer, eliminated altogether, and, if appropriate, until the display becomes correct.

A revealing variant also not infrequently occurs:

2b. Transaction proceeds until an incorrect display becomes appropriately *incorrect*.

One can allude here to the established, expected behaviors of "the village idiot" and other aberrant types of person. In a later context, Pygmalion-in-the-class-room literature, will be discussed, that is, the general notion that student performances come to conform to previously established teacher expectations.

PROPOSITION 3. RATES IN THE ELIMINATION OF ERROR. Transactions usually proceed for any newcomer until displays of any commonplace know-hows are both appropriate and correct or until such displays are eliminated. It appears almost self-evident that, with respect to commonplace know-hows, appropriateness is for a newcomer hard come by, correctness much less so. This is to say that, with respect to commonplace know-hows, what is primarily at issue is the transaction of the newcomer's role relationships and his or her place in the organized interacting group that brings off the event in question. This can be examined empirically.

Education or schooling, whatever the case may be, proceeds through interaction. Among interactions, there occur stretches of trouble-free enactment and, when trouble arises, interludes of transaction. The latter is marked by stumbles and consequent repair work. The nature of that repair work reveals what the trouble was about, what the error was. Thus, this proposition addresses the incidence of different kinds of trouble:

3. In any event, as the transactions by which a newcomer becomes an old hand proceed, and insofar as commonplace know-how is involved, the relative frequency of stumbles and consequent repair work decreases, as follows:

	Early ⟶ Late			
As to the appropriateness of displays	hi	hi	hi	lo
As to the correctness of displays	hi	lo	lo	lo

Figure 4.

Stumbles are the very heart of interactional constraint. At the outset of this volume, it was noted that in face-to-face interaction, any listener frequently can stop a speaker in midsentence, with or without conscious intent. This is what a stumble is — the breakdown of synchrony that does the stopping. It was further noted that joint action is required to reestablish the talk, to reconstitute it, or comfortably to dissolve it. This is what the repair work is — the joint action that gets the interaction back on course. Note that stumbles never quite disappear in human interaction. All established, routinized interaction requires joint self-monitoring. Old hands slip or have obstreperous days. Regulation follows, and it proceeds through stumbles and consequent repair work.

PROPOSITION 4. EQUIVALENCE AND NONEQUIVALENCE. I have been dealing with the propertylike nature of commonplace know-hows: who can properly do what with whom? Specifically, when a newcomer interacts with an old hand, appropriate displays are selective in some predictable pattern; both may appropriately display some given item; neither may appropriately display a second item; the newcomer but not the old hand may display a third; the old hand but not the newcomer, a fourth. All these vary predictably according to the complex role relationships forming between these two persons. Displays analytically combine to form four types of exchange: open, paced, selective, and pro forma. These, in turn, analytically combine to form two functionally salient types of relationships, of equivalence and nonequivalence.

A rather large array of propositions here suggest themselves, dealing generally with commonplace know-hows and how these enter the shaping of sex roles (selective exchanges predominantly), relationships between age groups and generations (paced exchanges predominantly), the marking of class differences or ethnic identities (possibly pro forma exchanges), and so on. I pass all the above by and name but one proposition. Note that in education or schooling, among the predictable forms of selective displays just named, two are symmetrical, wherein both may display an item or neither may, and the remaining two, wherein one but not the other may display an item, are asymmetrical. This proposition concerns, in these terms, the transaction of those functionally salient relationships of equivalence and nonequivalence:

4. Where a newcomer with an old hand are transacting a relationship of equivalence, symmetrical and asymmetrical patterns of display of commonplace know-hows occur, with each alternately predominating until some stable mix of symmetrical and asymmetrical displays is reached. Where they are transacting a relationship of nonequivalence, asymmetrical patterns of display of those know-hows increasingly predominate without definable limit.

This contrast is a reflection of the absence and presence, respectively, of pro forma exchange. The contrast also reflects, now in explicit behavioral terms, the contrast in tacit leading-and-following as opposed to avoidance behaviors (Propositions 1a and 1b), and the fact that across relationships of equivalence, "learning" occurs, but across relationships of nonequivalence, each party keeps what he or she has.

PROPOSITION 5. COMMONPLACE KNOW-HOWS AND ROLE. I have been dealing throughout this section with commonplace know-how. This volume addresses a larger problem, which is the search for ways to describe analytically a community in the act of educating and schooling itself. This involves, as well, know-hows not at all commonplace. It may be, however, that the total system of education and schooling is shaped to some very large degree through the handlings of displays of solely commonplace know-hows. Thus, this proposition, which may prove pivotal and which admits of empirical examination, can be stated:

5. In any event, as between any newcomer and any old hand, roles are typically transacted in the context of displays of commonplace know-hows and only rarely in the context of displays of other kinds of know-how.

Among other things, this means that whenever roles become troublesome, the parties fall back to displays of commonplace know-hows, and through these displays, the transaction with respect to roles proceeds.

Stated otherwise, as newcomers arrive to participate in any event, and as they become old hands and as more newcomers arrive, the total organizational shape of the interacting group is perpetually re-created through the handlings of commonplace know-hows. Inappropriate displays of these commonplace know-hows make roles and role relations visible, and appropriate displays of them keep roles real.

If it can further be shown that complex know-hows, like commonplace know-hows, are regularly propertylike, and that interactional role relationships render displays of these appropriate or inappropriate, then this general notion becomes plausible — namely, that the shape of the total process is formed through the handlings of these commonplace matters as discussed.

The exploration of these possibilities can be opened, at least, by the empirical examination of two propositions.

PROPOSITION 6. COMPLEX KNOW-HOWS AND EQUIVALENCE. I earlier noted (see Propositions 1a and 1b) that, where a newcomer with an old hand are transacting toward a relationship of equivalence, they also establish regular patterns of tacit leading-and-following between them. Where such patterns exist, these two evidently have established a little social system whereby they can jointly control what they talk about and do. Conversely, where a newcomer and old hand are transacting a relationship of nonequivalence, they establish a pattern of avoidance, without leading-and-following. In general, they do not jointly talk or otherwise jointly act and indeed have no established vehicle to do so, except sporadically. Further, if a newcomer is to come competently to join in displays of know-hows that are not commonplace and that are complex, as, for example, the telling of an origin myth or the diagnosing of a misbehaving car, that clearly requires consistently focused displayings. This involves old hand with newcomer and over many occasions of an event which, in turn, requires effective joint control over shifts in topic of conversation and germane bodily action. Thus, in education or schooling, this preposition applies:

6. In any event, and across several occasions of that event, where an old hand with a newcomer are well along toward establishing a relationship of equivalence, joint displays of complex know-hows occur. Where a relationship of nonequivalence is being established, displays of this kind do not occur.

It would appear that complex know-hows are, in this indirect sense at least, propertylike: the relationships of equivalence and nonequivalence (otherwise established) act as small systems of interactional constraint, allowing and disallowing the entailed displays. Additionally, many complex know-hows — those entailed in vocational specializations, for example — are quite markedly propertylike and even negotiable.

Cultural premises (as described in Part I) are not only complex but unverbalized and normally unverbalizable. Proposition 6 would apply with respect to these with the same or greater force and certainty.

PROPOSITION 7. COMPLEX KNOW-HOWS AND RATE OF ELIMINATION OF ERROR. Proposition 3 dealt with the incidence of different kinds of trouble in displays of commonplace know-hows, as these troubles are made visible by the occurrences of stumbles and consequent repair work, and as these decrease over time as the newcomer becomes an old hand. Here, with respect to displays of complex know-hows, the pattern is evidently a mirror image. The correctness of displays is hard to come by; the appropriateness, less so, principally because the latter work is done in other contexts or is already finished.

7. In any event and where complex know-hows are entailed, as the transactions by which a newcomer becomes an old hand proceed, the relative frequency of stumbles and consequent repair work decreases, as follows in Figure 5.

	Early ———→ Late			
As to the appropriateness of displays	hi	lo	lo	lo
As to the correctness of displays	hi	hi	hi	lo

Figure 5.

PROPOSITION 8. SCHOOLING AND HIDDEN CURRICULUMS. We have moved from commonplace know-hows to complex ones, as displays of these are handled in any community. In all communities where it is required that one not competent to join in displaying complex know-hows become competent, usually that transactional work unfolds in the kinds of events called schooling. The propositions so far named require empirical examination in any or all education and schooling events. I now shift to schooling. Later, I shall return to the whole.

Some events in a community entail schooling; these always include the explicit instruction of some participants by others. I think of some of the events that unfold in institutions, such as jails, churches, asylums, schools, and colleges. I also think of Hopi initiations and events of this kind everywhere. In these, two kinds of know-how are being displayed. First, there are commonplace know-hows, which are to be displayed appropriately and correctly. Second, there are other know-hows that are not commonplace and that are often complex, principally the content of the instruction itself. These know-hows are also to be displayed appropriately and correctly. The first involves information that is immediately necessary in the organizing of the group that brings off the event. The second is principally information that is deemed useful at some other time and some other place.

The first — handlings of commonplace know-hows — is the "hidden curriculum." The second — the handlings of know-hows that are not commonplace — is the "manifest curriculum." In events that entail schooling, the transition of newcomer into old hand follows two careers — one for the hidden curriculum and one for the manifest curriculum.

With respect to the hidden curriculum, a child newcomer to kindergarten becomes an old hand kindergartner over the course of several weeks or months. When he or she enters first or second grade, the transition occurs in much less time. The transition in later grades requires only days, even hours or minutes, for all that remains to be learned are minor variations of well-established patterns. There are, along the way, points of only slightly slowed transition from newcomer to old hand, as for freshmen entering high school or college and for first-year graduate students. The facts are similar for persons who repeatedly go to jail or to mental hospitals. In all these contexts, careers unfold: the newcomer enters, there follows a relatively brief period of transition, and this is followed by a long stretch of participation as an established old hand. Then another, briefer transition and another long stretch as an old hand, and so on. All this occurs with respect to the hidden curriculum.

With respect to the commonplace know-hows of the hidden curriculum, coming to participate as an old hand means coming to participate well in established routines. This is principally to say that, according to the interactional roles the participant has helped establish for himself and his counterparts, he has come to make no inappropriate displays, correctness being easily come by.

With respect to the manifest curriculum, on the other hand, the career is different. For any given topic, the career forms a series which consists of a period principally of transaction of some duration, followed by a brief plateau of sure enactment, followed by another extended period of transaction, and another plateau, and so on. With respect to the manifest curriculum, some participants (students, prisoners, patients) are chronically newcomers, with only brief interludes otherwise. During these brief interludes, participating as an old hand means participating well in the established routines. This is principally to say, the newcomer-become-old hand has come to make no incorrect displays, appropriateness being relatively easily come by.

The key question raised by the two curriculums that coexist in schooling events is this: Do the operations of hidden curriculum *control* the operations of the manifest curriculum? A beginning, at least, can be made through empirical examination of a single proposition.

A hidden curriculum of some kind and a manifest curriculum of some kind are both being "taught" in any schooling event. These are revealed through analytic description. Particularly, these are revealed as some array of routines that regularly unfolds in such an event.

Parts of a hidden curriculum are revealed when one identifies a pivotal actor (the teacher in a classroom, or an old Fox Indian telling "Winter Stories") and when one identifies two routines that regularly unfold side-by-side and by which displays of commonplace know-hows are ordered. One of these unfolds between the pivotal actor and one set of participants; the other between the same pivotal actor and another set of participants. The two sets of participants might be male and female, rich and poor, etc. The mere existence of such pairs of routines in a schooling event — irrespective of the nature of the routines — is itself an item of hidden curriculum unfolding in that place. All the participants are effectively engaged in enacting those routines, and by those enactments, all are, at some level of partial awareness, enacting those entailed contrasts in their identifications of themselves and each other and in their interactional role relationships.

Simultaneously, the manifest curriculum is revealed not only in what the people are talking about, but in certain qualitative features of the entailed routines by which the talk proceeds. For example, as instruction proceeds a routine may unfold where the pivotal actor and some set of participants alternatively engage in cognitively complex talk, and a second routine may coexist between the pivotal actor and some second set of others wherein instances of cognitively complex talk are regularly cut off and regularly followed by cognitively simple talk.

The key question is whether the hidden curriculum controls the manifest curriculum. More particularly, the question is: If such controls were operating, what special features would be evident, in the set of routines unfolding? Thus, we have this proposition:

8. In any schooling event, the participants who are variously aggregated (according to contrasting interactional roles) in the context of displaying commonplace know-hows, are aggregated in like fashion in the context of displaying complex know-hows.

In Propositions 3 and 5, the reader saw that what appears to be principally at issue in handlings of commonplace know-hows was appropriateness (role), and that the organization of the group which constitutes an event may be perpetually re-created in and through these handlings of solely commonplace know-how. This is what the hidden curriculum is, and this is what the hidden curriculum does: it creates and sustains organization. Proposition 8 suggests that the resulting organization then orders the handlings of displays of complex know-hows. If true, the hidden curriculum controls, in this sense at least, the manifest curriculum.

PROPOSITION 9. HIDDEN CURRICULUMS AND EQUIVALENCE. If the schooling event is so organized so that the pivotal actor has transacted through the operations of hidden curriculum a relationship of equivalence with one set of participants and a relationship of nonequivalence with a second set, then contrasts in the routines through which the manifest curriculum unfolds can be quite stark, such as the contrasts in side-by-side routines suggested above. In schooling events, the principal purpose, usually stated, is to generate competence in the handlings of complex know-hows. Consider then, this proposition:

> 9. In any schooling event, where a relationship of equivalence exists between a pivotal actor and one set of participants, the routines that order the manifest curriculum will be functional to the principal purpose at hand, thereby generating competence. Where a relationship of nonequivalence exists between the pivotal actor and a second set of participants, these routines will be markedly dysfunctional to that principal purpose.

Of course, such contrasting routines are expressions in elaborated behavioral terms of the contrasting patterns of leading-and-following noted earlier (see Propositions 1a, 1b, 4, and 6).

Thus, more generally, if there regularly unfold two parallel pairs of routines, the pivotal actor interacting contrastingly in the unfolding of both the hidden and manifest curricula (with males and females, for example), then it would seem probable that the hidden curriculum is controlling the manifest one. This might be found with respect to male and female, affluent and poor, black and white, and so on, as those identities might be enacted through pairs of routines in some place.

I earlier alluded to and will later discuss the Pygmalion literature data that strongly suggest that the hidden curriculum does tend to control the manifest curriculum. Many persons have noted that there is more than chance congruence between identities of, on the one hand, rich v. poor, white v. black, and, on the other hand, the interactional roles that tend to occur principally in schooling events, as in the case of high achievers v. low achievers. What matters to research in any particular place, however, is whether this happens, and if it does, precisely how it is brought off.

PROPOSITION 10. MICRO AND MACRO. I return to the whole — a community in the act of educating and schooling itself — and to the question of whether, in doing this, the community is somehow re-creating itself perpetually.

An overall theory of education and schooling must analytically describe the fact that know-hows get distributed through the population of any community, not randomly, but rather, selectively and according to a predictable pattern. Many know-hows are propertylike, and education and schooling is, in effect, a process of censorship of an unusual kind. It is always jointly brought off, and is usually inadvertent.

The discussions to this point have treated the phenomena of education and schooling only at the level of face-to-face interaction. This is not accidental, for obviously that is where interactional constraints operate. A theory of education and schooling informed by that notion must find ways to describe analytically those constraints in operation.

Yet, it seems logically necessary that the principal job of a system of education and schooling in any community is perpetually to re-create that community's "template for work." One must, in such analytic description, somehow get from the micro level, which has preoccupied us to this point, to the community-wide macro level. To this final task, I now turn.

The work system it was said is the community's job-doing system; it is a description of the community in the act of getting and consuming food and shelter and coping with other communities. This system, by the mode of analytic description here adopted, consists of: a surface structure called the social organization, which varies as circumstances vary, pragmatically, but within limits; an infrastructure, referred to here as the template for work, which does not change; and a monitoring process, transaction, which constrains variation in the surface within limits established by the infrastructure.

I established earlier a functional sorting, noting that some events are "education" and some are "schooling." Education events are those wherein the interaction between old hands and newcomers resemble on-the-job training. The participants are doing something; the know-hows are entailed in getting that done; a newcomer becomes an old hand as he comes to join in those displays appropriately and correctly. In short, what the old hands regularly do is the curriculum awaiting a newcomer to that event. The social organization — that part of it unfolding in that event — is the curriculum in events of this kind.

One aspect, then, of the problem of getting back and forth between analytic descriptions of micro and macro levels is a problem of translation or rephrasing in these education events, from a description of social organization to description of the routines that order face-to-face interaction. It would appear that this is not difficult.

In contrast, schooling events are those where, in the content of talk and other action, there is included information or skills deemed to be useful at some other time and place. What the old hands do is again the curriculum, but in schooling events, the curricula are two — a manifest curriculum and a hidden one.

With respect to schooling events, getting back and forth between descriptions at micro and macro levels is very difficult. The presumption is strong and the implication most crucial that the hidden curriculum in these schooling events *is* the work system's template for work. But the problem is translating the description of one into a description of the other with sufficient clarity to determine whether that presumption is empirically correct.

The first aspect of the problem, then, is simply describing twice what the old hands do in the events called education. In a macro level description of what they do, as social organization, one would normally describe a division of labor, a system of authority, and rewards and punishments. In a micro level description of what they do, as a curriculum, one describes the same behaviors as some array of routines, in terms of the behavioral units and functional concepts here outlined. All this is time consuming and taxing, but no imponderables are evident.

On the other hand, how one goes about the second aspect of the problem, as presented in schooling events, is far less clear. Since the hidden curriculum deals centrally with organization, specifically with interactional role relations, it seems possible to focus principally on that dimension of the template that is parallel — those descriptions called social structure by anthropologists. The units of description in both instances are roles; the problem is how to discern whether the roles in a description of social structure of the community at large are or are not "the same" as the interactional roles found in a description of the old hands in an event displaying commonplace know-hows. The two sets of roles are not identical; it is a problem of pattern replication.

In the context of this outline of a reference model, I can only name the problem and offer three observations. First, role attributes that appear in a description of social structure, such as black and white or rich and poor, correlate with high achiever and low, smart and dumb, and other such interactional roles to be observed in schooling events far more frequently than chance would allow. The second and third observations relate to whether the hidden curriculum in schooling events is in fact the template for work. In serious and less serious literature, similar observations frequently occur such as, "Schools are museums of virtue." This is to say, the intuitive sense keeps surfacing. The result is that, in schooling, as opposed to other educational contexts, the hidden curriculum is somehow lagging behind the times or "purer." Finally, in every community and at some junctures across total life careers in every community, the educational tasks are put into the hands of persons who are otherwise out of the community's work, i.e., teachers and professors, old men, priests, wardens, psychiatrists. It is a little-examined but probable fact that such persons, simply because they are out of the community's work, tend to enact the infrastructure rather than the vacillating surface structure of the work system of their respective communities.

I must leave these imponderables and phrase the concern in a final proposition that, one hopes, admits of empirical examination, even though such examination clearly requires resolution of those imponderables. The proposition is phrased in two parts:

10a. In any schooling event in any community, there unfolds a manifest curriculum and a hidden curriculum; the content of the latter is the infrastructure of the community's work system, its template for work.

This is to say that, through transactions between old hands and newcomers in schooling events, the hidden curriculum is taught, unawares, and thereby that template for work is perpetually re-created. The principal job of a community's system of education and schooling would appear to be the perpetual re-creation of that community's template for work. This task falls, as it appears, specifically to that part of the system called schooling.

10b. Where that template for work sorts members of the community into large aggregates of population that are ranked, the hidden curriculum in schooling events contains routines wherein persons enact relations of equivalence and, across such rankings, of nonequivalence; these in turn constrain displays of complex know-hows in patterns that contrast sharply.

In some communities, this may refer to white and black, rich and poor in terms of the template for work and to high and low achievers, smart and dumb in terms of the hidden curriculum.

In some very imprecise sense, all this is surely true. Brophy and Good (1974) summarized a large number of studies from educational research literature, all of which dealt with how teachers relate differently to low and high achievers. The language treats teachers and their students. Note, however, that in every item, if the nouns were changed to "guards" and "prisoners" or "psychiatrists" and "patients," and if high and low achievers were appropriately redefined, the behaviors reported, though perhaps unexamined to date in these contexts, would still be plausible. Brophy and Good found the following:

1. *Waiting less time for lows to answer.* Teachers have been observed to provide more time for high achievers to respond than for low achievers.
2. *Not staying with lows in failure situations.* In addition to waiting less time for lows to begin their response, the teachers have been found to respond to incorrect answers by lows by giving them the answer or by calling on another student to

answer the question. High achievers in failure situations are much more likely to ask a teacher to repeat a question, provide a clue, or to ask them a new question. Thus, teachers have been found to accept mediocre performance from lows but to work with and demand better performance from highs.

3. *Rewarding inappropriate behavior of lows.* In some studies, teachers have been found to praise marginal or inaccurate responses from these students.

4. *Criticizing lows more frequently than highs.* Somewhat at odds with the above finding, teachers have been found to criticize lows proportionately more frequently than highs when they provide wrong answers. This is indeed a strong finding, for it suggests that risk-taking behavior and general initiative on the part of lows is being discouraged.

5. *Praising lows less frequently than highs.* Also in contrast to point 3, some research has shown that, when lows provide correct answers, they are less likely to be praised than are highs, even though they provide fewer correct responses.

6. *Not giving feedback to public responses of lows.* Teachers in some studies have been found to respond to answers by lows (especially correct answers) by calling on another student to respond.

7. *Paying less attention to lows.* Studies have shown that teachers attend more closely to highs (and, as we noted above, provide more feedback). Some data exist to suggest that teachers smile more often and maintain greater eye contact with highs than with lows. Studies also show that teachers miss many opportunities to reinforce lows simply because they do not attend to their behavior.

8. *Calling on lows less often.* Teachers have been found to call on high achievers more frequently than on lows. The difference in public participation becomes more sharply differentiated with increases in grade level.

9. *Differing interaction patterns of highs and lows.* Interestingly, contact patterns between teachers and lows are different in elementary and secondary classrooms. In elementary classrooms, highs dominate public response opportunities, but highs and lows receive roughly the same number of private teacher contacts. In secondary classrooms, highs become even more dominant in public settings, but lows begin to receive more private contacts with the teacher.

10. *Seating lows farther from the teachers*: Seating pattern studies have sometimes found that lows tend to be placed away from the teacher, thus creating a physical barrier. Random placement seems to reduce the physical isolation of lows and hinders the development of sharp status differences among peers.

11. *Demanding less from lows.* This includes giving these students easier tests (and letting the students know it) or simply not asking the student to do academic work. Also, sometimes if a low achiever masters the elementary aspects of a unit, he may be neglected until the elementary aspects of the next unit are dealt with.

In 1968, *Pygmalion in the classroom* by Rosenthal and Jacobson had a large impact in educational circles. It demonstrated that the beliefs teachers entertain as to the varying levels of ability of their students set in motion transactions so that the students come to perform academically according to those levels. In the experiment, as reported in the study, initial beliefs about the students were implanted by false (randomly assigned) information. The study had obvious implications for education of the children of the poor, and a host of studies were mounted to replicate the result. In almost all cases, the results were not replicated. Recently, Finn (1972) has reviewed that array of attempted replications, argued that the statistical procedures doomed them, and mounted an analogous small study himself, using multivariate statistical analysis, wherein the initial Pygmalion results were in part confirmed. It should be noted in passing that multivariate analysis permits simultaneous handling of multiple independent and multiple dependent variables; and would thus appear to permit statistical analysis of what to an ethnographer begins to resemble the real world. That world is partly grasped in the observational studies that follow — all of which emerged in those intervening months, addressing variations on the Pygmalion theme.

Rist (1970 and, see Part II) did an ethnography of a kindergarten (black teacher, black students), in which he noted that in the very early weeks the teacher had sorted the children into ability groups. He asked himself what information the teacher then had with which to accomplish that sorting, discovered that she had various information as to the children's social classes and little else, and found that she had sorted them by social class (specifically, the very poor against the rest). There was no movement of children between the ability groups during the year, and the children performed at levels to which they were assigned. The sorting remained basically unchanged over two succeeding years.

Analogously, Rosenfeld (1971 and, see Part II), on the basis of four years of teaching in a predominantly black ghetto school in Harlem, traces similar self-fulfilling prophesies by which students come to conform to the expectations of the teachers, who are predominantly white. By virtue of his position and by doing ethnography, he was further able to intervene in his own classroom. He observed and plotted the social organization of the students (their alliances and oppositions, etc.), allowed those groupings to operate at academic tasks, and generally retransacted roles. Their scores on standardized achievement tests increased across the range of subject areas but this change was read by the staff as the result of a trick of some mysterious kind.

Still further, Leacock (1971) compared schools of respectively lower and middle class students, including black and white students, and found that expectation and performance levels varied as to economic class but not with regard to race. Talbert (1970, also Part II) also examined patterns of spatial movement toward the periphery of the classroom by children in two kindergartens. Specifically, she studied how these movements were affected by teacher behaviors and how these spatial locations in turn affected interaction. All this varied as to sex and through time during the school year.

In these Pygmalion studies, there consistently runs the theme that schools have failed, as indeed these particular schools conspicuously have by any humane measures. The question, however, is whether such failures are aberrations of some kind or whether, from some understanding of the general nature of education and schooling, one could predict precisely what is reported in these studies. Evidently, the latter is true.

In most places, most of the time, with respect to most aspects of culture, societies do replicate themselves over the generations. Hidden curricula are at least dimly seen as they unfold in all these studies of failure. They can also be seen unfolding just as conspicuously in "good" schools. What appears to be happening is that the society is reproducing itself with regard to caste, class, sex roles — warts and all — and through actions that, in some substantial part, the actors themselves are only dimly aware of. These are even actions that they would often deplore if they were fully aware of them. One could as easily say that schooling, as seen here, awesomely succeeds.

SUMMARY

To recapitulate, as briefly and precisely as is now possible:

Any community must re-create itself, daily and across the succession of generations; insofar as this is occurring, the community is well described by the notion of interactional constraint.

If description is shaped by the notion of interactional constraint, a community is analytically described and redescribed as three systems of such constraint.

The job-doing system is the work system; this includes a surface structure (the social organization), which varies within limits; an infrastructure (the template for work), which normally does not vary; and a monitoring process (transaction), by which variation in the first is constrained within limits established by the second.

Insofar as a community does recreate itself unchanged, the central question is: what re-creates the template for work? The probable answer is that the community's system of education and schooling, specifically that subclass of events called schooling, re-create it in this manner:

In any schooling event, there unfolds a manifest curriculum, which consists of routines wherein complex know-hows are selectively displayed, and a hidden curriculum, which consists of routines wherein commonplace know-hows are selectively displayed; the hidden curriculum is concerned with organization — interactional roles.

In any schooling event in any community, old hands enact the template for work (not the varying social organization). The template for work is the hidden curriculum, and through the unfolding of the routines that together form the hidden curriculum, the newcomers to any schooling event are inducted into this system of role relations. This system is a replica in microcosm of the community's template for work.

The hidden curriculum controls the manifest curriculum, establishes constraints as to who will and who will not come to join competently in displays of complex know-hows.

In all this, it is functionally salient that large aggregates of persons are sorted and hierarchically ranked by the template for work. This is a hidden curriculum expressed as relations of equivalence within such subgroups and of nonequivalence between those groups. By this contrast especially, vocational specializations and life careers generally are shaped.

In short, in this manner, in any schooling event in any community, the template for work is enacted; it becomes thereby a hidden curriculum. And through constraints inherent in transactions between old hands and newcomers, the template gets exactly replicated. Through the succession of generations, this process becomes a perpetual recreation of the work system and of the community itself.

Through the operations of such indirect constraints, the work system would continue basically unchanged in the absence of rather massive disruptions or very long-lasting shifts of circumstance in the community or its environs. Perhaps the best demonstrated form of the latter is from Marx. Probably the key reason shifts in relationship to the means of production have the ranging systemic effects they have is because the shifts systematically alter who comes together with whom in that critical large class of events called schooling, where the template for work is perpetually re-created and where that infra-structure is always "under construction."

PERIPHERAL MATTERS: PSYCHES; SOCIAL CHANGE

The reference model, whose outline has proceeded, suggests one mode of description. By using it, any community is analytically described as a system of interactional constraints. Any community is described and redescribed three times, as three linked systems of interactional constraints. One of these descriptions is the cultural theory of education and schooling we are reaching out to create.

Such descriptions may distress many, for it will seem to them that the descriptions are simply "wrong." And it will probably seem that the sources of the distress are two: psyches have been somehow caused to disappear from the scene, and social change is likewise nowhere in evidence. Commonsense experience tells us, correctly, that people and societies are not like this. Yet, descriptions such as here proposed are not necessarily false. They may indeed be accurate descriptions even though, quite obviously, they are not complete. Other redescriptions of the community are always possible, and the sources of distress would suggest that two complementary redescriptions are necessary to deal with social change and psyches.

The two necessary redescriptions would parallel the two descriptions of the community — as a work system and as a system of education and schooling. (I leave aside, as before, play and ritual.) These two rediscriptions would move respectively at the macro level, wherein hierarchically organized sets of events are described in aggregate, and at the micro level, wherein particular events are described severally. And, in further parallel, whereas the descriptions earlier suggested were both formed by the overarching notion of interactional constraint, both redescriptions must, be formed by a historically related notion of servomechanism. By this notion, applied to human behavior, a person is seen as a goal-seeking entity that operates through negative feedback (Powers 1974). The four descriptions together describe the community as a cybernetic system and are to be logically compatible.

By the term "change," I mean any instance where the members of a community were seen to behave one way yesterday, another way today, and presumably yet another way tomorrow. Inquiries launched on this subject often seek to discover the circumstances that evoke such social change.

By the term "psyche," I mean that real or imagined entity that is construed to exist inside any individual human, principally inside the skull. Inquiries launched on this subject often seek to discover its internal workings and organization.

It seems evident that, within the mode of analytic description followed until now, there is no place for psyches; any prior information about the psyches of persons involved do not help one to see the patterns of interaction behaviors that are critically at issue, and seeing those patterns of interaction provides no nontrivial information about the psyches involved. It seems equally evident that, within that mode of analytic description, there is no place for social change; where such changes are ongoing, the patterns of interaction at issue are there at one moment and not there, or altered, at another. Information derived from mapping those patterns allows one to note that change has occurred, but otherwise leaves one speechless.

The key arena within which the logical linkage between the two pairs of descriptions is most clearly visible is "transaction." The earlier descriptions were shaped by the notion of interactional constraints. At the macro level, one maps the results of transaction and the limits within which transactions operate. At the micro level, one maps the action by which variation beyond those limits is constrained. Two redescriptions are to be shaped by the notion of servomechanism to reveal the goal-seeking whereby the transactions are put in motion in the first place. At the macro level, one would describe goal-seeking behaviors by the powerful and otherwise influential whereby the processes of social change are generated. At the micro level, one would describe activity inside the psyches of persons who interact.

Following Powers, a servomechanism[1] contains four principal sets of parts: (1) it must have a goal, a preferred condition of things outside itself, and a way of keeping track of what that goal is; (2) it must have a way of knowing what the conditions outside itself in fact are; (3) it must have a way of noting when those actual conditions do not match the preferred conditions; and (4) it must have a way of affecting those outside conditions and thus acting when and only when the actual conditions depart from the preferred conditions. I am told that the human nervous system is a mass of linked "servos," and that a human organism is one very complex "servo."

I turn to the two redescriptions. In any community, persons find each other in those kinds of situations called events and there act. To look inside those events, one at a time, and to describe those servos doing that, is to describe the community at a micro level. This can be called a description of the community as a socialization system.

The comments that follow are very narrow. I look toward a description of a community as a socialization system solely from the perspective of that other preoccupying description of the community as a system of education and schooling. If one thinks of socialization functionally, one necessarily thinks of someone learning something; and one necessarily thinks of sequences of someone learning this fact on the basis of having learned that fact.

The other preoccupying description, guided by the notion of interactional constraint, cannot deal with learning simply because it does not and cannot deal with individuals at all. Analytically, one cannot "follow that man," and it follows that it is impossible to say with any analytic seriousness that any individual learned anything.

How does a servo learn? And what does a servo learn? It is perhaps not too fictitious, as a start, to imagine a servo newcomer about whom two things are true: he is altogether innocent of any information about germane know-hows and the appropriateness and correctness of their display, and his sole goal is that there be no stumbles. At some level of awareness he has in his mind a preferred condition, that talk or other interchange be comfortably stumble-free. He can perceive when the actual condition departs from this. He can act, perhaps at first by trial and error and later with sureness, so that the actual condition can be made to fit the preferred one. The movement from trial and error to sureness is that servo newcomer learning. And what has the newcomer learned? He now knows standards of appropriateness and correctness to be used in displaying the entailed know-hows; in other words, he has now additional preferred conditions, more goals. He has come to make the goals of old hands his own goals.

[1] I am particularly indebted here to personal communication with Raoul Naroll, and I hope he will not be offended by my gross oversimplification and inevitable errors.

This having occurred, the newcomer is no longer quite so fictitious. He now knows, with respect to the entailed know-hows of an event, about appropriateness (thus, who he is, in terms of roles) and correctness (thus, the involved knowledge and skill). He is now, to some degree, forearmed upon entering as a newcomer the next event new to him. It is evident, though little explored, that some role learnings are prerequisites for other role learning. It is evident, and very exhaustively explored, that some knowledge learnings are prerequisites for others (for a more salient example, see the works of Piaget and Piagetians); and analogously, there are prerequisites for skill learnings.

In this sense, the principal function of the socialization system is to create "readiness." When a community is described socializing itself, it is creating contrasting readinesses, contrasting among different persons and contrasting for the same person at different times. From the narrow vantage point of the preoccupation of this volume, these are readinesses to receive items from the community's pool of know-hows when these get selectively distributed — different ones to different persons, and different ones to the same person at different times, principally in terms of social identities. These know-hows come and go across total lifetimes.

I turn to social change events, being now described as hierarchically arranged aggregates. To describe goal-seeking humans or servos, acting in aggregated events in pursuit of goals, is to describe regularities in accumulating and deploying influence and power. Economists and political scientists so describe communities. Call this a description of the community as a power system. The direct sources of social change, those behaviors that put social change in motion and move it along, are well identified through description of a community as a system wherein economic and political power is being accumulated and deployed.

It seems evident that human entities behaving in such fashions are well described as servos. That is, persons with preferred conditions in their minds are able to perceive actual conditions, and, where the latter departs from the first, are able to act in ways that affect those actual conditions. It seems equally evident that, with organization, groups and very large groups of groups can act corporately. That is to say, some persons, namely, those in the higher levels in pyramidally organized events and, specifically, those in such positions in those specific events that affect the actions of others in other events, are more able than others to affect the actual conditions. This is power.

From the vantage of the preoccupations of this volume, all this need not be further elaborated. A question that more directly bears on the preoccupations of this volume is: What effects does social change have on that aspect of the community described as education and schooling? And what effects do education and schooling have on social change?

In any community at any time, there is change. The critical question always is whether such change is systemic, that is, irreversible. A description of a community as a work system includes as one facet of that, a surface structure, a social organization. Any second description at a later time would depict a somewhat modified social organization, since social organization normally varies. But a description of the community as the related infrastructure — as a template for work — and then a second description later would both depict the same template. The infrastructure normally does not vary. However, it may and this provides the definition of systemic change: where the infrastructure changes, social change is irreversible — systemic. Where the infrastructure does not change, social change is not systemic.

How, then, does the change relate to education and schooling in any community? And how does education and schooling relate to change? The flow of change through the community possibly moves as follows: Exercises of power lead always to modified social organization. This in turn may lead to modified hidden curricula in events called schooling, and in turn to a modified template for work. More probably, the hidden curricula do not change, and the template for work is recreated unchanged. The first in systemic change; the second, not. Change in both cases flows through those events called schooling. The empirical questions now become: Which changes in social organization modify hidden curricula and which do not?

One bit of the answer is reasonably clear. The changes reflected in modified social organization can be piecemeal. In one event, change moves in one direction; in another, in an opposite direction; in a third, there is no change. The template for work describes the averaged-out, cumulative experience, a kind of group memory. It follows then that the social changes that come to be reflected in changes in the template for work must be consistent and massive. They must affect many events in the same ways.

Certain current developments that are unfolding in US cities on a rather large scale invite examination, for they may be systematic, or they may not be. Moves toward racial desegregation in the schools is one such development. The presumption seems strong that these changes, to date, are not systemic. In part, the changes are not proving to be systemic because they are not massive. They directly affect only those events that occur in only one kind of place — the schools — and they occur in only some of them; in fact, they occur in an exceedingly small proportion of that wider class of events (in schools and elsewhere) here called schooling. In addition, for this and other reasons, if the roles white and black tend to become, in the interactions organized as hidden curricula, high achievers and low achievers, and if role relations across those classes tend to become relationships of nonequivalence, then presumably the infrastructure is not being changed. The role identities and the ranking of the roles and the relationships between them evidently are not being changed. If so, this social change is not systematic. All the above, of course, is a way of phrasing the questions, and is not to be confused with answers to those questions. It is a matter inviting empirical reexamination in the terms suggested.

The current developments with respect to sex roles are more ambiguous. Here, at least, the criterion of massiveness is probably met. Many events, and perhaps virtually all schooling events, are being affected to some degree and in roughly the same directions. The key question, again, is: What is happening in hidden curricula? Surface appearances suggest two things. First, very dimly, role identities are being enacted without change; it is still behaviorally evident that interchanges are male-to-male, female-to-female, male-to-female. Possibly, with the general loosening-up in respect to homosexuality, a parallel pair of new role identities is emerging. (Of course, sorting everyone into only two genders is a social convention; many societies use three or four genders, as in cases where males assume female lifestyles but do not become female. This occurred with transvestites among Plains Indians and widely elsewhere. More rarely, women adopt male lifestyles.) To date behavioral evidence of such a change in identities in the unfolding of hidden curricula probably does not exist: In the acting out of the entailed routines, everyone is still male or female and nothing else, and these roles are always behaviorally evident. On the other hand, very probably, altered relations are becoming evident between those identities, and there is some loosening of the complex rankings as between them. Little girls now appear to say "shit" about as often and in the same contexts as do little boys. Such displays of commonplace know-hows are what hidden curricula are made of. Role identities, then, are probably not changing, but role relations probably are, within these hidden curricula. If so, the infrastructure of the work system is being re-created in altered form. This social change is systemic and irreversible in the sense that the infrastructure will not snap back on its own accord, though, of course, it could again be changed by similar developments in the reverse direction. All this, again, is a way of phrasing the empirical questions, not to be confused with the empirical answers to those questions.

Closely parallel developments appear underway with respect to role relations across the generations and among age groups generally.

I shift back to descriptions shaped by the notion of interactional constraint. The mapping of change in these terms, at micro levels inside hidden curricula, can be abstractly sketched. To see this change, it is necessary to look at the patterns of "selective exchange," as between the sexes, or the patterns of "paced exchange," as between age groups, as these unfold in the routines that constitute hidden curricula. Changes in hidden curricula are made visible when either of these constraining patterns of exchange are opened for renegotiation by the parties. Renegotiation is first evidenced by an increased incidence of inappropriate displays, thus, of stumbles and consequent repair work.

Two parallel sets of patterns in such renegotiations invite empirical attention. First, where role identities contrast by age, a pattern of paced exchange may give way to an episode of renegotiation marked by inappropriate displays and stumbles, and finally, back to a pattern of paced exchange, modified from the original or not, as the case may be. Similarly, where role identities contrast by sex, a pattern of selective exchange, followed by renegotiation, and then, a move back to selective exchange modified from the original or not. In human experience, very generally, it seems plausible that renegotiations occur more frequently between age groups and where patterns of paced exchange prevail more generally. But episodes of renegotiation are longer and more troublesome between the sexes and where patterns of selective exchange prevail more generally. All this is one pattern.

The second pattern in such renegotiations is where, from an episode of renegotiation, there emerges, not the earlier pattern of paced or selective exchange, but instead, a pattern of pro forma exchange, and thereby, the parties settle into a relationship of nonequivalence. In human experience very generally, it appears that this increasingly happens as social systems become larger and more complex.

This pattern of pro forma exchange emerges in situations of impasse over role identities and role relationships. Where that pattern has come to prevail, parties tune each other out and coexist. To speak somewhat figuratively, it is rather easy in large and complex social systems to settle into a relationship of nonequivalence, and quite difficult to negotiate a way out.

To return again to the servos who interact, it seems possible to see yet further inside these processes whereby hidden curricula get changed. These transactions are occurring within an event at micro levels of description. To see inside them would turn us back to that other micro level description — the community as a socialization system. The actors who open and pursue such transactions are surely restless, goal-seeking creatures — servos. These servos are learning now, by *creating* stumbles and then finding out how to reduce those stumbles; what they are learning, insofar as hidden curricula are changing, are newly generated goals, new standards of preferred conditions. Stumbles are uncomfortable; yet some servos under some conditions do, as it appears, generate them. I do not believe this is well understood.

Social change, in sum, is or is not systemic. Recent and current domestic experience provides numerous instances of other social change, as, for example, in the space effort, the development of television, and the environmental protection movement. These very real changes are possibly being assimilated into unchanged hidden curricula; or possibly, the hidden curricula are changing, thus the infrastructure, and these changes are systemic. My intuition is that the changes are for the most part not systemic, but it is a matter for empirical investigation. In contrast to these changes, another kind of unplanned and unwanted change whose origins are not convincingly identified, would strongly appear to be systemic — the steadily increasing incidence of patterns of pro forma exchange and consequent relations of nonequivalence — "alienation," as it is sometimes called. This, too, is a matter for empirical investigation and perhaps, intervention.

In any human community, changes of these kinds are regularly being generated, but only some are systemic. The unfinished theoretical business pursuant to a cultural theory of education and schooling is to identify, predict, and explain the effects of social change on processes operating within the events called schooling. It may be that these schooling events regularly serve as the principal vehicle for the assimilation of discrete changes, and thereby as the principal brake against systemic change, in human communities generally — of course, for better and for worse.

4. ACTION ANTHROPOLOGY IN THE SCHOOLS

A cultural theory of education and schooling would, as one might suppose, paint a picture of powerfully conservative processes unfolding through the events called schooling. There are, to be sure, certain adaptive advantages in this. By analogy, in the realm of biological evolution there exists a barrier that precludes any information derived from experience from reaching the germ cells and being recoded there in the genetic code (the barrier that precludes the inheritance of acquired characteristics). That barrier did poorly by dinosaurs, but it seems to have done well by life more generally. Change is biologically adaptive, but the absence of change is biologically adaptive, also. Perhaps the events called education and, more stringently, those called schooling are in the realm of culture just such barriers — somewhat permeable, to be sure, but as it theoretically appears, powerful ones nonetheless. By extension of the analogy, education and schooling may do poorly by this or that community, but do well by communities in general.

I may be forgiven, or even applauded, for looking at all this as parochially as the dinosaurs in their later centuries must have. I wish my own community and others well, I confess, and, insofar as they are troubled, I find little comfort in what may happen to "community" in general.

There are to be derived from all that has preceded two principal pragmatic implications. First, it seems likely that we students of culture who have involved ourselves in education and schooling in pragmatic ways have rather badly underestimated the forces against which we have pitted wit and energy. Insofar as this cultural theory may prove generally correct, nothing significant can be made to occur by wish or exhortation, and very little can be made to occur through opening and closing the spigots through which flow materiel. Yet, virtually all pragmatic efforts, — professional training programs, curricular material developments and distributions, etc. — have consisted of thinly veiled versions of exhortation and turning spigots. And when great effort is expended and little result follows, the natural inclination is to find a culprit to blame, some kind of person or some kind of phenomenon. In either event, a scapegoat is sought — the parents, genes, neighborhoods, the teachers or wardens or psychiatrists, cultural deprivation, teenagers, the Establishment, or the counterculture. It seems tragically wasteful to underestimate real forces or to invent fantasies that distract and may hurt.

From the theory, one may derive a second implication. Insofar as the theory may be correct, the area and direction of necessary action seems clearly identified: changes are to be sought in those transactions and enactments that make up the routines, and which, in turn, are the hidden curricula in schooling. Principally, this would mean changes in role identities and role relations. Insofar as such changes can massively occur, the effects would, by the theory, flow wavelike, evidently without possible interception, through the society at large, and such changes would be systemic, and, therefore, irreversible.

Changes in hidden curricula are thinkable, but how are they to be brought off? The theory, insofar as it may be correct, contains one bit of further guidance. It suggests where such changes strategically would best begin. The changes must begin in the behaviors of old hands, rather than in the behaviors of the newcomers, and specifically in the actions of pivotal actors.

The theory, even in some future, well-elaborated condition, would appear to offer little further practical guidance as to how such changes in hidden curricula are to occur.

Over twenty years ago, Sol Tax, working with others, defined and named a kind of anthropology simultaneously to be pursued in the world of affairs and in the world of scholarship. Tax called it action anthropology. Action anthropology deals solely with information. It envisages a complex dialogue, wherein members of the client community provide the anthropologist with information as to their experience and aspirations, and the anthropologist provides the members of the community his or her best analytic readings at any moment as to the community's several options and the implications of each and also simultaneously reports these readings, as they seem to merit, to the scholarly community. The members of the client community react to the diagnoses and perhaps act upon the evident choices; the anthropologist makes new readings of the ensuing developments. The process continues over some extended, ill-defined duration.

This theory of education and schooling identifies critical behaviors — those hidden curricula — and identifies critical persons — those old hands who are also pivotal. Action anthropology suggests that, through a dialogue of some kind, those persons must receive information about those behaviors.

Action anthropology, as it was known twenty years ago, imagined a dialogue between such clients and an anthropologist. This would not promise to yield visible results in bringing off the changes here required for one obvious reason, namely, because there are few anthropologists and many clients — and changes, to effect systemic change, must be massive. Further, and more fundamentally, any recurring action in face-to-face interaction is thoroughly reciprocal and jointly a product of several parties; thus, any departure by one person from those patterns must carry through against stumbles and repair work, and generally against recip- rocal actions by others that tend, with or without conscious intent, to reestablish the status quo. It follows that the information must be unusu- ally compelling and unusually powerful. It seems evident that, somehow, the clients must be their own observers, that their observation must be observation of themselves behaving in the course of their work, and that such observation must continue through the course of their efforts to act on the observations.

The dialogue, then, must be between the client and the client's own records of his or her own behaviors.

The cultural theory of education and schooling, plus the idea of action anthropology, together suggest that anthropologists invest their scarce energies in helping critical persons in schools, jails, asylums, and in the events generally called schooling, to develop skills in the self-observation of their own critical behaviors. Thereby those persons will be enabled to undertake systematic self-monitoring, the parts they have played, and may choose to differently play, in shaping transactions and enactments between themselves and their counterparts.

A group associated with the Center for Studies of Cultural Trans- mission has been so engaged, specifically in schools. A few thousand teachers and education administrators have been taught ethnographic self-observation. Some of these busy people, probably numbering a few dozen, have continued to observe themselves at work with some regu- larity, with effects satisfactory to them but unknown in behavioral detail to us.

I report on that experience.

Teachers are professional persons; thus, they are duty-bound to be practical persons. It follows that their ethnographic activity must be bracketed before and after with activities other than ethnography. They begin by identifying some professional concern, some recurring "bad" thing they wish to change or some "good" thing they seek to protect. This concern must be phrased behaviorally at the outset as well as possible. The concern must be described as some identified actors engaged in some identified behaviors in some identified context. Then, ethnography can begin.

Teachers are also very busy persons. It follows that the ethnographic procedures must be well focused, yielding information that is not only accurate but also strategic about critical moments that recur and pointed about some specific feature of all that is going on at such moments. A busy person can hold strategic and pointed information in mind through the rush of events and use it. I shall return to the ethnographic procedures that yield information of this kind.

Ethnographic effort having run its course in the modes to be described, lines of possible action are indicated, but the ethnography itself does not advise. Thus, these professional persons end with evaluating values in terms of individual and group values and deciding whether to act. If the decision is to act, ethnography reenters the picture as self-monitoring, continuing observations as to whether the changes decided upon are, in fact, occurring.

In short, busy professional persons need to know and want to know about the "differences that are making a practical difference" in the places where they daily work and only that.

What follows is the heart of the activities, the ethnographic self-observation procedures themselves, drawn here in outline from an instructional manual (Gearing et al. 1975). The manual resulted from the efforts mentioned, and it guides recent and current efforts. The language that follows mentions teachers or professors and students, but, as noted, it is possible to read, in place of these, psychiatrists and patients, wardens and prisoners, etc.

Ethnographic self-observation by any particular teacher in his or her particular school and classroom usefully moves forward in orderly fashion through four operations. First, there is *informal observation*. The teacher has already identified a concern and translated that into behavioral terms. The purposes of informal observation are two: to note the occurrences of those behaviors of concern; and to note the contexts in which these occur. Informal observations normally proceed as the work of the classroom and the teacher's involvements in that work proceed. Cryptic note-taking is necessary.

Second, there is *preliminary mapping*. Recurring behaviors always occur in the context of routines, the teacher's selected behaviors of concern included. This mapping is a first attempt to detail routines. This requires two activities. First, the teachers ask, "What happens when . . . ?"

That is, who typically does what before the behavior of concern occurs? And who else typically does what else while it occurs? And who typically does what after it occurs? This mapping primarily draws on the memory, jogged as needed and loosely checked by informal observation. Second, preliminary mapping includes provisionally designing and using an ethnographic schedule. Such a schedule permits the focused observation and recording of all behaviors sorted as categories of behavior, including those behaviors of concern, others not of concern that alternatively may occur at those moments, and still others that occur before and after — all of which are sorted into categories. It permits recording who does those things and in what sequence such that the stream of behavior is captured. Self-observation now requires an audio record, if that is sufficient, or a video record, if that is required. This depends on the verbal or nonverbal nature of the behaviors. These records are made during the appropriate events and phases in the events. This preliminary mapping reveals problems with the question as asked, more than indicating its answers.

Third, there is *closer identification of categories*. Routines are made up solely of categories that have already been negotiated, largely unawares, jointly by the teacher and students. These include categories of behavior, which are some array of objectively unique behaviors being treated alike in contrast to another array, for example, real questions as opposed to rhetorical questions, and include as well categories of person, for example teacher as opposed to student and also male as opposed to female, or high performers as opposed to low. The identification of such categories is inductive; the teacher compiles a small corpus of anecdotal records of brief interchanges germane to the behaviors of concern and to what happens before and after, each anecdote being written out in as much behavioral detail as possible. The teacher then does running comparisons of sameness and difference, one behavior with another and possibly another, one set of actors with the next, etc., seeking out a classification system that works. The classes are emically correct when regularity in the routines begins to be revealed.

Fourth there is the *mapping of the routines*. On the basis of all the above, guided especially by point three, the teacher now revises the preliminary mapping of the routines, which is now meant to serve as a descriptive hypothesis, revises the ethnographic schedule, and observes a small number of audio or video records of the appropriate phases and events. The data confirm or deny the existence of the routines as mapped.

The typical result is to reveal the initial behavior of concern, which is now some category of behavior by some category of person, imbedded in one routine, one interactive chain that, once initiated, regularly unfolds. If that behavior of concern was deemed "bad," that routine and not the isolated action is revealed as the problem. Typically, too, a coexisting parallel behavior, imbedded in a parallel routine is revealed, and this is potentially the solution.

Ethnography proper ends here. The teacher's choice, to act or not, requires other considerations, including considerations of personal and public values. If the teacher chooses to act, this requires identifying that information that is strategic and pointed, those of the teacher's own behaviors that, if altered, would promise to lower the frequency of occurrence of the problem routine and raise the frequency of the solution routine. To so act, however, is not to solve the problem, but rather, is only to open a tacit renegotiation, a longish series of transactions among all the involved persons, teacher with student and student with student. To chart the progress of that renegotiation requires periodic monitoring, using new audio or video records and the above ethnographic schedule.

It is fully evident, but can be mentioned that, among all the routines that may become revealed, those that most emphatically call for change are the side-by-side routines in which teachers enact relations of equivalence with some, nonequivalence with others. Here, as throughout, the hidden curriculum controls the manifest curriculum. And here, uniquely, the explicit purposes of the institution itself and the prevailing explicit goals of the society at large are visibly violated. In our experience, the teacher typically is among those most troubled by the fact of such violation when it is revealed.

Ethnographic self-observation may, in special circumstances, be complemented by procedures at the very center of ethnographic activities as they are typically pursued by anthropologists — the compiling of narrative accounts of events as they unfold, without prior commitment. This special circumstance has to do with the teacher's time and charge; insofar as a teacher has special diagnostic and policy-making duties and has reasonable amounts of time free from other preoccupations, he or she may begin ethnographic activity by compiling narrative accounts.

Compiling a narrative account requires three operations: (1) watching and listening, while compiling very cryptic notes; (2) transcribing those notes with all the detail possible, putting purely behavioral records (the narrative proper) in one column, and various inferences, questions, and other commentary in a second column; then editing the record so as to catch slips in the above sorting and to capture omissions from memory; (3) and then, occasionally, processing the record itself in a manner that reveals patterns of inadvertent habitual inattention to certain kinds of phenomena.

The principal purpose of the time-consuming effort of so compiling a narrative account is this. It is not unusual that the teacher comes to see the activities unfolding in one classroom or several in some quite new and unexpected way, comes to ask a fresh, even startling, question, and, asking it, finds an answer.

All this, I believe, reflects the sort of thing that can realistically and usefully be done by anthropologists and others in schools and in other places where the events called schooling regularly occur. Such persons can convey, to critical persons professionally involved, observation skills that will reveal critical information, lay bare the differences that make a difference in their places of professional work. This reflects, I also believe, the only kind of thing that can realistically be done by anthropologists with the hope of broad effect, following the guidance of the cultural theory of education and schooling, insofar as it may prove to be in its general thrust empirically correct.

POSTSCRIPT

I have long been preoccupied in these pages with the possibility of generating one theory, a cultural theory of education and schooling. The sense might easily be conveyed that this theoretical development would best proceed by working on the theory empirically. I think not, and perhaps will be indulged in entering here this counterclaim. This theoretical development will best proceed by working on interesting *questions,* guided by the reference model insofar as it is useful, modifying and extending it as far as is possible, or simply tossing it aside as may be necessary. One does not look at the world through the reference model described; one looks at the world and allows that reference model to help, insofar as it can.

Of all questions, probably the most critical are those about *Homo sapiens*, questions about our basic nature as a species, and our contrasts with other primate species. When questions are generated from this perspective, the reference model seems sometimes to serve well; sometimes, not as well. When it serves well, fine, but when it does not, perhaps this is even better.

This species evolved out of primate forebears. And throughout the latest phases of its evolutionary history, all its members on all continents lived in small communities by hunting and gathering. Out of that primate ancestry, and under the conditions of life in small, foraging societies, *Homo sapiens* became what we now are. It would surely follow that there can be no better substantive orientation to research pursuant to this theory, no better way to shape particular hypotheses so that they may embrace promisingly salient matters, than for the researchers to allow themselves to be guided by the available corpus of knowledge about the lives of nonhuman primates and of those contemporary humans who live in small foraging societies. John Herzog (1973) has well summarized much of this corpus of knowledge. We select and paraphrase:

1. *The critical education importance of play.* The young of all primate species spend enormous amounts of energy in play and grow up socially and physically retarded if deprived of play. Young humans in most foraging societies spend most of their time in play and imitative activities.

2. *The scope of activity of young.* Young primates and these young humans explore in detail virtually their total surroundings, both the natural world and the world of adult activity, the latter being done by watching the affairs of adults and imitating them.

3. *The overriding educational importance of age peers.* After infancy, young primates and young humans in foraging societies spend most of their time with each other and in the activities suggested above develop critical proficiencies, including facility with the signal system and/or language of the group.

4. *The educational importance of infrequent stress.* Some critical competences, principally fearful identifications of dangerous things and situations, emerge full-blown out of brief and stressful events, both for young primates and young humans in small foraging societies.

5. *The obverse of all the above, the relative small amount of time invested in instruction.* Adult primates and adult humans in foraging societies, though they have great amounts of free time, rarely undertake deliberately to teach their young; but the young do, nevertheless, learn.

The most fascinating of all research pursuant to this theory would be to discover whether the theory describes well and predicts and explains the events through which baboons educate baboons or wolves educate wolves or to discover in what specific ways it does not. (These animals engage in the kind of events called education, but perhaps not in the other kind called schooling.)

Cybernetics is an epistomology; it deals centrally with information, its flow and entailed constraints. Information, it is often said, is always about differences, pure relations. Imagine two human parties waving to each other at some distance. As one thinks about the sequence of codings and recodings by which information flows in this event, the information does, in fact, seem to be solely about contrasts: a differentiated reflecting surface (a hand and arm) and its motions; this body motion recoded as light waves; those waves impinging on visual receptors, themselves perpetually in miniscule scanning motion searching out contrasts, and recoded as neurological firings; these are recoded as muscular contractions, the second party's reflecting surface in motion, etc.

But if all that information is purely relational, what about language itself? One of the above parties might verbalize the exchange: "I see you are waving to me," which utterance seems to be additionally, perhaps principally, occupied with naming things (I, you, me) and naming actions as if they were things (see, waving). At best, the named "things" become foreground, while the relations they reflect (those contrasts, not-I, not-you, etc.) become background. If all that other, nonverbal information is, as seems probable, purely relational, then this verbal utterance, being principally about things, is not a very accurate recoding of all that. The utterance, this recoding, is a construction about, not a replica of, that other information, and distortion has been introduced.

Perhaps all linguistically formulated thought should be deemed glosses of all other processings of information. By extension, perhaps all linguistically thought information, which is then linguistically conveyed between persons, must be deemed glosses of those glosses. And by still further extension, any scientific discourse that deals with such verbal interchange as data and that is itself couched in language, would be glosses about those glosses of those glosses.

I am speculating that the human species shares with many other animals similar, nonlinguistic devices for processing many kinds of information, and that all that information is solely about differences, is purely relational, and that this human species is no doubt blessed and confounded as well with this additional channel for messaging called speech. Speech recodes information about relations into information principally about things. In interaction, speech generates the culturally recognized "things" that the information is now supposed to be about; and those of this species who try to think straight and talk clearly about these matters scientifically are even further victimized.

Addressing this theory to baboons and wolves might help draw into focus the purely relational nature of information in this context, and thus, by contrast help researchers see the special features of this fourth channel in human communication, linguistically channelled information, thereby gaining a truly fresh perspective on education and schooling in human contexts.

From all such empirical effort pursuant to this theory, there is one byproduct of some very general implication. The Western folk imagery that makes it seem that individuals are the atoms of social behavior, which makes processes inside their respective heads seem to be the proximate causes of their behaviors, is not empirically "false." The folk image is, however, a cultural fact of great power; it takes over. Thus, a researcher may not resist it a little with any effect; the researcher must, if at all, resist it totally. Otherwise, that image simply becomes the mother image that shapes and constrains all other images, however much one may try to think nonpsychologically.

Cultural and social anthropology provide a revealing example. In spite of all the early anthropological talk about the superorganic, the items of anthropological observation and lower-level analysis — habits, customs, perhaps traits, maps, codes, canons of choice, values, affective states — had, by some compulsion, to be located somewhere. That somewhere, by the power of that folk image, usually became the heads of the actors or, often the head of that construct, the omniscient informant.

I am simply observing that, from the vantage of a radically *inter*psychic position, cultural and social anthropology, past and present, frequently has the markings of second-rate, seat-of-the-pants psychology. Of course, one may by design embrace an intrapsychic stance, as some anthropologists have done with distinction. But, if not, then it is necessary to be aware that the folk image is powerful. Resisting it a little is, to use a hackneyed simile, like letting the camel get his nose under the tent.

Perhaps for such reasons, there has been but little systematic and dogged exploration, even in anthropology, of the power of other thinkable imageries. Whether this apposite effort — this radically interpsychic *cultural* theory of education and schooling — is interesting and seems possible, readers can judge from these pages. Whether the effort will prove fruitful, we shall all judge, later.

References

ARGYLE, MICHAEL
  1972 "Non-verbal communication in human social interaction," in *Non-verbal communication*. Edited by Robert Hinde. Cambridge: Cambridge University Press.
ARGYLE, MICHAEL, *editor*
  1973 *Social encounters*. Chicago: Aldine.
ARGYLE, MICHAEL, JANET DEAN
  1965 Eye contact, distance and affiliation. *Sociometry* 28.
BAJEMA, C.
  1971 *Natural selection in human populations: the measurement of ongoing genetic evolution in contemporary societies*. New York: John Wiley.
  1972 Transmission of information about the environment in the human species: a cybernetic view of genetic and cultural evolution. *Social Biology* 19:224–226.
  1973 "Differential transmission of genetic and cultural information about the environment: a cybernetic view of genetic and cultural (non-genetic) evolution in animal species." Paper presented at the IXth International Congress of Anthropological and Ethnological Sciences, Chicago, Ill.
BARKER, ROGER
  1963 *The stream of behavior*. New Jersey: Appleton-Century-Crofts.
BARKER, ROGER, L. BARKER
  1961 "Behavior units for comparative study of culture," in *Studying personality cross-culturally*. Edited by B. Kaplan. Evanston, Ill.: Row, Peterson.
BARKER, ROGER, H. WRIGHT
  1951 *One boy's day: a specific record of behavior*. New York: Harper.
  1955 *Midwest and its children: the psychological ecology of an American town*. Evanston, Ill.: Row, Peterson.
BARTH, FREDRIK
  1966 *Models of social organization*. Occasional Paper No. 23. London: Royal Anthropological Institute of Great Britain and Ireland.
  1972 Analytical dimensions in the comparison of social organizations. *American Anthropologist* 74:206–220.

BATESON, GREGORY
1935   Culture contact and schizomogenesis. *Man* 35:178–183.
1936   *Naven*. Cambridge: Cambridge University Press.
1941   The frustration-aggression hypothesis and culture. *Psychological Review* 48:350–355.
1942a Some systematic approaches to the study of culture and personality. *Culture and Personality* 11:76–84.
1942b "Social planning and the concept of deutero-learning," *Symposia, conference on science, philosophy and religion in their relation to the democratic way of life*, volume two.
1944   "Culture determinants of personality," in *Personality and behavior disorders*, volume 2. Edited by J. McV. Hunt, 714–735. New York: Ronald.
1955   "A theory of play and fantasy," in *American Psychological Association Psychiatric Research Reports*, volume 2. Washington, D.C.: American Psychological Association.
1958   "Epilogue 1958," in *Naven* (second edition). Stanford, California: Stanford University Press.
1967   Cybernetic explanation. *American Behavioral Scientist* 10 (8).
1968   "Redundancy and coding," in *Animal communication: techniques of study and results of research*. Edited by Thomas A. Sebeok. Bloomington: Indiana University Press.
1972   *Steps to an ecology of mind*. New York: Ballantine Books.
BATESON, G., R. L. BIRDWHISTELL, N. W. BROSIN, C. F. HOCKETT, N. A. McQUOWN
1971   Microfilm collection of manuscripts on cultural anthropology. Series XV, nos. 95, 96, 97, 98. Chicago, Ill.: University of Chicago, Joseph Regenstein Library.
BATESON, GREGORY, JURGEN RUESCH
1968   *Communication: the social matrix of psychiatry*. New York: W. W. Norton.
BATY, R. M.
1972   *Reeducating teachers for cultural awareness: preparation for educating Mexican-American children in Northern California*. New York: Praeger.
BENEDICT, R.
1934   *Patterns of culture*. Boston: Houghton Mifflin.
BERLIN, B.
1968   *Basic color terms: their universality and evolution*. Berkeley, Calif.: University of California Press.
BERLIN, B., D. BREEDLOVE, P. RAVEN
1968   Covert categories and folk taxonomies. *American Anthropologist* 70:290–299.
BERNSTEIN, BASIL
1964   Elaborated and restricted codes: their social origins and some consequences. *American Anthropologist* 66:55–59.
BERREMAN, G. D.
1972   Social categories and social interaction in urban India. *American Anthropologist* 74.
BIRDWHISTELL, RAY
1952   *Introduction to kinesics: an annotation system for analysis of body motion and gesture*. Washington, D.C.: State Dept. Foreign Service Institute.

1970   *Kinesics and context.* Philadelphia: University of Pennsylvania Press.
BLACK, M., D. METZGER
1969   "Ethnographic description and the study of law," in *Cognitive anthropology.* Edited by S. Tyler. New York: Holt, Rinehart and Winston.
BOHANNAN, PAUL
1973   Rethinking culture. *Current Anthropology* 14 (4):357–362.
BRIGHT, JANE, WILLIAM BRIGHT
1969   "Semantic structures in Northwestern California and the Sapir-Whorf hypothesis," in *Cognitive anthropology.* Edited by Stephen Tyler. New York: Holt, Rinehart and Winston.
BRIM, O.
1968   "Socialization: adult socialization," in *International encyclopedia of the social sciences.* Edited by D. S. Sills. New York: Macmillan.
BROPHY, J. E., T. L. GOOD
1970   Teachers communication of differential expectations for children's classroom performance. *Journal of Educational Psychology* 61:365–374.
1974   *Teacher-student relationships: causes and consequences.* New York: Holt, Rinehart and Winston.
BROWN, R.
1974   *A first language.* Cambridge, Mass.: Harvard University Press.
BROWN, ROGER, ERIC LENNEBERG
1954   A study in language and cognition. *Journal of Abnormal and Social Psychology* 49:454–462.
BURNETT, JACQUETTA
1969   Ceremony, rites, and economy in the student system of an American high school. *Human Organization* 28:1–10.
1972   "Event analysis as a methodology for urban anthropology," in *Final report: cultural and structural determinants of occupational and educational problems of young Puerto Ricans in Chicago.* Urbana: Bureau of Education Research, University of Illinois.
BURTON, R.
1968   "Socialization: psychological aspects," in *International encyclopedia of the social sciences.* Edited by D. S. Sills. New York: Macmillan.
BYERS, PAUL
n.d.   "From biological rhythm to cultural pattern: a study of minimal units." Unpublished dissertation, Columbia University.
BYERS, PAUL, HAPPY BYERS
1972   "Non-verbal communication and the education of children," in *Functions of language in the classroom.* Edited by C. Cazden et al. New York: Columbia Teachers College Press.
CARROLL, THOMAS G.
1975   Structures of censorship, usually inadvertent: studies in a cultural theory of education. *Council on Anthropology and Education Quarterly* 6(2).
1976   "Work and play: a cognitive probe of the development of adult and child activity categories." Unpublished Ph. D. dissertation, SUNY at Buffalo.
CAZDEN, C.
1970   The situation: a neglected source of social class differences in language use. *Journal of Social Issues* 26:35–60.

234   *References*

CAZDEN, C., D. HYMES, VERA JOHNS
1971   *The function of language in the classroom.* New York: Columbia Teachers College Press.
CHAPMAN, S. CROSBY, GEORGE COUNTS
1924   "Why the school was established," in *Principles of education.* Boston: Houghton Mifflin
CHAPPLE, ELIOT
1970   *Culture and biological man.* New York: Holt, Rinehart and Winston.
CHAPPLE, ELIOT, CARELTON COON
1942   *Principles of anthropology.* New York: Holt.
CHILD, I.
1954   "Socialization," in *Handbook of social psychology.* Edited by G. Lindzey. Cambridge, Mass.: Addison-Wesley.
CHOMSKY, NOAM
1957   *Syntactic structures.* The Hague: Mouton.
1959   "Review of Skinner's verbal behavior," in *Readings in the psychology of language.* Edited by L. Jakobovits and M. Miron. Englewood Cliffs, N.J.: Prentice-Hall.
1963a "Formal properties of grammars," in *Handbook of mathematical psychology.* Edited by R. D. Luce and E. Galanter. New York: John Wiley.
1963b "Introduction to the formal analysis of natural languages," in *Handbook of mathematical psychology.* Edited by R. D. Luce and E. Galanter. New York: John Wiley.
1963c "Finitary models of language users," in *Handbook of mathematical psychology.* Edited by R. D. Luce and E. Galanter. New York: John Wiley.
1965   *Aspects of the theory of syntax.* Cambridge, Mass.: MIT Press.
1968   *Language and mind.* New York: Harcourt, Brace, Jovanovich.
1978   *Topics in the theory of generative grammar.* The Hague: Mouton.
CICOUREL, AARON V.
1972   "Basic and normative rules in the negotiation of status and role," in *Studies in social interaction.* Edited by David Sudnow. New York: The Free Press.
1973   *Cognitive sociology.* Glencoe, Ill.: The Free Press.
CLAUSEN, J.
1968   *Socialization and society.* Boston: Little, Brown.
COHEN, ROSALIE A.
1969   Conceptual styles, culture conflict, and nonverbal tests of intelligence. *American Anthropologist* 71:828–856.
COHEN, YEHUDI
1971   "The shaping of men's minds," in *Anthropological perspectives on education.* Edited by Murry Wax, Stanley Diamond and Fred Gearing. New York: Basic Books.
COLE, M., J. GAY
1972   Culture and memory. *American Anthropologist* 74:1066–1084.
COLE, MICHAEL, JOHN GAY, JOSEPH GLICK, DONALD SHARP
1971   *The cultural context of learning and thinking.* New York: Basic Books.
CONDON, W. S.
1968   Speech and body motion synchrony of the speaker-hearer. Pittsburgh, Pa.: Western Psychiatric Institute.

1970 Method of micro-analysis of sound films of behavior. *Behavior Research Methods and Instruments* 2:51–54.

CONDON, W. S., W. D. OGSTON
1966 Sound film analysis of normal and pathological behavior patterns. *Journal of Nervous and Mental Disease.* 143:338–347.
1967 A segmentation of behavior. *Journal of Psychiatric Research* 5: 221–235.

CONDON, W. S., L. W. SANDER
1974 Neonate movement is synchronized with adult speech: interactional participation and language acquisition. *Science* 183:99–101.

CONKLIN, H. C.
1955 Hanunoo color categories. *South-west Journal of Anthropology* 11 (4):339–344.

CRYSTAL, D.
1969 *Prosodic systems and intonation in English.* London: Cambridge University Press.

DANZIGER, K.
1970 *Readings in child socialization.* Oxford: Pergamon.

DUNCAN, S. D.
1972 Some signals and rules for taking speaking turns in conversations. *Journal of Personality and Social Psychology* 23:283–292.
1973a "Language, paralanguage and body motion in the structure of conversations." Paper presented at the IXth International Congress of Anthropological and Ethnological Sciences, Chicago, 1973.
1973b Toward a grammar for dyadic conversation. *Semiotica* 9:29–46.
1974 "On the structure of speaker-auditor interaction during speaking turns," in *Language in society.*

EKMAN, P., W. V. FRIESEN
1969 The repertoire of nonverbal behavior: categories, origins, usage, and coding. *Semiotica* 1:49–98.

ELKIN, F.
1960 *The child and society: the process of socialization.* New York: Random House.

ELKIN, F., G. HANDEL
1972 *The child and society.* New York: Random House.

EPSTEIN, E. H.
1971 Education and Peruanidad: internal colonialism in the Peruvian Highlands. *Comparative Educational Review* 15:188–201.

ERICKSON, FREDERICK
1973 *Inter-ethnic relations in urban institutional settings.* Final Technical Report, Center for Studies of Metropolitan Problems, NIMH MH 18230 and MH 21460.
n.d. Film and conference paper presented at the University Council in Educational Administration Conference, Buffalo, N. Y., April, 1973.
1974 "Gatekeeping encounters: a social selection process," in *Anthropology and public policy.* Edited by Peggy R. Sanday. New York: Academic Press.
1975 Gatekeeping and the melting pot: interaction in counselling encounters. *Harvard Education Review* 45 (1):44–70.

ERICKSON, FREDERICK, JEFFREY J. SHULTZ
i.p. *Talking to the man: social and cultural organization of communication in school counselling interviews.* New York: Academic Press.

EVANS-PRITCHARD, E. E.
1940   *The Nuer.* Oxford: Oxford University Press.
FINN, J. D.
1972   Expectations and the educational environment. *Review of Educational Research* 42:387–410.
FIRTH, RAYMOND T.
1964   "Social organization and social change," in *Essays on social organization and values.* Edited by R. Firth. London: Athlone Press.
FISCHER, J., A. FISCHER
1966   *The New Englanders of Orchard Town, U.S.A.* New York: John Wiley.
FORTES, M.
1938   Social and psychological aspects of education in Taleland. *Africa* (4):supplement.
FRAKE, CHARLES
1961   The diagnosis of disease among the Subanum of Mindanao. *American Anthropologist* 63:113–132.
FREEMAN, D.
1970   "Human nature and culture," in *Man and the new biology.* Canberra: Australian National University Press.
FRIEDRICH, P.
1972   "Social context and semantic feature: the Russian pronominal usage," in *Directions in socio-linguistics.* Edited by J. J. Gumperz and D. Hymes, 270–300. New York: Holt, Rinehart and Winston.
GAY, J., M. COLE
1967   *The new mathematics and an old culture.* New York: Holt, Rinehart and Winston.
GEARING, FREDERICK
1962   Priests and warriors. *American Anthropologist* 64(5).
1970   *The face of the fox.* Chicago: Aldine.
1973   "Where we are and where we might go: steps toward a general theory of cultural transmission." Council on Anthropology and Education Newsletter 4:(1).
1974   "Anthropology and education," in *Handbook of social and cultural anthropology.* Edited by John J. Honigmann. Chicago: Rand McNally.
GEARING, F., R. McC. NETTING, L. R. PEATTIE, editors
1960   *Documentary history of the Fox Project.* Chicago: Department of Anthropology, University of Chicago.
GEARING, FREDERICK, ALLAN TINDALL
1973   Anthropological studies of the educational process. *Annual Review of Anthropology* 2.
GEARING, FREDERICK, ALLAN TINDALL, ALLEN SMITH, THOMAS CARROLL
1975   Structures of censorship, usually inadvertent: studies in a cultural theory of education. *Council on Anthropology and Education Quarterly* 6(2).
GEARING, FREDERICK, WAYNE HUGHES, THOMAS CARROLL, WALTER PRECOURT, ALLEN SMITH
1975   "On observing well: self-instruction in ethnographic observation for teachers, principals, and supervisors." Buffalo: Department of Anthropology, SUNY at Buffalo.
GEERTZ, C.
1968   "Linguistic etiquette," in *Readings in the sociology of language.* Edited by J. A. Fishman. The Hague: Mouton.

GLADWIN, THOMAS
  1970   *East is a big bird*. Cambridge, Mass.: Harvard University Press.
GLASER, BARNEY G., ANSELM L. STRAUSS
  1967   *The discovery of grounded theory: strategies for qualitative research*.
         Chicago: Aldine.
GOFFMAN, E.
  1957   "Alienation from interaction." *Human Relations* 10:47–60.
  1959   *The presentation of self in everyday life*. Garden City, N. Y.: Anchor.
  1961a *Asylums*. Chicago: Aldine.
  1961b *Encounters*. Indianapolis: Bobbs-Merrill.
  1963   *Behavior in public places*. New York: The Free Press.
  1964   The neglected situation. *American Anthropologist* 66(2).
  1967   *Interaction ritual*. Garden City, N. Y.: Anchor.
  1971   *Relations in public*. New York: Basic Books.
GOLDSCHMIDT, WALTER
  1972   An ethnography of encounters: a methodology for the enquiry into the
         relation between the individual and society. *Current Anthropology*
         13(1):59–78.
GOODENOUGH, WARD
  1951   *Property, kin, and community on Truk*. New Haven: Yale University
         Publication in Anthropology No. 46. New York: Anchor.
  1965   Yankee kinship terminology: a problem in componential analysis.
         American Anthropologist 67 (5), Part 2.
  1969   "Rethinking status and role," in *The relevance of models in social
         anthropology*. Edited by M. Banton. London: Tavistock Publications.
  1970   *Description and comparison in cultural anthropology*. Chicago;
         Aldine.
GOODMAN, G.
  1971   "Man's place in the phylogeny of the primates as reflected in serum
         proteins," in *Classification and human evolution*. Edited by S. Wash-
         burn, 204–234. Chicago: Aldine:
GOSLIN, D., *editor*
  1969   *Handbook of socialization theory and research*. Chicago: Rand
         McNally.
GOULDNER, ALVIN W.
  1959   "Reciprocity and autonomy in functional theory," in *Symposium on
         sociological theory*. Edited by L. Gross. New York: Harper and Row.
GOULDNER, HELEN
  1971   "The natural history of the black child in the city." Final report OE
         6–2771, Washington, D.C.: US Office of Education.
GREENBERG, E.
  1970   *Political socialization*. New York: Atherton.
GREENSTEIN, F.
  1968   "Socialization: political socialization," in *International encyclopedia
         of the social sciences*. Edited by D. S. Sills, 551–555. New York:
         Macmillan.
GRINDAL, B. T.
  1972   *Growing up in two worlds: education and transition among the Sisala of
         Northern Ghana*. New York: Holt, Rinehart and Winston.
GUMPERZ, JOHN J.
  1969   "Social differences in verbal strategies." Paper presented at the Ameri-
         can Anthropological Association, New Orleans.

HALE, KENNETH
1973   "Deep-surface canonical disparities in relation to analysis and change: an Australian example." CTL 11. 401–458.
HALL, E. T.
1959   *The silent language.* Garden City, N. Y.: Doubleday.
1966   *The hidden dimension.* Garden City, N. Y.: Doubleday.
HALLOWELL, A. I.
1964   "Ojibwa ontology, behavior, and world view," in *Primitive views of the world.* Edited by S. Diamond. New York: Columbia Paperbacks.
HANDELMAN, D.
1973a   "Components of interaction in the negotiation of a definition of the situation." Paper presented at the IXth International Congress of Anthropological and Ethnological Sciences, Chicago, Illinois.
1973b   Gossip in encounters: the transmission of information in bounded social settings. *Man* 8(2):210–227.
HAYEK, F. A.
1942–1944   Scientism and the study of society. *Economica* 9:267–291; 10:34–63; 11:27–39.
HEIDER, ELEANOR P.
n.d.   "Universals and cultural specifics in human categorization." Unpublished paper presented at Conference on the Interface Between Culture and Learning. Honolulu, Hawaii: East-West Center.
HENRY, JULES
1955   "Culture, education and communication theory," in *Education and anthropology.* Edited by G. D. Spindler. Stanford, Ca.: Stanford University Press.
1957   "Attitude organization in elementary school classrooms," in *American Journal of Orthopsychiatry* 27:117–133.
1959   The problems of spontaneity, initiative, and creativity in suburban classrooms. *American Journal of Orthopsychiatry* 29:266–279.
1960   "A cross-cultural outline of education," in *Current Anthropology* 1: 267–305.
HERSKOVITS, M. J.
1947   *Man and his works.* New York.: Knopf.
HERZOG, JOHN D.
1962   Deliberate instruction and household structure: a cross-cultural study. *Harvard Educational Review* 32 (3):301–342.
1973   "Ethnology, natural childhood, and intentional socialization." Paper presented at the annual meeting of American Anthropological Association. New Orleans.
HILGER, M.
1960   *Field guide to the ethnological study of child life.* New Haven: Human Relations Area Files.
HOMANS, GEORGE
1950   "Norms and behavior," in *Role theory: concepts and research.* Edited by B. S. Biddle and E. J. Thomas. New York.: John Wiley.
1952   "Bringing men back in." Presidential address, American Sociological Association.
HOSTETLER, J. A., G. E. HUNTINGTON
1971   *Children in Amish society: socialization and community acculturation.* New York: Holt, Rinehart and Winston.

HOWARD, ALAN
  1970 *Learning to be Rotuman: enculturation in the South Pacific.* New York: Teachers College Press.
HSU, FRANCIS L. K.
  1961 "Kinship and ways of life," in *Psychological Anthropology.* Edited by Francis L. K. Hsu, 400–456. Homewood, Ill.: Dorsey Press.
  1961 *Psychological anthropology.* Edited by Francis L. K. Hsu. Homewood, Ill. Dorsey Press.
IBERALL, A. S.
  1972 *Toward a general science of viable systems.* New York.: McGraw Hill.
JOOS, M.
  1968 "The isolation of styles," in *Readings in the sociology of language.* Edited by J. Fishman. The Hague: Mouton.
KAPLAN, D., R. MANNERS
  1972 *Culture theory.* Englewood Cliffs, N. J.: Prentice Hall.
KATZ, FRED
  1968 *Autonomy and organization.* New York.: Random.
KEIFER, C. W.
  1970 The psychological interdependence of family, school and bureaucracy in Japan. *American Anthropologist* 72:66–75.
KENDON, ADAM
  1967 Some functions of gaze direction in social interaction. *Acta Psychologica* 26:22–63.
  1970 Movement coordination in social interaction: some examples described. *Acta Psychologica* 32:100–125.
  1972a "Some relationships between body motion and speech," in *Studies in dyadic communication.* Edited by A. Seigman and B. Pope. Elmsford, N. Y.: Pergamon Press.
  1972b Review of R. L. Birdwhistell's *Kinesics and context. American Journal of Psychology* 85:441–455.
  1973 Paper presented at the annual meeting of American Anthropological Association, New Orleans.
  1975 Some functions of the face in a kissing round. *Semiotica* 15(4): 99–334.
  1977 *Studies in the behavior of social interaction.* Studies in Semiotics 6 Bloomington: Indiana University.
  i.p. "The facing formation system: spatial organization in social encounters," in *Human territoriality.* Edited by A. E. Scheflen. Garden City, N. Y.: Doubleday.
KENDON, ADAM, ANDREW FERBER
  1973 "A description of some human greetings," in *Comparative ecology and behavior of primates.* Edited by R. P. Michael and K. J. H. Crook, London: Academic.
KENDON, A., R. M. HARRIS, M. R. KEY, *editors*
  1975 *The organization of behavior in face-to-face interaction.* The Hague: Mouton.
KING, A. RICHARD
  1967 *The school at Mopass: a problem of identity.* New York: Holt, Rinehart and Winston.
KING, G.
  1971 "The use of living species in the reconstruction of hominid behavioral evolution." Unpublished Ph.D. dissertation, University of California, Berkeley.

KLUCKHOHN, C.
1939   Theoretical bases of an empirical method of studying the acquisition of culture by individuals. *Man* 39:98–103.
1941   "Patterning as exemplified in Navaho Culture," in *Language, culture and personality: essays in memory of Edward Sapir*. Edited by L. Spier, A. I. Hallowell, and S. Newman. Menasha, Wisconsin: The Sapir Memorial Fund.
1947   Some aspects of Navaho infancy and early childhood. *Psychoanalysis and the Social Sciences* 1:37–86.

KOCHMAN, THOMAS
1973   *"Orality* and *literacy* as factors of 'black' and 'white' communicative behaviors." Paper presented at the annual meeting of American Anthropological Association, New Orleans.

KOESTLER, ARTHUR
1967   *The ghost in the machine*. New York: Macmillan.

KOHNE, R.
1970   Evolution of higher organism DNA. *Quarterly Review of Biophysics* 3:327–375.

KROEBER, A., C. KLUCKHOHN
1952   *Culture: a critical review of concepts and definitions*. Papers of the Peabody Museum of American Archaeology and Ethnology, Harvard University, 48(1).

KUHN, THOMAS
1962   *The structure of scientific revolutions*, Chicago: University of Chicago Press.

LABOV, WILLIAM
1968   *A study of the non-standard English of Negro and Puerto Rican speakers in New York City*. Final Report, Cooperative Research Project No. 3288. Washington, D.C.: US Office of Education.
1973   "The social setting of linguistic change," *Diachronic, areal, and typological linguistics*. Edited by H. N. Hoenigswald and R. E. Longacre, 195–251. The Hague: Mouton.

LACEY, C.
1973   "Some sociological concomitants of academic streaming in a grammar school," in *Cultural relevance and educational issues*. Edited by F. A. S. Ianni and E. Storey. New York: Little, Brown.

LEACOCK, E. B.
1971   "Theoretical and methodological problems in the study of schools," in *Anthropological perspectives on education*, 169–179. New York: Basic.

LEE, DOROTHY
1949   Being and value in a primitive culture. *Journal of Philosophy* 46(13).

LEIS, E. B.
1971   *Enculturation and socialization in an Ijaw village*. New York: Holt, Rinehart and Winston.

LEONARD-DOLAN, CAROLYN
1972   "A method for film analysis of ethnic communication style." Paper delivered at the annual meeting of the Society for Applied Anthropology, Montreal, Canada.

LeVINE, R.
1963   "Culture and personality," in *Biennial review of anthropology*. Edited by B. Siegel and A. Beals, 107–145. Stanford, California: Stanford University Press.

1969 "Culture, personality and socialization: an evolutionary point of view," in *Handbook of socialization on theory and research*. Edited by D. A. Goslin, 509–541. Chicago: Rand McNally.
1973 *Culture, behavior and personality*. Chicago: Aldine.

LeVINE, R., B. LeVINE
1966 *Nyansongo: a Gusii community in Kenya*. New York: John Wiley.

LINDQUIST, H. M.
1971 "World bibliography of anthropology and education with annotations," in *Anthropological perspectives on education*, 307–384. New York: Basic.

LOUNSBURY, FLOYD
1964 "A formal account of the Crow and Omaha-type kinship terminology," in *Explorations in cultural anthropology*. Edited by Ward Goodenough. New York: McGraw Hill.

LYONS, JOHN
1968 *Introduction to theoretical linguistics*. London and New York: Cambridge University Press.

MARETZKI, T., H. MARETZKI
1966 *Taira: An Okinawan village*. New York: John Wiley.

MATHIOT, M.
n.d. "Informational structure versus syntactic structure: segmentation criteria." Proceedings of the Symposium on Structures and Genres of Ethnic Literature, Palermo, Italy.

MAUSS, MARCEL
1954 *The gift*. (Translated by I. Cunnison.). Glencoe, Ill.: The Free Press.

MAYER, P., editor
1970 *Socialization: the approach from social anthropology*. London: Tavistock.

McNEIL, E.
1969 *Human socialization*. Belmont, Ca.: Brooks Cole.

McQUOWN, N. A.
1971a "Natural history method — a frontier method," in *Creative developments in psychotherapy*, volume one. Edited by Alvin R. Maher and Leonard Pearson. Cleveland: The Press of Case Western Reserve University.

McQUOWN, N. A., editor
1971b *The natural history of an interview*. Chicago: University of Chicago Library.

MEAD, M.
1928a *Coming of age in Samoa*. New York: Morrow.
1928b The role of the individual in Samoan culture. *Journal of the Royal Anthropological Institute of Great Britain and Ireland* 58:481–495.
1930a An ethnologist's footnote to totem and taboo. *Psychoanalytic Review* 17:297–304.
1930b *Growing up in New Guinea*. New York: Morrow.
1932 An investigation of the thought of primitive children with special reference to animism. *Journal of the Royal Anthropological Institute of Great Britain and Ireland* 62:173–190.
1935 *Sex and temperament in three primitive societies*. New York: Morrow.
1963 Socialization and enculturation. *Current Anthropology* 4:184–188.
1970 *Culture and commitment*. New York: Natural History.

1972   "Foreword," in *Introduction to socialization: human culture transmitted*. Edited by T. R. Williams, ix–xi. St. Louis: Mosby.

MEAD, MARGARET, editor
1937   *Cooperation and competition among primitive peoples*. New York: McGraw-Hill.

MERTON, ROBERT K.
1958   *Social theory and social structure*. Glencoe, Ill.: The Free Press.

METZGER, D., G. WILLIAMS
1966   Some procedures and results in the study of native categories: Tzeltal firewood. *American Anthropologist* 68:389–407.

MINTURN, L., J. HITCHCOCK
1966   *The Rājpūts of Khalapur, India*. New York: John Wiley.

MILLER, G. A., E. GALANTER., K. H. PRIBRAN
1960   *Plans and the structure of behavior*. New York: Holt, Rinehart and Winston.

MYERHOFF, BARBARA G.
1971   "Organization and ecstasy." Paper presented at the annual meeting of American Anthropological Association, New York.

NASH, M.
1972   Ethnicity, centrality and education in Pasir, Mas, Kelantan. *Comparative Educational Review*. 16:4–15.

NEEDLEMAN, JACOB
1963   "Systematic exploration and the science of psychoanalysis," in *Being in the world, selected papers of Ludwig Binswanger*. Edited by Jacob Needleman, New York: Basic.

NYDEGGER, W., C. NYDEGGER
1966   *Tarong: An Ilocos barrio in the Philippines*. New York: John Wiley.

OHNUKI-TIERNEY, EMIKU
1972   Spatial concepts of the Ainu of the Northwest Coast of Southern Sakhalin. *American Anthropologist*. 74:3.

PARSONS, THEODORE W.
1965   "Ethnic cleavage in a California school." Unpublished Ph.D. dissertation, Stanford University.

PASHKIN, A.
1972   *Kanuri school children: education and social mobilization in Nigeria*. New York: Holt, Rinehart and Winston.

PAULSTON, R. G.
1972a   Cultural revitalization and educational change in Cuba. *Comparative Educational Review* 16:474–485.

PAULSTON, R. G., editor
1972b   *Non-formal education: an annotated international bibliography*. New York: Praeger Special Studies.

PHILIPS, S. V.
1972   "Participant structures and communicative competence: Warm Springs children in community and classroom," in *Functions of language in the classroom*. Edited by C. B. Cazden, V. P. John, and D. Hymes. New York: Teachers College Press.

PIESTRUP, ANNE McC.
n.d.   "Black dialect interference and accommodation of reading instruction in first grade." Monograph IV. Berkeley: Language-Behavior Research Laboratory, University of California.

POWERS, W. T.
1974 *Behavior: the control of perception*. Chicago: Aldine.
PRECOURT, W.
1974 "Initiation ceremonies and secret societies as educational institutions: a cross-cultural study," in *Cross-cultural perspective on learning*. Edited by R. Brislin, S. Bochner, W. Lonner. Beverly Hills, Ca.: Sage Publication.
PROST, JACK
1967 Bipedalism of man and gibbon compared using estimates of joint motion. *American Journal of Physical Anthropology* 26.
PROVENCHER, R.
1972 "Comparison of social interaction styles: urban and rural Malay culture," in *The anthropology of urban environments*. Edited by Thomas Weaver and Douglas White. The Society for Applied Anthropology Monograph 11.
RATTRAY, R. S.
1932 "The education of girls," in *The tribes of hinterland*. Oxford: Clarendon Press.
RINNERT, CAROL
1973 "Different kinds of 'kinds of' in American English." Paper presented at the annual meeting of the American Anthropological Association, New Orleans.
RIST, RAY C.
1970 Student social class and teacher expectation: the self-fulfilling prophecy in ghetto education. *Harvard Educational Review* 40:411–451.
ROMNEY, K., R. ROMNEY
1966 *The Mixtecans of Juxtlahuaca, Mexico*. New York: John Wiley.
ROSENFELD, G.
1971 "Shut those thick lips!" *A study of slum school failure*. New York: Holt, Rinehart and Winston.
ROSENSTIEL, A.
1971 "The changing focus of native education in Alaska." *Arctic and Alpine Research* 3:187–197.
ROSENTHAL, R., L. JACOBSON
1968 *Pygmalion in the classroom*. New York: Holt, Rinehart and Winston.
SACHS, HARVEY
n.d. Unpublished lectures.
SACHS, H., E. A. SCHEGLOFF, G. JEFFERSON
1974 A simplest systematics for the organization of turn taking for conversation. *Language* 50:696–735.
SANKOFF, GILLIAN
1971 Quantitative analysis of sharing and variability in a cognitive model. *Ethnology* 10 (1):389–408.
1972 Cognitive variability and New Guinea social organization: the Buang Dgwa. *American Anthropologist* 74:555–566.
SARICH, V.
1970 "Primate systematics with special reference to Old World monkeys," in *Old World monkeys*. Edited by S. Napier and P. Napier, 175–226. New York: Academic Press.
SCHEFLEN, ALBERT E.
1964 The significance of posture in communication systems. *Psychiatry* 27: 316–331.

1966   "Natural history method in psychotherapy: communicational research," in *Methods of research in psychotherapy*. Edited by L. A. Gottschalk and A. H. Auerbach, 263–289. New York: Appleton-Century-Crofts. (Reprinted in *Creative developments in psychotherapy*. Edited by A. R. Mahrer and L. Pearson. Cleveland: The Press of Case Western Reserve University, 1971.)

1968   Human communication: behavioral programs and their integration in interaction. *Behavioral Science* 13:44–55.

1973   *Communicational structure: analysis of a psychotherapy transaction.* Bloomington: Indiana University Press.

SCHEGLOFF, EMANUEL
1968   Sequencing in conversational openings. *American Anthropologist* 70(6):1075–1095.

SCHEGLOFF, E., H. SACHS
1973   Opening up closings. *Semiotica* 8:289–327.

SCRIBNER, S., M. COLE
1973   Cognitive consequences of formal and informal education. *Science* 182:553–559.

SHIMAHARA, N.
1970   Enculturation — a reconsideration. *Current Anthropology* 11:143–154.

1971   *Burakumin: a Japanese minority and education.* The Hague: Martinus Nijhoff.

SHULTZ, JEFFREY
1974   "The search for co-membership: an analysis of conversations among strangers." Unpublished Ph.D. dissertation, Harvard Graduate School of Education.

SINDELL, P. S.
1969   Anthropological approaches to the study of education. *Review of Educational Research* 39:593–605.

SINGLETON, JOHN
1967   *Nichu: a Japanese school.* New York: Holt, Rinehart and Winston.

SLOBIN, D. I.
1971   *Psycholinguistics.* Glenview, Ill.: Scott, Foresman.

SMITH, ALLEN
1976   Structures of censorship, usually inadvertent: studies in a cultural theory of education. *Council on Anthropology and Education Quarterly* 6(2).

SMITH, HENRY L.
1956   *Linguistic science and the teaching of English.* Cambridge: Harvard University Press.

SOSKIN, W. F., VERA P. JOHN.
1963   "The study of spontaneous talk," in *The stream of behavior*. Edited by Barker. New York: Appleton-Century-Crofts.

SPINDLER, G. D., *editor*
1963   *Education and culture.* New York: Holt, Rinehart and Winston.

SPRADLEY, JAMES, DAVID W. McCURDY
1972   *The cultural experience: ethnography in complex society.* Chicago: Science Research Associates.

STEWARD, J. H.
1951   *Theory of culture change: the methodology of multilinear evolution.* Urbana: University of Illinois Press.

SULLIVAN, HARRY STACK
1940   *Conceptions of modern psychiatry.* New York: W. W. Norton.
TALBERT, CAROL
1970   Interaction and adaption in two Negro kindergartens. *Human Organization* 29:103–114.
1973   "Anthropological research models," in *Research in the teaching of English.* Official Bulletin of the National Council of Teachers of English 7(2):190–211.
TAX, S.
1952   Action anthropology. *America Indigena.*
THOMAS, R. K., A. L. WAHRHAFTIG
1971   "Indians, hillbillies, and the education problem," in *Anthropological perspectives on education.* Edited by M. L. Wax, S. Diamond, and F. O. Gearing, 230–251. New York: Basic.
TINDALL, B. ALLAN
1972   "Organizing physical education for change: an anthropological perspective." Unpublished manuscript.
1973   "The hidden curriculum in sport." Paper presented at the North Eastern Anthropological Association meetings. Burlington, Vt.
1975   Explorations of a troublesome agenda based on the non-sharing of property-like information. *Council on Anthropology and Education Quarterly* 6(2).
TOPFER, SIGRID
1974   "Social identity categories in an American classroom." Unpublished Ph.D. dissertation.
TRAGER, G. L.
1964   Paralanguage: a first approximation. *Studies in Linguistics* 13:1–12.
TRIPP, SUSAN
1969   *On sociolinguistic rules: alternation and concurrence in directions in sociolinguistics.* Edited by D. Hymes and J. J. Gumperz. New York: Holt, Rinehart and Winston.
TSCHOPIK, H.
1938   Taboo as a possible factor involved in the obsolescence of Navaho pottery and basketry. *American Anthropologist* 40:257–262.
TURNER, TERENCE
1973   Piaget's structuralism. *American Anthropologist* 75(2):251–373.
1974   "Structure, system and semantics: a reformation of the general structural properties of kinship systems and terminologies." Paper presented at the Conference on Culture and Cognition, Geneseo, New York.
TURNER, VICTOR
n.d.   "Liminality: play, flow, and ritual: an essay in comparative symbology." Unpublished paper.
1969   *The ritual process: structure and anti-structure.* Chicago: Aldine.
UNDERHILL, RUTH
1936   *Autobiography of a Papago woman.* Washington, D.C.: American Anthropological Association.
VALENTINE, C. A.
1971   Deficit, difference, and bicultural models of Afro-American behavior. *Harvard Educational Review*, 41:137–151.
VAN GENNEP, ARNOLD
1960   *The rites of passage.* (Originally published in 1908. Translated by

Monica Vizedom and Gabrielle L. Chaffee.) Chicago: Chicago University Press.
WALLACE, A. F. C.
1970   *Culture and personality* (second edition). New York: Random.
WARD, M. C.
1971   *Them children: a study in language learning.* New York: Holt, Rinehart and Winston.
WARREN, RICHARD L.
1967   *Education in Rebhausen.* New York: Holt, Rinehart and Winston.
WASHBURN, S.
1972a Evolution of human behavior. *Social Biology* 19:163–170.
1972b "Primate studies and human evolution," in *Primate Studies in Biomedical Research.* Edited by G. Bourne. New York: Academic Press.
WATZLAWICK, P.
1967   *Pragmatics of human communication.* New York: W. W. Norton.
WAX, MURRAY L., ROSALIE H. WAX, ROBERT V. DUMONT, Jr.
1964   "Formal education in an American Indian community." Society for the Study of Social Problems Monograph 1. Kalamazoo, Mich.: The Society for the Study of Social Problems.
WEAVER, THOMAS, DOUGLAS WHITE
1972   "Anthropological approaches to urban and complex societies," in *The Anthropology of urban environments.* The Society for Applied Anthropology Monograph 11. Washington, D.C.: Society for Applied Anthropology.
WEISS, PAUL
1958   *Modes of being.* Carbondale, Ill.: University of Illinois Press.
WHITING, J.
1968   "Socialization: anthropological aspects," in *International encyclopedia of the social sciences.* Edited by D. S. Sills. New York: Macmillan.
WHITING, J., I. CHILD
1953   *Child training and personality.* New Haven: Yale University Press.
WHITING, J., I. CHILD, W. LAMBERT
1966   *Field guide for a study of socialization*, New York: John Wiley.
WHYTE, W. F.
1949   The social structure of the restaurant. *American Journal of Sociology* 54(4):469–471.
WILLIAMS, THOMAS R.
1958   The structure of the socialization process in Papago Indian society. *Social Forces* 36:251–256.
1959   The evolution of a human nature. *Philosophy of Science* 26:1–13.
1969   *A Borneo childhood: enculturation in Dusun society.* New York: Holt, Rinehart and Winston.
1972a *Introduction to socialization: human culture transmitted.* St. Louis: Mosby.
1972b "The socialization process: a theoretical perspective," in *Primate socialization.* Edited by F. Poirier, 207–260. New York: Random.
1974a "Introduction," in *Psychological anthropology.* Edited by T. R. Williams. The Hague: Mouton.
1974b "On the origin of the socialization process," in *Psychological anthropology.* Edited by T. R. Williams. The Hague: Mouton.

WILSON, A., V. SARICH
   1969   "A molecular time scale for human evolution." *Proceedings of the National Academy of Sciences* 63:1088–1093.
WOLCOTT, H. F.
   1967   Anthropology and education. *Review of Educational Research* 37:82–92.
YAKER, H. M.
   1972   "The schizophrenic perception of time: a syntactical analysis of time language," in *The future of time: man's temporal environment.* Edited by H. Yaker, H. Osmond, and F. Cheek. New York: Anchor.
ZARETZKY, I. L.
   1972   "The language of spiritualist churches," in *Culture and cognition: rules, maps, and plans.* Edited by James Spradley. New York: Chandler.

List of Contributors

CRAIG JACKSON CALHOUN of the University of North Carolina, Department of Sociology, Chapel Hill, North Carolina.

THOMAS CARROLL of the Department of Education at Clark University, Worcester, Massachusetts.

WOODROW W. CLARK, JR., Institute for Study of Social Change, University of California at Berkeley, Berkeley, California.

WILLIAM S. CONDON of the Boston School of Medicine, Boston, Massachusetts.

STARKEY DUNCAN of the Counseling and Psychotherapy Center of the University of Chicago, Chicago, Illinois.

FREDERICK ERICKSON, Institute for Research on Teaching, Michigan State University, East Lansing, Michigan.

PAUL GARVIN of the Department of Linguistics and Center for the Study of Cultural Transmission, the State University of New York at Buffalo, Buffalo, New York.

FREDERICK GEARING of the Department of Anthropology and Center for the Study of Cultural Transmission, the State University of New York at Buffalo, Buffalo, New York.

WARD GOODENOUGH of the University Museum and Department of Anthropology of the University of Pennsylvania, Philadelphia, Pennsylvania.

PATRICIA GROGAN-HURLICH, Seattle, Washington.

JOHN J. GUMPERZ of the Department of Anthropology of the University of California at Berkeley, Berkeley, California.

ROBERT J. HAVIGHURST, Professor Emeritus of the Department of Education and Human Development, University of Chicago, Chicago, Illinois.

JOHN D. HERZOG of the Department of Foundations of Education at Northeastern University, Boston, Massachusetts.

WAYNE D. HUGHES, Vice-Principal, Starpoint Secondary Schools, Pendleton, New York.

ADAM KENDON of the Department of Anthropology at Australian National University, Canberra, Australia.

A. RICHARD KING of the Faculty of Education at the University of Victoria, Victoria, British Columbia, Canada.

JEAN CARTER LAVE of the School of Social Sciences at the University of California at Irvine, Irvine, California.

MADELEINE MATHIOT of the Department of Linguistics and Center for the Study of Cultural Transmission, the State University of New York at Buffalo, Buffalo, New York.

NORMAN A. MCQUOWN of the Department of Anthropology of the University of Chicago, Chicago, Illinois.

WALTER E. PRECOURT of the Department of Anthropology at the University of Kentucky, Lexington, Kentucky.

LETA RICHTER of Buffalo, New York.

RAY C. RIST of U.S. National Institute of Education, Washington, D.C.

GERARD ROSENFELD of the Department of Anthropology, the State University of New York at Buffalo, Buffalo, New York; temporarily, University of Botswana, Gaborone, Botswana, Africa.

JOHN SINGLETON of the International and Development Education Program in the School of Education at the University of Pittsburgh, Pittsburgh, Pennsylvania.

ALLEN SMITH of the High/Scope Education Research Foundation, Ypsilanti, Michigan.

CAROL TALBERT, Co-ordinator of Community Service and Continuing Education, New Mexico State University, Grants, New Mexico.

B. ALLAN TINDALL, deceased, formerly of the Department of Physical Education at the University of California at Berkeley, Berkeley, California.

SIGRID TÖPFER of the Department of Soziologie at the University of Konstanz, Konstanz, Germany.

THOMAS R. WILLIAMS of the Department of Anthropology at Ohio State University, Columbus, Ohio.

Index of Names

Index of Subjects

Aborigines: Australian cultural pluralism, 46–47
Achievement: school research reported, 210–213
Action anthropology, 221–227
Affective education: not considered by Gearing, 51
Agendas: critical comment, 68, 84; defined, 11, 36–37; in education, 21–29; paradigmatic model, 131–134; research reported on Black English, 108–109, 110; types, 12–15, 36. *See also* Exchanges; Open agendas; Stable agendas; Troublesome agendas
Analytic dimensions, 180–189
Analytic units: research methodology, 116–125
Anglo-Saxon culture: imposition on primitive peoples, 46–47
Appropriate displays: functional concepts, 181–182, 200–201, 204
Asylums (Goffman), 104
Australia: cultural pluralism, 46–47

Barriers. *See* Constraints
Basketball, 60
Behavior: likened to dance, 2–3, 191
Behavioral units, 176–180; research methodology, 116–125
Biology, human: related to culture, 159–166
Bureaucratic contexts: encounters, 16, 29, 74, 133

Chimpanzees: behavior compared to humans, 160
Cognitive sociology (Cicourel), 100

Comembership, particularistic, 90–92
Commonplace know-how, 202–203
Communities: organization, 173–176, 193–198
Complex information, 17, 30–32, 36, 134, 203–204; critical comment, 148–150
Constraints: affecting diffusion of knowledge, 2, 10, 45, 96, 138–139; affecting non-human areas, 174–175; analytic description of behavior, 2, 4–5, 175–176, 213
Correct displays: functional concepts, 181–182, 200–201, 204
Cross-cultural outline of education (Henry), 57
Cultural pluralism: and application of Gearing's theory, 46–47
Cultural premises, 17–18, 32–34, 36; critical comment, 50, 102–103, 140–141; defined, 37; paradigmatic model, 134; research project on Black English, 110–111
Cultural transmission: Gearing's theory questioned, 155–166; researches on, 151–155
Culture and commitment (Mead), 61
Curriculum, hidden: schooling, 204–207, 209, 210, 213, 214
Cybernetics: idiom borrowed, 2, 5, 10, 48, 81, 158, 228

Dancelike behavior, 2–3, 191
Digital information, 30–31, 188
Distribution of knowledge: patterns, 12, 17, 35–36, 130–131, 133, 138–139
Dyads. *See* Public dyads

Propertylike knowledge, 36; affecting agendas, 13–14; affecting exchanges, 183; paradigmatic model, 131–132
Protocols, 18, 33–34; critical comment, 50; defined, 37
Psyches: ignored by Gearing, 214–217
Public dyads, 25–26; critical comment, 80, 82–83, 96; defined, 11, 37
Pygmalion in the classroom (Rosenthal and Jacobson), 211

Racial desegregation: schools, 218
Racial differences: research reported, 87–92
Random diffusion of knowledge: lack queried, 1–2; meaning queried, 49, 69, 138n
Reenactment. *See* Social change
Reference model (Gearing), 173–227
Research: in education, 32
Response. *See* Initiation and response
Restaurants: staff behavior, 29
Restraints. *See* Constraints
Rethinking culture (Bohannon), 81n
Ritual process, The (Turner), 143
Role learning, 19, 26–27, 134
Routines: behavioral units, 178–179, 181–182, 192–193; defined, 176, 177

Schooling. *See* Education and schooling
Selective exchanges, 184, 185, 219–220
Self-fulfilling prophecies: pupil ability, 210–213
Servomechanisms: applied to behavior, 215, 216–217, 220
Sex roles: social change, 219
Sharing: items of information, 23, 30, 34, 62–63
Skills. *See* Knowledge and skills
Social change: Gearing's further views, 214–221; prevented by education, 19, 34–35, 36, 111, 135, 171; promotion of, 221–227; theory criticized, 50, 52n, 60, 74–76, 105n
Social identity, 24; affecting agendas, 13–14, 70–71, 85, 86–87, 100; affecting exchanges, 183, 184–185, paradigmatic model, 131–133; "smart and dumb", 106
Social system: paralleled by education system, 18–19, 34–35

Socialization: critical comments, 151–166
Specialized information, 31–32
Speech: synchronized behavior, 2–4, 190–191
"Spelling baseball", 63
Stable agendas: bureaucratic contexts, 16, 29; critical comment, 49–50, 100; and cultural premises, 17–18; defined, 14, 37; distribution of information, 17; initiation and response, 15–16; subtypes, 15
Structure: as behavioral units, 177–180; and function, 175–177
Studies in the behavior of face-to-face interaction (Indiana University), 95
Stumbles: behavior analysis, 84, 178, 201
Supernatural, 59
Synchronized behavior, 2–4, 190–191

Tacit behavior patterns, 15, 27–28, 133
Tailoring: research reported in Liberia, 147–148, 150
Talk. *See* Speech
Template for work, 195, 209, 210, 213, 214
Terminology: use by Gearing criticized, 50, 53–54, 64–71, 82–87, 145
Theory development: critical comment, 72–74, 103–104
Transactions, 26–28; critical comment, 66–68, 85–87; defined, 11, 37, 178
Troublesome agendas: and cultural premises, 17–18; critical comment, 70–71, 145; defined, 14, 38; distribution of information, 17; initiation and response, 15–16; microethnographic study reported, 87–92
Turns, 25; critical comment, 79, 80, 83–84; defined, 11, 38; initiation and response, 15–16
Typologic information, 30–31, 188

United States: cultural pluralism, 46–47

Vai: research in Liberia reported, 147–148, 150

Where we are and where we might go (Gearing), 51, 68
Work system: community organization, 194–198